CAMBRIDGE

Brighter Thinking

A Level Further Mathematics for OCR A

Statistics Student Book (AS/A Level)

Vesna Kadelburg, Ben Woolley, Paul Fannon and Stephen Ward

CAMBRIDGE
UNIVERSITY PRESS

University Printing House, Cambridge CB2 8BS, United Kingdom

One Liberty Plaza, 20th Floor, New York, NY 10006, USA

477 Williamstown Road, Port Melbourne, VIC 3207, Australia

314–321, 3rd Floor, Plot 3, Splendor Forum, Jasola District Centre, New Delhi – 110025, India

79 Anson Road, #06–04/06, Singapore 079906

Cambridge University Press is part of the University of Cambridge.

It furthers the University's mission by disseminating knowledge in the pursuit of
education, learning and research at the highest international levels of excellence.

www.cambridge.org
Information on this title: www.cambridge.org/9781316644409 (Paperback)
www.cambridge.org/9781316644263 (Paperback with Cambridge Elevate edition)

© Cambridge University Press 2017

First published 2017

20 19 18 17 16 15 14 13 12 11 10 9 8 7 6 5 4 3 2 1

Printed in the United Kingdom by Latimer Trend

A catalogue record for this publication is available from the British Library

ISBN 978-1-316-64440-9 Paperback
ISBN 978-1-316-64426-3 Paperback with Cambridge Elevate edition

Additional resources for this publication at www.cambridge.org/education

Cambridge University Press has no responsibility for the persistence or accuracy
of URLs for external or third-party internet websites referred to in this publication,
and does not guarantee that any content on such websites is, or will remain,
accurate or appropriate.

....

....

This resource is endorsed by OCR for use with specification AS Level Further Mathematics A (H235)
and specification A Level Further Mathematics A (H245). In order to gain OCR endorsement,
this resource has undergone an independent quality check. Any references to assessment and/
or assessment preparation are the publisher's interpretation of the specification requirements
and are not endorsed by OCR. OCR recommends that a range of teaching and learning
resources are used in preparing learners for assessment. OCR has not paid for the production
of this resource, nor does OCR receive any royalties from its sale. For more information about
the endorsement process, please visit the OCR website, **www.ocr.org.uk.**

Contents

Introduction

You have probably been told that mathematics is very useful, yet it can often seem like a lot of techniques that just have to be learned to answer examination questions. You are now getting to the point where you will start to see where some of these techniques can be applied in solving real problems. However, as well as seeing how maths can be useful we hope that anyone working through this book will realise that it can also be incredibly frustrating, surprising and ultimately beautiful.

The book is woven around three key themes from the new curriculum:

Proof

Maths is valued because it trains you to think logically and communicate precisely. At a high level, maths is far less concerned about answers and more about the clear communication of ideas. It is not about being neat – although that might help! It is about creating a coherent argument that other people can easily follow but find difficult to refute. Have you ever tried looking at your own work? If you cannot follow it yourself it is unlikely anybody else will be able to understand it. In maths we communicate using a variety of means – feel free to use combinations of diagrams, words and algebra to aid your argument. Once you have attempted a proof, try presenting it to your peers. Look critically (but positively) at some other people's attempts. It is only through having your own attempts evaluated and trying to find flaws in other proofs that you will develop sophisticated mathematical thinking. This is why we have included lots of common errors in our 'work it out' boxes – just in case your friends don't make any mistakes!

Problem solving

Maths is valued because it trains you to look at situations in unusual, creative ways, to persevere and to evaluate solutions along the way. We have been heavily influenced by a great mathematician and maths educator George Polya, who believed that students were not just born with problem solving skills – they were developed by seeing problems being solved and reflecting on their solutions before trying similar problems. You may not realise it but good mathematicians spend most of their time being stuck. You need to spend some time on problems you can't do, trying out different possibilities. If after a while you have not cracked it then look at the solution and try a similar problem. Don't be disheartened if you cannot get it immediately – in fact, the longer you spend puzzling over a problem the more you will learn from the solution. You may never need to integrate a rational function in future, but we firmly believe that the problem solving skills you will develop by trying it can be applied to many other situations.

Modelling

Maths is valued because it helps us solve real-world problems. However, maths describes ideal situations and the real world is messy! Modelling is about deciding on the important features needed to describe the essence of a situation and turning that into a mathematical form, then using it to make predictions, compare to reality and possibly improve the model. In many situations the technical maths is actually the easy part – especially with modern technology. Deciding which features of reality to include or ignore and anticipating the consequences of these decisions is the hard part. Yet it is amazing how some fairly drastic assumptions – such as pretending a car is a single point or that people's votes are independent – can result in models that are surprisingly accurate.

More than anything else, this book is about making links. Links between the different chapters, the topics covered and the themes above, links to other subjects and links to the real world. We hope that you will grow to see maths as one great complex but beautiful web of interlinking ideas.

Maths is about so much more than examinations, but we hope that if you take on board these ideas (and do plenty of practice!) you will find maths examinations a much more approachable and possibly even enjoyable experience. However, always remember that the results of what you write down in a few hours by yourself in silence under exam conditions is not the only measure you should consider when judging your mathematical ability – it is only one variable in a much more complicated mathematical model!

How to use this book

Throughout this book you will notice particular features that are designed to aid your learning. This section provides a brief overview of these features.

In this chapter you will learn how to:
- break down complicated questions into parts that are easier to count, and then combine them together
- count the number of ways to permute a set of objects

Before you start…		
A Level Mathematics Student Book 1, Chapter 9	You should know how to work with the factorial function.	1 Evaluate $\frac{7!}{5!}$
A Level Mathematics Student Book 1, Chapter 17	You should know how to work with basic probability.	2 What is the probability of rolling a prime number on a fair dice?

Learning objectives
A short summary of the content that you will learn in each chapter.

Before you start…
Points you should know from your previous learning and questions to check that you're ready to start the chapter.

WORKED EXAMPLE
The left-hand side shows you how to set out your working. The right-hand side explains the more difficult steps and helps you understand why a particular method was chosen.

Key point
A summary of the most important methods, facts and formulae.

PROOF
Step-by-step walk-throughs of standard proofs and methods of proof.

Explore
Ideas for activities and investigations to extend your understanding of the topic.

WORK IT OUT
Can you identify the correct solution and find the mistakes in the two incorrect solutions?

Tip
Useful guidance, including ways of calculating or checking answers and using technology.

Each chapter ends with a **Checklist of learning and understanding** and a **Mixed practice exercise**, which includes **past paper questions** marked with the icon .

In between chapters, you will find extra sections that bring together topics in a more synoptic way.

Focus on …
Unique sections relating to the preceding chapters that develop your skills in proof, problem solving and modelling.

Cross-topic review exercise
Questions covering topics from across the preceding chapters, testing your ability to apply what you have learned.

You will find **practice paper questions** towards the end of the book, as well as a **glossary** of key terms (picked out in colour within the chapters), and **answers** to all questions. Full **worked solutions** can be found on the Cambridge Elevate digital platform, along with a **digital version** of this Student Book.

Maths is all about making links, which is why throughout this book you will find signposts emphasising connections between different topics, applications and suggestions for further research.

⏮ Rewind

Reminders of where to find useful information from earlier in your study.

📷 Focus on ...

Links to problem-solving, modelling or proof exercises that relate to the topic currently being studied.

⏭ Fast forward

Links to topics that you may cover in greater detail later in your study.

ⓘ Did you know?

Interesting or historical information and links with other subjects to improve your awareness about how mathematics contributes to society.

Colour-coding of exercises

The questions in the exercises are designed to provide careful progression, ranging from basic fluency to practice questions. They are uniquely colour-coded, as shown here.

---

1 Evaluate:

   a i $5!$ **ii** $6!$ **b i** $2 \times 4!$ **ii** $3 \times 5!$ **c i** $6! - 5!$ **ii** $6! - 4 \times 5!$

2 Find the number of arrangements of the letters ALGEBRA.

3 Find the number of permutations of the letters STATISTICIAN.

8 $X \sim U(n)$ and $\text{Var}(X) = \text{E}(X) + 4$. Find n.

10 Find the number of ordered subsets of 1 1 1 2 2 2 of size four.

11 Explain why the number of arrangements of x copies of object A and y copies of object B is $^{x+y}C_x$.

Black – drill questions. These come in several parts, each with subparts i and ii. You only need attempt subpart i at first; subpart ii is essentially the same question, which you can use for further practice if you got part i wrong, for homework, or when you revisit the exercise during revision.

Green – practice questions at a basic level.

Blue – practice questions at an intermediate level.

Red – practice questions at an advanced level.

Purple – challenging questions that apply the concept of the current chapter across other areas of maths.

Yellow – designed to encourage reflection and discussion.

A – indicates content that is for A Level students only

AS – indicates content that is for AS Level students only.

🖩 – indicates a question that requires a calculator.

1 Counting principles and probability

In this chapter you will learn how to:

- break down complicated questions into parts that are easier to count, and then combine them together
- count the number of ways to permute a set of objects
- count the number of ways you can choose objects from a group
- apply these tools to problems involving probabilities.

Before you start…

A Level Mathematics Student Book 1, Chapter 9	You should know how to work with the factorial function.	1	Evaluate $\dfrac{7!}{5!}$
A Level Mathematics Student Book 1, Chapter 17	You should know how to work with basic probability.	2	What is the probability of rolling a prime number on a fair dice?

Making maths count

Counting is the one of the first things you learn in Mathematics and at first it seems very simple. If you were asked to count how many people there are in your school, this would not be too tricky. If you were asked how many chess matches need to be played if everyone is to play everyone else, this is a little more complicated. If you were asked how many different football teams could be chosen, you might find that the numbers become far too large to count without using some mathematical techniques.

One of the main uses of this type of counting is in calculating probabilities. You already have tools such as tree diagrams and Venn diagrams, but some problems are easier to solve by counting all the possibilities. The methods can be applied to fields as diverse as games of chance, genetics and cryptography.

Although in the exam all the questions will be set in the context of probability, you need to learn about various counting techniques first, before applying them to probability problems in Section 8.

Section 1: The product principle and the addition principle

Counting very small groups is simple. You need to break down more complicated problems into counting small groups. But how do you combine these together to come up with an answer to the overall problem? The answer lies in the product principle and the addition principle, which can be demonstrated by considering order choices from the menu shown.

Mains

Pizza
Hamburger
Paella

Desserts

Ice cream
Fruit salad

Anna would like to order a main course *and* a dessert. She could make six different orders – three choices for the main course and for each choice she makes there, two choices for dessert, so she multiplies the individual possibilities.

Bob would like to order *either* a main course *or* a dessert. He could make five different orders – one of the three main courses or one of the two desserts so he adds the individual possibilities.

You can use the notation n(A) to mean the number of ways of making a choice about A.

The product principle tells us that when you wish to select one option from A AND one option from B you multiply the individual possibilities together.

 Key point 1.1

Product principle: $n(A \text{ AND } B) = n(A) \times n(B)$

The addition principle tells us that when you wish to select one option from A *or* one option from B you add the individual possibilities together.

The addition principle has one caveat. You can only use it if there is no overlap between the choices for A and the choices for B. For example, you *cannot* apply the addition principle to counting the number of ways of getting an odd number or a prime number on a dice. If there is no overlap between the choices for A and for B the two events are mutually exclusive.

 Key point 1.2

Addition principle:

$$n(A \text{ OR } B) = n(A) + n(B)$$

if A and B are mutually exclusive.

The hardest part of applying the addition or product principles is breaking the problem down into relevant parts. It is often useful to rewrite questions to emphasise whether what is required is 'AND' or 'OR'.

WORKED EXAMPLE 1.1

An examination has ten questions in section A and four questions in section B. Calculate how many different ways there are to choose questions if you must choose:

a one question from each section
b a question from either section A or section B.

a *Choose one question from A (10 ways)*
       AND one from B (4 ways).

Describe the problem accurately.

       Number of ways = 10 × 4
                       = 40

'AND' means you should apply the product principle.

Continues on next page ...

b Choose one question from A (10 ways)

OR one from B (4 ways)

Number of ways = 10 + 4

= 14

> Describe the problem accurately.

> 'OR' means you should apply the addition principle.

In the context of Worked example 1.1 you cannot have a repeat selection of an object. However, there are situations where you might be able to do so.

WORKED EXAMPLE 1.2

In a class there is an award for best mathematician, best sportsperson and nicest person. People can receive more than one award. In how many ways can the awards be distributed if there are twelve people in the class?

Choose one of twelve people for the best mathematician (12 ways)

AND one of the twelve for best sportsperson (12 ways)

AND one of the twelve for nicest person (12 ways).

$12 \times 12 \times 12 = 1728$

> Describe the problem accurately.

> Apply the product principle.

EXERCISE 1A

1 If there are 10 ways of doing *A*, 3 ways of doing *B* and 19 ways of doing *C*, with *A*, *B* and *C* mutually exclusive, calculate how many ways there are of doing:

    a **i** both *A* and *B*   **ii** both *B* and *C*

    b **i** either *A* or *B*   **ii** either *A* or *C*.

2 If there are four ways of doing *A*, seven ways of doing *B* and five ways of doing *C*, with *A*, *B* and *C* mutually exclusive, calculate how many ways there are of doing:

    a all of *A*, *B* and *C*   **b** exactly one of *A*, *B* or *C*.

3 Show many different paths there are in this diagram:

    a from A to C

    b from C to E

    c from A to E.

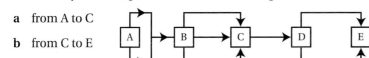

4 John is planting out his garden and needs a new rose bush and some dahlias. There are twelve types of rose and four varieties of dahlia in his local nursery. How many possible selections does he have to choose from if he wants exactly one type of rose and one type of dahlia?

5 A lunchtime menu at a restaurant offers five starters, six main courses and three desserts. State how many different choices of meal you can make if you would like:

    a a starter, a main course and a dessert

    b a main course and either a starter or a dessert

    c any two different courses.

6 Five men and three women would like to represent their club in a tennis tournament. In how many ways can one mixed doubles pair be chosen?

7 A Mathematics team consists of one student from each of Years 7, 8, 9 and 10. There are 58 students in Year 7, 68 in Year 8, 61 in Year 9 and 65 in Year 10.

    a How many ways are there of picking the team?

    Year 10 is split into three classes: 10A (21 students), 10B (23 students) and 10C (21 students).

    b If students from 10B cannot participate in the challenge, how many ways are there of picking the team?

8 Student ID codes consist of three letters chosen from A to Z, followed by four digits chosen from 1–9. Repeated characters are permitted. How many possible ID codes are there?

9 A beetle walks along the struts from the bottom to the top of an octahedral sculpture, visiting exactly two of the middle points (A, B, C or D), How many possible routes are there?

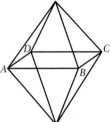

10 Professor Small has 15 different ties (7 blue, 3 red and 5 green), 4 waistcoats (red, black, blue and brown) and 12 different shirts (3 each of red, pink, white and blue). He always wears a shirt, a tie and a waistcoat.

    a How many different outfits can he use until he has to repeat one?

    Professor Small never wears any outfit that combines red with pink.

    b How many different outfits can he make with this limitation?

11 State how many different three-digit numbers can be formed using the digits 1, 2, 3, 5, 7:

    a at most once only   **b** as often as desired.

12 State how many ways:

    a that four distinguishable toys can be put into three distinguishable boxes

    b that three distinguishable toys can be put into five distinguishable boxes.

Section 2: Permutations

A permutation (sometimes called an arrangement) is an ordering of a list of objects. For example, a flag has four horizontal stripes: one each of the colours red, yellow, green and black. If you want to count how many different possible flags you have, you need to find the number of permutations of the colours. You can use this as a generic example to illustrate how to think about permutations.

There are four options for the colour of the top stripe, three options for the colour of the next one (because one of the colours has already been used), two options for the third stripe and one option for the last one. Using the 'product principle', the number of possible options for each are multiplied together, so the total number of permutations is $4 \times 3 \times 2 \times 1 = 24$. The number of ways n different objects can be permuted is equal to the product of all positive integers less than or equal to n; you have already met the notation for this expression: $n!$

 Key point 1.3

$$n! = n(n-1)(n-2)\ldots \times 2 \times 1$$

The number of permutations (arrangements) of n distinct objects is $n!$

WORKED EXAMPLE 1.3

A test has twelve questions. How many different arrangements of the questions are possible?

Permute twelve items.	Describe the problem accurately.
Number of permutations $= 12! = 479\,001\,600$.	Use the formula from Key point 1.3.

In most examination questions you will have to combine the idea of permutations with the product and addition principles:

WORKED EXAMPLE 1.4

A seven-digit number is formed by using each of the digits 1 to 7 exactly once. How many such numbers are even?

Pick the final digit to be even (3 ways) AND then permute the remaining six digits (6! ways).	Describe the problem accurately.
$3 \times 720 = 2160$ possible even numbers	Apply the product principle.

This example shows the very common situation in counting where you are given a constraint – in this case you have to end with an even digit.

WORKED EXAMPLE 1.5

How many permutations of the letters of the word SQUARE start with three vowels?

Permute the three vowels at the beginning (3! ways) AND permute the three consonants at the end (3! ways).	Describe the problem accurately.
Number of ways $= 3! \times 3! = 36$	Apply the product principle.

EXERCISE 1B

1 Evaluate:

    a i $5!$ **b i** $2 \times 4!$ **c i** $6! - 5!$

      ii $6!$ **ii** $3 \times 5!$ **ii** $6! - 4 \times 5!$

2 Evaluate:

    a i $8!$ **b i** $9 \times 5!$ **c i** $12! - 10!$

      ii $11!$ **ii** $9! \times 5$ **ii** $9! - 7!$

3 Find the number of ways of arranging:

    a 6 CDs   **b** 8 photographs   **c** 26 books.

4   **a** How many ways are there of arranging seven textbooks on a shelf?

    b In how many of those permutations is the single biggest textbook in the middle?

5   **a** How many five-digit numbers can be formed by using each of the digits 1–5 exactly once?

    b How many of those numbers are divisible by five?

6 A class of 16 pupils and their teacher are queuing outside a cinema.

    a How many different permutations are there?

    b How many different permutations are there if the teacher has to stand at the front?

7 A group of nine pupils (five boys and four girls) are lining up for a photograph, with all the girls in the front row and all the boys at the back. How many different permutations are there?

8 How many permutations of the letters of the word 'SQUARE' start with a consonant?

9   **a** How many six-digit numbers can be made by using each of the digits 1–6 exactly once?

    b How many of those numbers are smaller than 300 000?

10 A class of 30 pupils is lining up in 3 rows of 10 for a class photograph. How many different arrangements are possible?

11 A baby has nine different toy animals. Five of them are red and four of them are blue. She arranges them in a line so that, in terms of colour, they are symmetrical. How many different arrangements are possible?

Section 3: Combinations

Suppose that three pupils are to be selected out of a class of eleven to attend a meeting with the head teacher. How many different groups of three can be chosen? In this example you need to choose three pupils out of eleven. They are not to be arranged in any specified order. Therefore, the selection of Ali, Bill and then Cathy is the same as the selection of Bill, Cathy and then Ali. This sort of selection is called a combination. In general the number of ways of choosing r distinct objects out of n is given the symbol $\binom{n}{r}$, $_nC_r$ or ^nC_r said as 'n choose r'.

> **Rewind**
>
> In A Level Mathematics Student Book 1, Chapter 17, you already met this symbol in the context of Pascal's triangle and the binomial expansion.

Most of the time you can find the value of $\binom{n}{r}$ on your calculator.

However, you can now also justify the formula you met in the context of binomial expansions and binomial probabilities.

In the head teacher examples, there are 11 ways to select the first pupil, 10 ways to select the second and 9 ways to select the third; this makes the total of $11 \times 10 \times 9$ selections. However, there are $3! = 6$ different permutations of any three selected pupils, so you have counted each selection six times. Therefore the number of distinct selections is in fact $\dfrac{11 \times 10 \times 9}{3!} = 165$.

The expression $\dfrac{11 \times 10 \times 9}{3!}$ can also be written as $\dfrac{11!}{8!3!}$.

You may recognise this as the formula for the binomial coefficient $\binom{11}{3}$.

This reasoning can be generalised to count selections from any size group.

🔑 Key point 1.4

The formula for the number of ways of choosing r objects from n objects is:

$$\binom{n}{r} = \frac{n!}{r!(n-r)!}$$

This will appear in your formula book.

💡 Tip

🖩 You can also calculate $\binom{n}{r}$ on your calculator, usually via an ^nC_r option.

Although you do not need to be able to prove this formula, you might find the following proof interesting. It highlights how counting arguments can be used to prove algebraic formulae.

PROOF 1

Total number of arrangements can be thought of as

Pick a set of size r

AND

Permute those r objects

AND

Permute the remaining $n-r$ objects

So

$$n! = \binom{n}{r} \times r! \times (n-r)!$$

Rearranging:

$$\binom{n}{r} = \frac{n!}{r!(n-r)!}$$

Write an expression for the total number of arrangements in terms of selecting a subset and then arranging the selected part and the remaining part.

Use the fact that the total number of arrangements is $n!$ and apply the product principle to the previous analysis.

WORKED EXAMPLE 1.6

A group of twelve friends wants to form a team for a five-a-side football tournament.

a In how many different ways can a team of five be chosen?

b Rob and Amir are the only goalkeepers and they cannot play in any other position. If a team has to contain exactly one goalkeeper, how many possible teams are there?

a Choosing 5 players from 12.

$$\text{Number of ways} = \binom{12}{5}$$

$$= 792$$

> Describe the problem accurately.

b Pick a goalkeeper, then fill in the rest of the team.

> Decide on a strategy.

Amir is in goal (1 way)

> Describe the problem accurately.

   AND

   choose four other players (? ways)

OR

Rob is in goal (1 way)

   AND

   choose four other players (? ways).

$$\text{Number of ways with Amir in goal} = \binom{10}{4}$$

> With Amir picked there are four remaining slots, but Rob cannot be picked so ten players remain.

$$\text{Number of ways with Rob in goal} = \binom{10}{4}$$

$$\text{Total number of ways} = 1 \times \binom{10}{4} + 1 \times \binom{10}{4}$$

> Apply the addition principle and the product principle.

$$= 210 + 210$$

$$= 420$$

EXERCISE 1C

1 Evaluate:

a i $\binom{7}{2}$ **b i** $3 \times \binom{6}{3}$ **c i** $\binom{5}{0} \times \binom{9}{5}$ **d i** $\binom{5}{2} + \binom{9}{5}$

  ii $\binom{12}{5}$ **ii** $10 \times \binom{6}{5}$ **ii** $\binom{10}{8} \times \binom{3}{1}$ **ii** $\binom{6}{0} + \binom{7}{3}$

2 a i In how many ways can six objects be selected from eight?

  ii In how many ways can five objects be selected from nine?

 b i In how many ways can either three objects be selected from ten or seven objects be selected from twelve?

  ii In how many ways can either two objects be selected from five or three objects be selected from four?

 c i In how many ways can five objects be selected from seven and three objects be selected from eight?

  ii In how many ways can six objects be selected from eight and three objects be selected from seven?

3 An exam paper consists of 15 questions. Students can select any 9 questions to answer. How many different selections can be made?

4 Suppose you are revising for seven subjects, and you study three subjects in one evening. You might study a subject on more than one evening.

   a In how many ways can you select three subjects to do on Monday evening?

   b If you have to revise Maths on Tuesday, in how many ways can you select the subjects to do on Tuesday evening?

5 In the 'Pick 'n' Mix' lottery, players select 7 numbers out of 39. How many different selections are possible?

6 There are 16 boys and 12 girls in a class. Three boys and two girls are needed to take part in the school play. In how many different ways can they be selected?

7 A football team consists of one goalkeeper, four defenders, four midfielders and two forwards. A manager has three goalkeepers, eight defenders, six midfielders and five forwards in the squad. In how many ways can she pick the team?

8 A school is planning some trips over the summer. There are twelve places on the Greece trip, ten places on the China trip and ten places on the Disneyland trip. Each pupil can go on only one trip. If there are 140 pupils in the school, and assuming that they are all able to go on any of the 3 trips, in how many ways can the spaces be allocated?

9 Out of 26 teachers in a school, 4 are needed to accompany a school theatre trip.

   a In how many ways can the four teachers be chosen?

   b How many selections are possible if Mr Brown and Mrs Brown cannot both go on the trip?

10 A committee of 3 boys and 3 girls is to be selected from a class of 14 boys and 17 girls. State how many ways the committee can be selected if:

   a Anna has to be on the committee

   b the committee has to include Bill or Emma, but not both.

11 Sam's sweet shop stocks seven different types of 2p sweets and five different types of 5p sweets. If you want at most one of each sweet, state how many different selections of sweets can be made when spending:

   a exactly 6p   **b** exactly 7p   **c** exactly 10p   **d** at most 5p.

12 An English examination has two sections. Section A has five questions and section B has four questions. Four questions must be answered.

   a How many different ways are there of selecting four questions to answer if there are no restrictions?

   b How many different ways are there of selecting four questions if there must be at least one question answered in each section?

13 Ten points are drawn on a sheet of paper so that no three lie in a straight line.

   a State how many different triangles can be drawn by connecting three points.

   b State how many different quadrilaterals can be drawn by connecting four points.

14 A group of 45 students are to be seated in 3 rows of 15 for a school photograph. Within each row, students must sit in alphabetical order according to name, but there is no restriction determining the row in which a student must sit. How many different seating permutations are possible, assuming no students have identical names?

Section 4: The exclusion principle

The exclusion principle is a trick for counting what you are interested in by counting what you are not interested in. This typically is needed when counting a situation where a certain property is prohibited.

> **Key point 1.5**
>
> Exclusion principle:
>
> Count what you are *not* interested in and subtract it from the total.

As an example, suppose a five-digit code is formed by using each of the digits 1 to 5 exactly once. If you wanted to count how many such codes do *not* end in '25' you could consider all possible options for the last two digits.

WORKED EXAMPLE 1.7A

How many five-digit codes formed by using each of the digits 1 to 5 exactly once do *not* end in '25'?

Pick the final digit from $\{1,2,3,4\}$ (4 ways)

   AND

   permute the remaining four digits (4! ways)

OR

pick the final digit as 5 (1 way)

   AND

   pick the penultimate digit from $\{1,3,4\}$ (3 ways)

   AND permute the remaining three digits (3! ways).

$(4 \times 4!) + (1 \times 3 \times 3!) = 114$

> Describe the problem accurately.

> Use the product and addition principles.

An alternative way to solve the same problem is to use the exclusion principle.

WORKED EXAMPLE 1.7B

How many five-digit codes formed by using each of the digits 1 to 5 exactly once do not end in '25'?

Count permutations of five-digit codes (5! ways)

then EXCLUDE cases where the last two digits are '25' (1 way)

   AND

   permute the remaining three digits (3! ways))

$5! - 1 \times 3! = 114$

> Describe the problem accurately.

> Use the product and exclusion principles.

A very common use of the exclusion principle occurs when you are asked to count a situation containing an 'at least' or 'at most' restriction.

WORKED EXAMPLE 1.8

Theo has eight different jigsaws and five different bears. He chooses four toys. In how many ways can he make a selection with at least two bears?

Count combinations of four toys from thirteen $\left(\binom{13}{4}\text{ways}\right)$ .... Describe the problem accurately.

then EXCLUDE combinations with

$$\text{no bears AND four jigsaws}\left(\binom{5}{0}\times\binom{8}{4}\right)$$

OR

$$\text{one bear AND three jigsaws}\left(\binom{5}{1}\times\binom{8}{3}\right)$$

Number of ways $= \binom{13}{4} - \left(\binom{5}{0}\times\binom{8}{4}+\binom{5}{1}\times\binom{8}{3}\right)$ .... Apply the exclusion principle.

$$= 365$$

EXERCISE 1D

1 How many numbers between 101 and 800 inclusive are not divisible by five?

2 How many permutations of the letters of the word JUMPER do not start with a 'J'?

3 A bag contains twelve different chocolates, four different mints and six different toffees. Three sweets are chosen. State how many ways there are of choosing:

    a all not chocolates   **b** not all chocolates.

4 State how many permutations of the letters of KITCHEN:

    a do not begin with KI   **b** do not have K and I in the first two letters.

5 A committee of five people is to be selected from a class of twelve boys and nine girls. How many such committees include at least one girl?

6 In a word game there are 26 letter tiles, each with a different letter. How many ways are there of choosing seven tiles so that at least two of them are vowels?

7 A committee of six is to be selected from a group of ten men and twelve women. In how many ways can the committee be chosen if it has to contain at least two men and one woman?

8 Seven numbers are chosen from the integers between 1 and 19 inclusive. State how many selections have:

    a at most two even digits   **b** at least two even digits.

9 How many permutations of the letters DANIEL do not begin with D or do not end with L?

Section 5: Selections where order matters

Sometimes there are occasions where you want to choose a number of objects from a bigger group but the order they are chosen in matters. For example, finding the possibilities for the first three finishers in a race or forming numbers from a fixed group of digits. The strategy for dealing with these situations is to first choose from the larger group and then permute the chosen objects.

🔍 Explore

According to the *Guinness World Records*, at the time of writing the largest number that has ever been assigned any meaning comes from the field of counting. It is called 'Graham's number' and it is so large that it is not feasible to write it out in normal notation even using all the paper in the world, so a new system of writing numbers had to be invented to describe it. Explore about the topic Graham's Number is used in – it is called Ramsey Theory. Investigate the notation used – it is called tetration.

WORKED EXAMPLE 1.9

A class of 28 pupils needs to select a committee consisting of a class representative, treasurer, secretary and football captain. Each post needs to be taken by a different person. In how many different ways can the four posts be filled?

Choose 4 from 28 $\left(\binom{28}{4} \text{ ways}\right)$

AND permute those 4 (4! ways).

> Describe problem accurately. Select four people and then allocate them to different jobs. Note that this is the same as selecting four people and then permuting them.

Number of ways $= \binom{28}{4} \times 4!$

$= 491\,400$

> Apply the product principle.

There is a shortcut for this reasoning. The symbol for the number of selections of size r from a group of n distinct objects is $^{n}P_{r}$ (sometimes written as $_{n}P_{r}$). This can be evaluated on your calculator. You can also generalise the reasoning from Worked example 1.9 to find a formula for $^{n}P_{r}$. You choose r objects and then arrange them. This means that $^{n}P_{r} = {}^{n}C_{r} \times n!$, leading to Key point 1.6.

🔑 Key point 1.6

The number of permutations of a subset of size r from a set of n distinct objects is:

$$^{n}P_{r} = \frac{n!}{(n-r)!}$$

EXERCISE 1E

1 Find the number of permutations of:

    a four distinct objects out of ten   **b** six distinct objects out of seven.

2 Find the number of ways of selecting when order matters:

    a three objects out of five   **b** two objects out of fifteen.

3 In a 'Magic sequence' lottery draw there are 39 balls numbered 1–39. Seven balls are drawn at random. The result is a sequence of seven numbers which must be matched in the correct order to win the grand prize. How many possible sequences can be made?

4 A teacher needs to select 4 pupils from a class of 24 to receive 4 different prizes. How many possible ways are there to award the prizes?

5 How many three-digit numbers can be formed from the digits 1–9 if no digit can be repeated?

6 Eight athletes are running a race. In how many different ways can the first three places be filled?

7 An identification number consists of two letters followed by four digits chosen from 0 to 9. No digit or letter can appear more than once. How many different identification numbers can be made?

8 Three letters are chosen from the word PICTURE and arranged in order. How many of the possible permutations contain at least one vowel?

9 Eight runners compete in a race. In how many different ways can the three medals be awarded if James wins either a gold or a silver?

10 A class of 18 needs to select a committee consisting of a President, a Secretary and a Treasurer. How many different ways are there to form the committee if one student, Ellie, does not want to be President?

Section 6: Keeping objects together or separated

How many anagrams of the word 'SQUARE' have the Q and U next to each other? How many have the vowels all separated? When such constraints are added to the problem you need some clever tricks to deal with them.

The first type of problem you look at is where objects are forced to stay together. The trick is to imagine the letters in the word SQUARE as being on tiles. If the Q and the U need to be together, you are really dealing with five tiles, one containing QU:

You must also remember that the condition is satisfied if Q and U are in the other order:

WORKED EXAMPLE 1.10

How many permutations of the word 'SQUARE' have the Q and the U next to each other?

Permute the five 'tiles' (S, QU, A, R, E) (5! ways)

AND

permute the letters QU on the 'double tile' (2! ways).

Number of ways = 5! × 2! = 240

Describe the problem accurately.

Apply the product principle.

 Key point 1.7

If a group of items have to be kept together, treat them all as one object. Remember that there might be permutations within this group too.

Another type of constraint is that objects have to be kept apart. It is tempting to treat this as the opposite of objects being kept together, and this is indeed the case if you are separating only two objects. However, the opposite of three objects staying together includes having two of them together and the third one apart. So when dealing with this situation you need to focus on the gaps that the critical objects can fit into. Consider the question of how many permutations of the word SQUARE have none of the vowels together. You first permute all of the consonants. One such permutation is:

$\_Q\_R\_S\_$

There are four gaps in which you can put the vowels. You only need to choose three of them, and then decide in what order to insert the vowels.

WORKED EXAMPLE 1.11

How many permutations of the word 'SQUARE' have none of the vowels together?

Permute three consonants (3! ways)

AND choose three out of the four gaps $\left(\binom{4}{3} \text{ways} \right)$

AND permute the three vowels to put into the gaps (3! ways).

Total number of ways = 3! × 4 × 3! = 144

Describe the problem accurately.

Apply the product principle.

 Key point 1.8

If some of the objects have to be kept apart, permute the remaining objects and then insert the separated objects into the gaps.

EXERCISE 1F

1 In how many ways can 15 people be arranged in a line if 2 of these people – Jack and Jill – have to stand together?

2 Students from three different classes are standing in the lunch queue. There are six students from 10A, four from 10B and four from 10C. In how many ways can the queue be arranged if students from the same class have to stand together?

3 In how many ways can six distinguishable Biology books and three distinguishable Physics books be arranged on the shelf if the three Physics books are always next to each other?

4 In a photo there are three families – six Greens, four Browns and seven Grays – arranged in a row. The Browns have had an argument among themselves so they refuse to stand next to each other. How many different permutations are permitted?

5 In a cinema there are 15 seats in a row. State how many ways seven friends can be seated in the same row if:

   a there are no restrictions

   b they all want to sit together.

6 Five women and four men stand in a line.

   a In how many arrangements will all four men stand next to each other?

   b In how many arrangements will all the men stand next to each other and all the women stand next to each other?

   c In how many arrangements will all the men be apart?

   d In how many arrangements will all the men be apart and all the women be apart?

Section 7: Permuting objects with repetitions

If you are permuting a group of objects where some are identical you need a different formula to find the number of arrangements.

🔑 Key point 1.9

If there are n objects with r_A of type A, r_B of type B, r_C of type C etc. then the number of permutations is:

$$\frac{n!}{r_A!\, r_B!\, r_C!\ldots}$$

WORKED EXAMPLE 1.12

Find the number of arrangements of the letters MATHEMATICS.

$\dfrac{11!}{2!2!2!} = 4\,989\,600$ There are eleven letters, of which there are two Ms, two Ts and two As. All other letters occur once. You could put in a 1! in the denominator to represent these, but it would not change the value.

EXERCISE 1G

1 Find the number of arrangements of the letters ABACUS.

2 Find the number of arrangements of the letters ALGEBRA.

3 Find the number of permutations of the letters STATISTICIAN.

4 Find the number of permutations of the letters MIDDLE that begin and end with a vowel.

5 Find the number of arrangements of the letters ABRACADABRA that begin and end with an A.

6 Find the number of permutations of the letters QUEEN that have the Q followed directly by the U.

7 Find the number of arrangements of the letters THESIS that have the T and the H next to each other.

8 Find the number of arrangements of the letters BATTLE that:

    a begin and end with a vowel   **b** begin and end with a consonant.

9 Find the number of arrangements of the digits 1 1 2 2 3 3 that begin and end with an odd number.

10 Find the number of ordered subsets of 1 1 1 2 2 2 of size four.

11 Explain why the number of arrangements of x copies of object A and y copies of object B is $^{x+y}C_x$.

Section 8: Counting principles in probability

Counting principles can be used to calculate probabilities in some problems that would be extremely difficult in any other way. To find the probability of an event labelled A occurring you compare the number of ways in which A occurs with the total number of ways any event can occur.

 Key point 1.10

$$P(A)=\frac{\text{number of outcomes in which } A \text{ occurs}}{\text{total number of possible outcomes}}$$

This only works if all the outcomes are equally likely.

> 💡 **Tip**
>
> In questions like Worked example 1.13 you will often see phrases such as '…randomly chosen…'. In this context it means chosen so that all possible outcomes are equally likely. You will find in future chapters that 'random' is not the same as 'equally likely' and there are actually many possible distributions which are described as random.

WORKED EXAMPLE 1.13

A committee of four is randomly chosen from six girls and five boys. What is the probability that the committee contains exactly three girls?

Total number of committees $=\begin{pmatrix}11\\4\end{pmatrix}$

$=330$

First decide how many different committees can be made up.

Choosing 3 girls from 6 and 1 boy from 5 can be done in $\begin{pmatrix}6\\3\end{pmatrix}\times\begin{pmatrix}5\\1\end{pmatrix}=100$ ways.

Then see how many committees have exactly three girls.

$P(\text{exactly 3 girls})=\dfrac{100}{330}=\dfrac{10}{33}$

Find the ratio.

EXERCISE 1H

1 A set of four alphabet blocks bearing the letters A, R, S and T are dropped in a line at random. What is the probability that they spell out one of the words STAR, RATS or ARTS?

2 Consider the word PARTING. What is the probability that a sequence of four letters chosen from this word contains the letter P?

3 **a** A team of 11 is chosen randomly from a squad of 18. What is the probability that both the captain and the vice captain are selected?

    b Two of the squad are goalkeepers, and precisely one must be chosen. If neither of the goalkeepers is captain or vice captain, what now is the probability that both the captain and the vice captain are selected?

4 A team of five students is to be chosen at random to take part in a debate. The team is to be chosen from a group of six history students and three philosophy students. Find the probability that:

    a only history students are chosen   **b** all three philosophy students are chosen.

5 Six boys sit at random in six seats arranged in a row. Two of the boys are brothers. Find the probability that they:

    a sit at the ends of the row   **b** sit next to each other.

6 A rugby team consists of eight forwards, seven backs and five substitutes. They all line up at random in one row for a picture. State the probability:

    a that the forwards are all next to each other   **b** that no two forwards are next to each other.

Checklist of learning and understanding

- The **product principle** states that if you have two choices you can count the total number of outcomes when you are interested in both the first choice *and* the second choice being made by multiplying together the number of outcomes for each choice.
- The **addition principle** states that the number of outcomes when you are interested in either the first choice *or* the second choice being made is the sum of the number of outcomes for each choice.
- The number of **permutations** of n distinct objects is $n!$.
- A **combination** is a selection of r out of n distinct objects in which the order does not matter. There are

  $$\binom{n}{r} = \frac{n!}{r!(n-r)!}$$ such selections.

- The **exclusion principle** says that to find the number of permutations that do *not* have a certain property, find the number of permutation that *do* have the property and subtract it from the number of all possible permutations.
- The number of permutations of a subset of size r from a set of n distinct objects is:

  $$^{n}P_{r} = \frac{n!}{(n-r)!}$$

- If a group of items have to be kept together, treat them all as one object. Remember that there might be permutations within this group too.
- If some of the objects have to be kept apart, permute the remaining objects and then insert the separated objects into the gaps.
- If there are n objects with r_A of type A, r_B of type B, r_C of type C etc. then the number of permutations is: $\frac{n!}{r_A! r_B! r_C! \ldots}$

- You can use counting ideas to work out a probability: $P(A) = \dfrac{\text{number of outcomes in which } A \text{ occurs}}{\text{total number of possible outcomes}}$

Mixed practice 1

1 **a** Seven athletes take part in the 100 m final of the Olympic games. In how many ways can three medals be awarded?

   b Usain uses his answer to part **a** to claim that the probability of the medals going to Ana, Betty and Ciara is $\frac{1}{35}$.

   i Explain how Usain found this figure.

   ii What is the flaw in Usain's logic?

2 **a** In how many ways can five different letters be put into five different envelopes?

   b Five addressed letters are placed into five addressed envelopes at random. Find the probability that the letters are all in the correct envelopes.

3 Ten people stand in a queue, in any order, including three friends: Amy, Bruno and Calum. What is the probability that Amy, Bruno and Calum occupy the first three places in the queue?

4 **a** How many three-digit numbers contain no zeros?

   b A random three-digit number (from 100 to 999) is chosen. Find the probability that it contains no zeros.

5 What is the probability that a randomly chosen permutation of the word 'CAROUSEL' starts and ends with a consonant?

6 What is the probability that a randomly chosen permutation of the word 'SCHOOL' starts with an O?

7 A group of 15 students contains 7 boys and 8 girls.

   a In how many ways can a committee of five be selected if it must contain at least one boy?

   b What is the probability that a randomly chosen committee contains at least one boy?

8 Abigail, Bahar, Chris, Dasha, Eustace and Franz are sitting next to each other in a cinema.

   If they were to sit at random, what would be the probability that Bahar and Eustace are not sitting next to each other?

9 A committee of five is to be selected from a group of twelve children. Find the probability that the two youngest children are not both in the randomly chosen committee.

10 A car registration number consists of three different letters followed by five digits chosen from 1 to 9 (the digits can be repeated).

   a How many different registration numbers can be made?

   b What is the probability that the number plate starts with SUM?

11 A van has eight seats, two at the front, a row of three in the middle and a row of three at the back. On two journeys the same eight people sit randomly in the seats in the van. Each person can drive. What is the probability that they sit in the same positions during these two journeys?

12 Ten people are to travel in one car (taking four people) and one van (taking six people). Only two of the people can drive. On two journeys the same ten people sit randomly in the available seats. What is the probability that they sit in the same vehicle during these two journeys? (The permutation of the passengers in each vehicle is not important.)

13 Five girls – Anna, Beth, Carol, Dasha and Elena – stand in a line.

    a State how many permutations are possible in which:

      i Anna is at one end of the line   **ii** Anna is not at either end.

    b What is the probability that, in a randomly chosen arrangement, Anna is at the left of the line or Elena is on the right, or both?

14 Five different sweets are shared randomly between Daniel and Alessia, with all splits equally likely. What is the probability that:

    a Alessia gets all the sweets

    b both Daniel and Alessia get at least one sweet?

15 In a doctor's waiting room, there are 14 seats in a row. Eight people are waiting to be seen.

    a In how many ways can they be seated?

    b Three of the people are all in the same family and they want to sit together. How many ways can this now happen?

    c The family no longer have to sit together, but there is someone with a very bad cough who must sit at least one seat away from anyone else. If all arrangements are equally likely, what is the probability that this happens?

16 A group of 7 students sit in random order on a bench.

    i **a** Find the number of orders in which they can sit.

        b The 7 students include Tom and Jerry. Find the probability that Tom and Jerry sit next to each other.

    ii The students consist of 3 girls and 4 boys. Find the probability that

        a no two boys sit next to each other,

        b all three girls sit next to each other.

                                          © OCR, AS GCE Mathematics, Paper 4732, June 2011

17 A bag contains 9 discs numbered 1, 2, 3, 4, 5, 6, 7, 8, 9.

    i Andrea chooses 4 discs at random, without replacement, and places them in a row.

      a How many different 4-digit numbers can be made?

      b How many different **odd** 4-digit numbers can be made?

    ii Andrea's 4 discs are put back in the bag. Martin then chooses 4 discs at random, without replacement.

    Find the probability that

    a the 4 digits include at least 3 odd digits,

    b the 4 digits add up to 28.

                                  © OCR, AS GCE Mathematics, Paper 4732, January 2012

2 Discrete random variables

In this chapter you will learn how:

- to calculate the mean and variance of a discrete random variable
- a linear transformation of the variable changes the mean and variance
- to use the formulae for expectation and variance of a special distribution called the uniform distribution
- to recognise when it is appropriate to use a uniform distribution
- to use the formula for expectation and variance of the binomial distribution
- to find probabilities, expectation and variance for a new distribution called the geometric distribution
- to recognise when it is appropriate to use a geometric distribution.

Before you start...

A Level Mathematics Student Book 1, Chapter 17	You should know how to use the rules of probability.	1 Two events A and B are independent. If $P(A) = 0.4$ and $P(B) = 0.3$ find $P(A$ AND $B)$.
A Level Mathematics Student Book 1, Chapter 17	You should know how to find probabilities of discrete random variables.	2 $P(X = x) = kx$ for $x = 1, 2, 3$. Find the value of k.
A Level Mathematics Student Book 1, Chapter 16	You should know how to find the mean, variance and standard deviation of data, including familiarity with formulae involving sigma notation.	3 Find the variance of 2, 5 and 8.

What are discrete random variables?

A **random variable** is a variable that can change every time it is observed – such as the outcome when you roll a dice. A **discrete random variable** can only take certain distinct values. In A Level Mathematics Student Book 1, Chapter 17, you covered the **probability distributions** of discrete random variables – a table or rule giving a list of all possible outcomes along with their probabilities.

Many real-world situations follow probability distributions – such as the velocity of a molecule in a waterfall or the amount of tax paid by an individual. It is extremely difficult to make a prediction about a single observation, but it turns out that you can predict remarkably accurately the overall behaviour of many millions of observations. In this chapter you see how you can calculate the mean and variance of a discrete random variable.

 Tip

Discrete variables don't have to take integer values, but the possible distinct values can be listed (though the list might be infinite). For example, if X is the standard UK shoe size of a random adult member of the public, X takes values 2, 2.5, 3, 3.5 up to 15.5 and is a discrete random variable.

If Y is the exact foot length of a random adult member of the public (in centimetres), Y takes values in the interval [20, 35] and is a continuous random variable. You will work with continuous random variables in Chapter 7.

Section 1: Average and spread of a discrete random variable

The most commonly used measure of the average of a random variable is the **expectation**. This is also called the mean of the random variable. It is a value representing the mean result if the variable were to be measured an infinite number of times.

Key point 2.1

The expectation of a random variable X is written $E(X)$ or μ and calculated as
$$\mu = E(X) = \sum x_i p_i$$
Where x_i and p_i are the possible values of X and their associated probabilities.

This will appear in your formula book.

You do not need to be able to prove this result, but you might find it helpful to see the following justification.

The mean of n pieces of discrete data is

$$\bar{x} = \frac{1}{n}\sum f_i x_i$$

Start from the definition of the mean of a sample. f_i is the frequency of the observation x_i.

$$= \sum\left(\frac{f_i}{n}\right)x_i$$

Since $\frac{1}{n}$ is the same for each term in the sum you can take it into the sum.

Now imagine n getting larger and larger. $\frac{f_i}{n}$ will tend towards the probability of x_i happening, so $\bar{x}$ will tend towards $\sum x_i p_i$.

You must use the definition of the expectation at some point in the proof.

As n tends to infinity, $\bar{x}$ tends to μ. Hence $\mu = \sum x_i p_i$.

WORKED EXAMPLE 2.1

The random variable X has a probability distribution as shown in the table. Calculate $E(X)$.

x	1	2	3	4	5	6
$P(X=x)$	$\frac{1}{10}$	$\frac{1}{4}$	$\frac{1}{10}$	$\frac{1}{4}$	$\frac{1}{5}$	$\frac{1}{10}$

$$E(X) = 1\times\frac{1}{10}+2\times\frac{1}{4}+3\times\frac{1}{10}+4\times\frac{1}{4}+5\times\frac{1}{5}+6\times\frac{1}{10}=\frac{7}{2}$$

Use the values from the distribution in the formula.

Tip

The expectation of a random variable does not need to be a value that the variable can actually be. In particular, many people think that 'expectation' is the most likely value, but this is not necessarily the case.

 Did you know?

Standard deviation – the square root of variance – is a much more meaningful representation of the spread of the variable. So why do you bother with variance at all? The answer is purely to do with mathematical elegance. It turns out that the algebra of variance is far neater than the algebra of standard deviation.

As well as knowing the average of a random variable, you might also be interested in how far away from the average the outcome might be. The **variance, σ^2 or Var(X)**, of a random variable is a value representing the degree of variation that would be seen if the variable were to be repeatedly measured an infinite number of times. It is a measure of how spread out the variable is.

 Key point 2.2

The **variance** of a random variable X is written Var(X) and calculated as

$$\sigma^2 = \text{Var}(X) = \sum(x_i - \mu)^2 p_i = \sum x_i^2 p_i - \mu^2$$

This will appear in your formula book.

 Fast forward

You will see in Section 2 how you find expectations of other functions of X.

The quantity $\sum x_i^2 p_i$ is the expectation of X^2, read as 'the mean of the squares'. This variance formula can also be written as Var(X) = $E(X^2) - E(X)^2$, and is often read as 'the mean of the squares minus the square of the mean'.

WORKED EXAMPLE 2.2

Calculate Var(X) for the probability distribution in Worked example 2.1

From Worked example 2.1, $E(X) = 3.5$

$E(X^2) = 1^2 \times \dfrac{1}{10} + 2^2 \times \dfrac{1}{4} + 3^2 \times \dfrac{1}{10} + 4^2 \times \dfrac{1}{4} + 5^2 \times \dfrac{1}{5} + 6^2 \times \dfrac{1}{10}$ ⋯⋯ Use the values from the distribution in Key point 2.1

$\quad = 14.6$

$\text{Var}(X) = E(X^2) - [E(X)]^2$

$\quad = 14.6 - 12.25$

$\quad = 2.35$

A probability distribution can also be described by a function.

WORKED EXAMPLE 2.3

W is a random variable that can take values -0.5, 1.5, 2.5 and k where $k > 0$.

$$P(W = w) = \frac{w^2}{29}$$

a Find the value of k.

b Find the expected mean of W.

c Find the standard deviation of W.

Continues on next page ...

a $\dfrac{(-0.5)^2}{29}+\dfrac{1.5^2}{29}+\dfrac{2.5^2}{29}+\dfrac{k^2}{29}=1$

$0.25+2.25+6.25+k^2=29$

$k^2=20.25$

$k=4.5$ since $k>0.$

Use the fact that the probabilities must add up to 1.

b $E(W)=-0.5\times\dfrac{(-0.5)^2}{29}+1.5\times\dfrac{1.5^2}{29}+2.5^2\times\dfrac{2.5^2}{29}+4.5\times\dfrac{4.5^2}{29}$

≈ 3.79

Using Key point 2.1

c $E(W^2)=(-0.5)^2\times\dfrac{(-0.5)^2}{29}+1.5^2\times\dfrac{1.5^2}{29}+2.5^2\times\dfrac{2.5^2}{29}+4.5^2\times\dfrac{4.5^2}{29}$

≈ 15.7

To find the standard deviation you first need to find the variance which means you need to find $E(W^2)$ and use Key point 2.2.

$\operatorname{Var}(W)=15.7-3.79^2\approx 1.28$

So $\sigma\approx\sqrt{1.28}\approx 1.13$

Although you only write down 3 s.f. in the working, you should use the full accuracy from the calculator to find the final answer.

WORK IT OUT 2.1

Find the variance of X, the random variable defined by the following distribution.

x	0	1	2
$P(X=x)$	0.2	0.3	0.5

Which is the correct solution? Can you identify the errors made in the incorrect solutions?

Solution 1	$E(X)=\dfrac{0+1+2}{3}=1$ $E\left(X^2\right)=\dfrac{0^2+1^2+2^2}{3}=\dfrac{5}{3}$ $\operatorname{Var}(X)=\dfrac{5}{3}-1^2=\dfrac{2}{3}$
Solution 2	$E(X)=1\times0.3+2\times0.5=1.3$ $E\left(X^2\right)=1\times0.3+4\times0.5=2.3$ $\operatorname{Var}(X)=2.3-1.3^2=0.61$
Solution 3	$E(X)=0\times0.2+1\times0.3+2\times0.5=1.3$ $E\left(X^2\right)=0^2\times0.2^2+1^2\times0.3^2+2^2\times0.5^2=1.09$ $\operatorname{Var}(X)=1.09-1.3^2=-0.6$

EXERCISE 2A

1 Calculate the expectation, variance and standard deviation of each of the following random variables:

a i

x	1	2	3	4
$P(X=x)$	0.4	0.3	0.2	0.1

ii

x	8	9	10	11
$P(X=x)$	0.4	0.3	0.2	0.1

b i

x	10	20	30	40
$P(X=x)$	0.4	0.3	0.2	0.1

ii

x	80	90	100	110
$P(X=x)$	0.4	0.3	0.2	0.1

c i

w	0.1	0.2	0.3	0.4
$P(W=w)$	0.4	0.1	0.25	0.25

ii

v	0.1	0.2	0.3	0.4
$P(V=v)$	0.5	0.3	0.1	0.1

d i $P(X=x)=\dfrac{x^2}{14}, x=1, 2, 3$

ii $P(X=x)=\dfrac{1}{x}, x=2, 3, 6.$

2 A discrete random variable X is given by $P(X=x)=k(x+1)$ for $x=2, 3, 4, 5, 6$.

a Show that $k=0.04$.

b Find $E(X)$.

3 The discrete random variable V has the following probability distribution and $E(V)=5.1$.

v	1	2	5	8	p
$P(V=v)$	0.2	0.3	0.1	0.1	q

a Find the values of p and q.

b Find $P(X>\mu)$.

4 A discrete random variable X has its probability given by

$P(X=x)=k(x+3)$, where x is 0, 1, 2, 3.

a Show that $k=\dfrac{1}{18}$.

b Find the exact value of $E(X)$.

5 The probability distribution of a discrete random variable X is defined by

$P(X=x)=kx(4-x), x=1, 2, 3.$

a Find the value of k.

b Find $E(X)$.

c Find the standard deviation of X.

6 A fair six-sided dice, with sides numbered 1, 1, 2, 2, 2, 5 is thrown. Find the mean and variance of the score.

7 The following table shows the probability distribution of a discrete random variable X.

x	0	1	2	3
$P(X = x)$	0.1	p	q	0.2

a Given that $E(X) = 1.5$, find the values of p and of q.

b Find the standard deviation of X.

8 A biased dice with four faces is used in a game. A player pays five counters to roll the dice. The following table shows the possible scores on the dice, the probability of each score and the number of counters the player receives in return for each score.

Score	1	2	3	4
Probability	$\frac{1}{2}$	$\frac{1}{4}$	$\frac{1}{5}$	$\frac{1}{20}$
Number of counters player receives	4	5	15	n

Find the value of n in order for the player to get an expected return of 3.25 counters per roll.

9 Two fair dice are thrown. The random variable D is the difference between the larger and the smaller score, or zero if they are the same.

a Copy and complete the following table to show the probability distribution of D.

d	0	1	2	3	4	5
p	$\frac{1}{6}$	$\frac{5}{18}$				

b Find $E(D)$.   c Find $Var(D)$.   d Find $P(D > E(D))$.

10 a In a game a player pays an entrance fee of £n. He then selects one number from 1, 2, 3 or 4 and rolls three unbiased four-sided dice. If his chosen number appears on all three dice he receives four times his entrance fee. If his number appears on exactly two of the dice he receives three times the entrance fee. If his number appears on exactly one dice he receives £1. If his number does not appear on any of the dice he receives nothing.

Copy and complete the probability table.

Frequency of chosen number	0	1	2	3
Profit (£)	$-n$			
Probability	$\frac{27}{64}$			

b The game organiser wants to make a profit over many plays of the game. Given that he must charge a whole number of pence, what is the minimum amount the organiser must charge?

Section 2: Expectation and variance of transformations of discrete random variables

Linear transformations

You might have noticed a link between question 1 parts **a** and **b** in Exercise 2A. The distributions were very similar but in part **b** all the x values were multiplied by 10. This is an example of a transformation. All the averages and the standard deviations were also multiplied by 10 but the variances were multiplied by 100.

The most common type of transformation is a linear transformation. This is where the new variable (Y) is found from the old variable (X) by multiplying by a constant and/or adding on a constant. You might do this if you change the units of measurement. This kind of change is also known as **linear coding**.

If you know the original mean and variance and how the values were transformed, you can use a shortcut to find the mean and variance of the new distribution, as shown in Key point 2.3.

Key point 2.3

If $Y = aX + b$ then

$$E(Y) = aE(X) + b$$

$$Var(Y) = a^2Var(X)$$

This means that the standard deviation of Y, σ_Y, is $|a|\sigma_X$. This makes sense as multiplying the values by a does change how spread out they are, but adding on b does not change the spread.

WORKED EXAMPLE 2.4

A random variable X has expectation 7 and variance 100. Y is a transformation of X given by $Y = 100 - 2X$. Find:

a the expectation of Y
b the standard deviation of Y.

a $E(Y) = 100 - 2 \times E(X)$
$\qquad = 100 - 2 \times 7$
$\qquad = 86$

> This is just a direct application of Key point 2.3.

b $Var(Y) = (-2)^2 Var(X)$
$\qquad = 4 \times 100$
$\qquad = 400$
$\qquad \sigma_Y = \sqrt{400} = 20$

> To find the standard deviation you need to first find the variance of Y, using Key point 2.3.

Tip

It is easy to get confused with the minus sign in the previous transformations. Remember that both variances and standard deviations are always positive.

EXERCISE 2B

1 If $E(X) = 9$ and $\text{Var}(X) = 25$ find $E(Y)$ and $\text{Var}(Y)$ if:

a **i** $Y = 3X$ **ii** $Y = 4X$

b **i** $Y = X - 1$ **ii** $Y = X + 2$

c **i** $Y = 2X + 1$ **ii** $Y = 3X - 5$

d **i** $Y = 10 - 3X$ **ii** $Y = 8 - 2X$

e **i** $Y = \dfrac{X - 1}{4}$ **ii** $Y = \dfrac{X + 5}{10}$

2 The random variable X has $\mu = 10$ and $\sigma = 3$. Find:

a $E(2X)$ **b** $\text{Var}(2X)$.

3 Stephen goes on a 30 mile bike ride every weekend. The distance until he stops for a picnic is modelled by X, where $E(X) = 20$ and $\text{Var}(X) = 16$.

Y is the amount of distance remaining after his picnic. Find $E(Y)$ and $\text{Var}(Y)$.

4 The rule for converting between degrees Celsius (C) and degrees Fahrenheit (F) is:

$$F = 1.8C + 32.$$

When a bread oven is operating its temperature has an expectation of $200\,°C$ with standard deviation $5\,°C$. Find the expectation and standard deviation of the temperature in degrees Fahrenheit.

5 The random variable X has expectation 10 and variance 25. If $Y = aX + b$ find the values of a and b so that the expectation of Y is 0 and the standard deviation is 1.

6 X is a discrete random variable where $E(X) = 10$ and $E(X^2) = 200$. Y is a transformation of X such that $Y = X + 2$. Find $E(Y)$ and the standard deviation of Y.

7 A discrete random variable X has equal expectation and standard deviation. Y is a transformation of X such that $Y = aX - b$. Prove that it is only possible for the expectation of Y to equal the variance of Y if $b \leqslant \dfrac{1}{4}$.

8 The St Petersburg Paradox describes a game where a fair coin is tossed repeatedly until a head occurs. You win 2^n pounds if the first head occurs on the nth toss. How much should you pay to play this game?

Section 3: The discrete uniform distribution

You have already met some special distributions that occur so often that they are named – the binomial and the normal distributions. Another very common distribution is the **discrete uniform distribution**. A discrete uniform distribution is a fixed number, n, of equally spaced numerical outcomes with constant and equal probability of occurring. Any discrete uniform distribution can be linearly transformed to the discrete uniform distribution of the whole numbers from 1 to n, which is given the symbol $U(n)$ (see Key point 2.4). For example, $U(6)$ gives the distribution of the outcomes on a fair ordinary dice.

🔑 Key point 2.4

If $X \sim U(n)$ then $P(X = x) = \dfrac{1}{n}$ for $x = 1, 2 \ldots n$.

If you identify a random variable as following a uniform distribution you can immediately write down the expectation and variance (see Key point 2.5).

Key point 2.5

If $X \sim U(n)$ then $P(X = x) = \dfrac{1}{n}$ for $x = 1, 2 \dots n$ and $E(X) = \dfrac{n+1}{2}$

and $\text{Var}(X) = \dfrac{n^2 - 1}{12}$.

Although you do not need to be able to prove this, you might find it interesting to see the following proof of these facts. It uses the fact that

$$\sum_{1}^{n} r = \frac{n(n+1)}{2} \text{ and } \sum_{1}^{n} r^2 = \frac{n(n+1)(2n+1)}{6}.$$

PROOF 2

Prove Key point 2.5: If $X \sim U(n)$ then $E(X) = \dfrac{n+1}{2}$ and $\text{Var}(X) = \dfrac{n^2 - 1}{12}$.

$E(X) = \displaystyle\sum_{r=1}^{n} r \times \frac{1}{n}$

r denotes the possible values of X, which are 1, 2, ..., n.

$= \dfrac{1}{n} \displaystyle\sum_{r=1}^{n} r$

$\dfrac{1}{n}$ is a constant, so it can be taken out of the sum.

$= \dfrac{1}{n} \dfrac{n(n+1)}{2}$

Use the result for the sum of the first n positive

$= \dfrac{n+1}{2}$

integers: $\displaystyle\sum_{r=1}^{n} r = \frac{n(n+1)}{2}$

$E(X^2) = \displaystyle\sum_{r=1}^{n} r^2 \times \frac{1}{n}$

All the values of X need to be squared.

$= \dfrac{1}{n} \displaystyle\sum_{r=1}^{n} r^2$

$= \dfrac{1}{n} \left(\dfrac{n(n+1)(2n+1)}{6} \right)$

Use the result for $\displaystyle\sum_{r=1}^{n} r^2$

$= \dfrac{(n+1)(2n+1)}{6}$

$\text{Var}(X) = E(X^2) - \left[E(X)\right]^2$

Use the formula for variance.

$= \dfrac{(n+1)(2n+1)}{6} - \left[\dfrac{n+1}{2}\right]^2$

$= \dfrac{n+1}{2} \left(\dfrac{2n+1}{3} - \dfrac{n+1}{2} \right)$

$= \dfrac{n+1}{2} \left(\dfrac{4n+2}{6} - \dfrac{3n+3}{6} \right)$

$= \dfrac{n+1}{2} \times \dfrac{n-1}{6}$

$= \dfrac{n^2 - 1}{12}$

In Section 2 you saw how to find the expectation and variance of a linear transformation of a discrete random variable. The expectation and variance of a linear transformation of a discrete uniform distribution can be found in the same way.

WORKED EXAMPLE 2.5

The discrete random variable Y is equally likely to take any even value between 10 and 20 inclusive. Find the variance of Y.

$Y = 2X + 8$ where $X \sim U(6)$

> The values of Y are 10, 12, 14... 20. These can be written as $Y = 2X + 8$, where $X = 1, 2, ... 6$
>
> So Y is a linear transformation of $X \sim U(6)$.

$Var(X) = \dfrac{35}{12}$

> Applying Key point 2.5.

$Var(Y) = 2^2 Var(X) = \dfrac{35}{3}$

> Applying Key point 2.3.

EXERCISE 2C

1   Find the mean and variance of the following distributions.

   a **i** $U(5)$ **ii** $U(8)$

   b **i** $U(2x)$ **ii** $U(x-1)$

2   A fair spinner has sides labelled 2, 4, 6, 8, 10. Find the expected mean and standard deviation of the results of the spinner.

3   A fair dice has sides labelled 0, 1, 2, 3, 4, 5. Find the expectation and standard deviation of the outcome of the dice.

4   **a** The random variable Y is equally likely to take any integer value between $-n$ and n. Show that this can be written as $aX + b$ where $X \sim U(2n + 1)$.

   b Hence find the variance of Y.

5   A string of 100 Christmas lights starts with a plug then contains a light every 4 cm from the plug.

   One light is broken. Assuming all bulbs are equally likely to break, what is the expected mean and variance of the distance of the broken light from the plug?

6   The random variable X is equally likely to take the value of any odd number between 1 and 99 inclusive. Find the variance of X.

7   The discrete random variable Y takes values $m, m + 1, m + 2... m + n$. Assuming equal probability for each value, find the expectation and variance of Y.

8   $X \sim U(n)$ and $Var(X) = E(X) + 4$. Find n.

9   A random number, X, is chosen from the fractions: $\dfrac{1}{n}, \dfrac{2}{n}, \dfrac{3}{n}, ..., 1$

   Prove that $E(X) > \dfrac{1}{2}$ but $Var(X) < \dfrac{1}{12}$.

10   $X \sim U(n)$. Prove that $6Var(X)$ is always divisible by $E(X)$.

Section 4: Binomial distribution

You have already studied probabilities associated with the binomial distribution. However, if you have identified a binomial situation you can immediately write down the expectation and variance (see Key point 2.6).

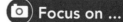 **Focus on ...**

These will be proved in Focus on ... Proof 1.

 Key point 2.6

If $X \sim B(n,p)$ then $E(X) = np$ and $Var(X) = np(1-p)$

This will appear in your formula book.

WORKED EXAMPLE 2.6

Find the expected value and the standard deviation in the number of '6's when 20 dice are rolled.

If X is the number of '6's rolled then $X \sim B\left(20, \dfrac{1}{6}\right)$

You can identify $n = 20$ and $p = \dfrac{1}{6}$.

$E(X) = 20 \times \dfrac{1}{6} \approx 3.33$

Using Key point 2.6.

$Var(X) = 20 \times \dfrac{1}{6} \times \dfrac{5}{6} = \dfrac{25}{9}$

Using Key point 2.6.

So the standard deviation will be $\sqrt{\dfrac{25}{9}} = \dfrac{5}{3} \approx 1.67$

EXERCISE 2D

Remember to round your answer to three significant figures when using the calculator.

1 Find the expected mean and standard deviation of each of the following variables

    a **i** $Y \sim B\left(100, \dfrac{1}{10}\right)$ **ii** $X \sim B\left(16, \dfrac{1}{2}\right)$

    b **i** $X \sim B(15, 0.3)$ **ii** $Y \sim B(20, 0.35)$

    c **i** $Z \sim B\left(n-1, \dfrac{1}{n}\right)$ **ii** $X \sim B\left(n, \dfrac{2}{n}\right)$

2 A coin is biased so that when it is tossed the probability of obtaining heads is $\dfrac{2}{3}$. The coin is tossed 4050 times. Let X be the number of heads obtained. Find:

    a the expected mean of X **b** the standard deviation of X.

3 A biology test consists of eight multiple choice questions. Each question has four answers, only one of which is correct. At least five correct answers are required to pass the test. Sheila does not know the answers to any of the questions, so answers each question at random.

    a What is the probability that Sheila answers exactly five questions correctly?

    b What is the expected number of correct answers Sheila will give?

    c What is the standard deviation in the number of correct answers Sheila will give?

    d What is the probability that Sheila manages to pass the test?

4 Given that $Y \sim B(12, 0.4)$, find:

    a the expected mean of Y **b** the standard deviation of $2Y$.

5 A coin is biased so that the probability of it showing tails is p. The coin is tossed n times. Let X be a random variable representing the number of tails. It is known that the expected mean of X is 19.5 and the variance is 6.825. Find the values of n and p.

6 In an experiment, a trial is repeated n times. The trials are independent and the probability p of success in each trial is constant. Let X be the number of successes in the n trials. The expected mean of X is 12 and the standard deviation is 2. Find n and p.

Section 5: The geometric distribution

If a footballer is practising taking free kicks you might be interested in how many free kicks she takes until she scores. This is the type of situation that is often modelled by another named distribution – the **geometric distribution**. It involves the same kind of trials as those you have been using with the binomial distribution, but it models the random variable 'number of trials up to and including the first success'.

The geometric distribution is commonly used in situations where the following conditions hold:

- There are trials where all outcomes can be classified into two distinct categories (often called 'success' and 'failure').
- The trials are independent.
- The probability of a success, p, is constant for each trial.
- There is no upper limit to the number of trials.

The only parameter you need to know is p. If X follows a geometric distribution then it is written as $X \sim \text{Geo}(p)$.

WORKED EXAMPLE 2.7

A footballer is practising free kicks. The number of free kicks that the footballer takes, up to and including her first goal, is modelled using a geometric distribution.

    a State two assumptions that would lead to the use of a geometric distribution in this situation.

    b Comment on the validity of these assumptions in the context of this situation.

a The footballer must be able to take an unlimited number of free kicks.

  The outcome of each free kick should not affect the outcome of future free kicks.

> You could use any of the conditions from the list, but notice that they have been put into the context of the situation.

b Although the footballer might get bored or run out of time it is likely that she will score before then so the assumption that she can take an unlimited number of free kicks is a good modelling assumption.

  The footballer might learn from her mistakes or get frustrated by her failures. Either way, it seems likely that the outcome of each free kick might affect future free kicks so this is not a good modelling assumption.

> You could accept or reject most assumptions – what is important is providing clear, convincing reasoning.

To get the probability of X taking any particular value, x, you use the fact that there must be $x - 1$ consecutive failures (each with probability $q = 1 - p$) followed by a single success.

Key point 2.7

If $X \sim \text{Geo}(p)$ then $P(X = x) = p(1-p)^{x-1}$ for $x = 1, 2, 3 \ldots$

This will appear in your formula book.

It can be quite useful to apply similar ideas to get a result for $P(X > x)$. For this situation to occur you must have started with x consecutive failures, therefore:

Key point 2.8

$P(X > x) = (1-p)^x$.

If you identify a variable as following a geometric distribution you can write down the expectation and variance.

Key point 2.9

If $X \sim \text{Geo}(p)$ then:

$E(X) = \dfrac{1}{p}$

$\text{Var}(X) = \dfrac{(1-p)}{p^2}$.

WORKED EXAMPLE 2.8

a A normal six-sided dice is rolled. What is the probability that the first '6' occurs:

  i on the fifth throw   **ii** after the fifth throw?

b What is the expected number of throws it will take until a '6' occurs?

X = 'Number of throws until the first six'	Define variables.
$X \sim \text{Geo}\left(\dfrac{1}{6}\right)$	Identify the distribution.
$P(X = 5) = \dfrac{1}{6} \times \left(\dfrac{5}{6}\right)^4 = 0.0804$ (3 s.f.)	Apply the formula for $P(X = x)$.
$P(X > 5) = \left(\dfrac{5}{6}\right)^5 = 0.402$ (3 s.f.)	Apply the formula for $P(X > x)$.
$E(X) = \dfrac{1}{\frac{1}{6}} = 6$	Apply the formula for $E(X)$.

EXERCISE 2E

1 Find the following probabilities:

a **i** $P(X = 5)$ if $X \sim \text{Geo}\left(\dfrac{1}{3}\right)$ **ii** $P(X = 7)$ if $X \sim \text{Geo}\left(\dfrac{1}{10}\right)$

b **i** $P(X \leqslant 5)$ if $X \sim \text{Geo}\left(\dfrac{1}{4}\right)$ **ii** $P(X < 4)$ if $X \sim \text{Geo}\left(\dfrac{2}{3}\right)$

c **i** $P(X > 10)$ if $X \sim \text{Geo}\left(\dfrac{1}{6}\right)$ **ii** $P(X \geqslant 20)$ if $X \sim \text{Geo}(0.06)$

d **i** The first boy born in a hospital on a given day is the fourth baby born (assuming no multiple births)

     ii A prize contained in one in five crisp packets is first won with the eighth crisp packet.

2 Find the expected mean and standard deviation of:

a **i** $\text{Geo}\left(\dfrac{1}{3}\right)$ **ii** $\text{Geo}(0.15)$

b **i** The number of attempts to hit a target with an arrow (there is a one in twelve chance of hitting the target on any given attempt)

     ii The number of times a dice must be rolled before a multiple of three is scored.

3 The probability of passing a driving test on any given attempt is 0.4. Solomon assumes that he has this probability of passing his test and that his attempts are independent of each other.

a Find the probability that Solomon passes the driving test on his third attempt.

b Find the expected average number of attempts Solomon needs to pass the driving test.

c How valid is the assumption that the attempts are independent of each other?

4 There are twelve green and eight yellow balls in a bag. One ball is drawn from the bag and replaced. This is repeated until a yellow ball is drawn.

a Find the expected mean and variance of the number of balls drawn.

b Find the probability that the number of balls drawn is at most one standard deviation from the mean.

5 Sophia is studying vehicles passing through a junction. Each morning she counts the number of vehicles up to and including the first motorbike. She calls this random variable M.

a State two assumptions which would lead to the use of a geometric distribution to model M in this situation.

b Comment on the validity of these assumptions in the context of this situation.

Sophia decides to model M using a $\text{Geo}(0.15)$ distribution.

c Based on her model, what is the expectation of M?

d Based on her model, find the probability that $M = 3$.

e Based on her model find the probability that at least five vehicles are observed before the first motorcycle is observed.

6 If $X \sim \text{Geo}(p)$ find the mode of X.

7 If $T \sim \text{Geo}(p)$ and $P(T = 2) = 0.21$ find the value of p.

8 $Y \sim \text{Geo}(p)$ and the variance of Y is three times as large as the mean of Y. Find the value of p.

9 **a** If $X \sim \text{Geo}\left(\dfrac{3}{4}\right)$ find the smallest value of x such that $P(X = x) < 10^{-6}$.

   b Find the smallest value of x such that $P(X > x) < 10^{-6}$.

10 Prove that the standard deviation of a variable following a geometric distribution is always less than the mean.

Checklist of learning and understanding

- The expectation of a random variable X is written $E(X)$ and calculated as:
$$E(X) = \sum x_i p_i$$

- The variance of a random variable X is written $\text{Var}(X)$ and calculated as:
$$\text{Var}(X) = E(X^2) - [E(X)]^2$$

  where:
$$E(X^2) = \sum x_i^2 p_i$$

- If $Y = aX + b$ then:
$$E(Y) = aE(X) + b$$
$$\text{Var}(Y) = a^2 \text{Var}(X)$$

- A uniform distribution models situations where all discrete outcomes are equally likely.

- If $X \sim U(n)$ then $P(X = x) = \dfrac{1}{n}$ for $x = 1, 2 \dots n$ and $E(X) = \dfrac{n+1}{2}$ and $\text{Var}(X) = \dfrac{n^2 - 1}{12}$.

- If $X \sim B(n, p)$ then $E(X) = np$ and $\text{Var}(X) = np(1 - p)$.

- A geometric distribution, $\text{Geo}(p)$, models the number of trials up to and including the first success in a situation with independent, constant probability trials.

- If $X \sim \text{Geo}(p)$ then $P(X = x) = (1 - p)^{x-1} p$, $P(X > x) = (1 - p)^x$, $E(X) = \dfrac{1}{p}$ and $\text{Var}(X) = \dfrac{(1 - p)}{p^2}$.

Mixed practice 2

1 A drawer contains three white socks and five black socks. Two socks are drawn without replacement. B is the number of black socks drawn.

   a Find the probability distribution of B.   **b** Find $E(B)$.

2 A fair six-sided dice is thrown once. The random variable X is calculated as half the result if the dice shows an even number or one higher than the result if the dice shows an odd number.

   a Create a table representing the probability distribution of X.

   b Find $E(X)$.   **c** Find $Var(X)$.

3 **a** $X \sim U(13)$. Find the expectation and variance of X.

   b Y is the discrete random variable that is equally likely to take any integer value between 14 and 26. Find $E(Y)$ and $Var(Y)$.

   c Z is the discrete random variable that is equally likely to take any even value between 2 and 26. Find $E(Z)$ and $Var(Z)$.

4 The random variable X follows this distribution:

x	1	2	3
p	a	b	0.6

   a If $E(X) = 2.5$ find the values of a and b.

   b Hence find $E(X^2)$ and show that $Var(X) = 0.45$.

5 X is a discrete random variable with $E(X) = 10$ and $Var(X) = 16$. Y is a transformation of X such that $Y = 12 - X$. Find $E(Y)$ and the standard deviation of Y.

6 When a four-sided spinner is spun, the number on which it lands is denoted by X, where X is a random variable taking values 2, 4, 6 and 8. The spinner is biased so that $P(X = x) = kx$, where k is a constant.

   i Show that $P(X = 6) = \dfrac{3}{10}$.   **ii** Find $E(X)$ and $Var(X)$.

© OCR, AS GCE Mathematics, Paper 4732, January 2013

7 The random variable X has expectation 12 and variance 100. If $Y = aX + b$ find the values of a and b so that the expectation of Y is 10 and the standard deviation is 20.

8 X is a discrete random variable that can take the values one or two.

   a If $E(X) = 1.2$ find the standard deviation of X.

   b Y is also a discrete random variable defined by $Y = 3X + 4$. Find $E(Y)$ and $Var(Y)$.

9 A fair dice is thrown until a six has been thrown or three throws have been made. T is the discrete random variable 'number of throws taken'.

   a Write down, in tabular form, the distribution of T.

   b Find $E(T)$.

   c Find the median of T.

   d The number of points awarded in the game, P, is $4 - T$. Find the variance of P.

10 **a** A four-sided dice is rolled twice. Write down, in a table, the probability distribution of S, the sum of the two rolls.

   b Find $E(S)$ and $Var(S)$.

   c A four-sided dice is rolled once and the score, X, is twice the result. Find the mean and variance of X.

11 The discrete random variable X follows the U(9) distribution. μ is the expectation of X and σ^2 is the variance of X. Find $P(\mu - \sigma < X < \mu + \sigma)$.

12 Approximately 1 in 30 people are carriers of the cystic fibrosis gene. In a sample of 1200 people state:

   a the expected number of carriers of the cystic fibrosis gene

   b the expected standard deviation in the number of carriers of the cystic fibrosis gene.

13 A squirrel drops nuts until one cracks. The probability of a nut cracking is 0.25. X is the number of drops required up until and including when one cracks.

   a State two assumptions required to model X with a geometric distribution. How likely are these assumptions to hold in this context?

   b If the required assumptions hold, find:

   i $E(X)$ **ii** $P(X > 2)$.

14 Sandra makes repeated, independent attempts to hit a target. On each attempt, the probability that she succeeds is 0.1.

   i Find the probability that

   a the first time she succeeds is on her 5th attempt,

   b the first time she succeeds is after her 5th attempt,

   c the second time she succeeds is before her 4th attempt.

Jill also makes repeated attempts to hit the target. Each attempt of either Jill or Sandra is independent. Each time that Jill attempts to hit the target, the probability that she succeeds is 0.2. Sandra and Jill take turns attempting to hit the target, with Sandra going first.

   ii Find the probability that the first person to hit the target is Sandra, on her

   a 2nd attempt,   **b** 10th attempt.

© **OCR, AS GCE Mathematics, Paper 4732, January 2013**

15 X is a discrete random variable satisfying $P(X = x) = kx$ for $x = 1, 2, 3 \ldots n$.

   Find, in terms of n:

   a k **b** $E(X)$ **c** $Var(X)$.

3 Poisson distribution

In this chapter you will learn:

- the conditions required for a Poisson distribution to model a situation
- the Poisson formula and how to calculate Poisson probabilities
- how to calculate the mean, variance and standard deviation of a Poisson variable
- how to use the distribution of the sum of independent Poisson distributions.

Before you start…

A Level Mathematics Student Book 1, Chapter 17	You should know how to work with the binomial distribution.	1 If $X \sim B(4, 0.25)$ find $P(X=2)$.
A Level Mathematics Student Book 2, Chapter 16	You should know how to work with conditional probability.	2 If $P(A \cap B) = 0.4$ and $P(B) = 0.6$ find $P(A\mid B)$.
Chapter 2	You should know how to find the expectation and variance of discrete random variables.	3 Find $E(X)$ and $Var(X)$ for the following distribution:

x	2	4
$P(X=x)$	0.4	0.6

What is the Poisson distribution?

When you are waiting for a bus there are two possible outcomes – at any given moment it either arrives or it doesn't. You can try modelling this situation using a binomial distribution, but it is not clear what an individual trial is. Instead you have an average rate of events – the average number of buses that arrive in a fixed time period.

There are many situations in which you know the rate of events within a given space or time, in contexts ranging from commercial, such as the number of calls through a telephone exchange per minute, to biological, such as the number of clover plants seen per square metre in a pasture. If the events can be considered independent of each other (so that the probability of each event is not affected by what has already been seen), the number of events in a fixed space or time interval can be modelled using the **Poisson distribution**.

Section 1: Using the Poisson model

The Poisson distribution is commonly used in situations where the following conditions hold:

- The events must occur randomly.
- The events must be independent of each other.
- The average rate of the events must be constant.

If this is the case, then the number of events, X, can be modelled by a Poisson distribution. If the average number of events in the period of interest is λ then you write this as $X \sim \text{Po}(\lambda)$.

Once you have identified that a Poisson distribution is a suitable model, you can use the formulae in Key point 3.1:

Key point 3.1

If $X \sim \text{Po}(\lambda)$ then:

$$P(X = x) = \frac{e^{-\lambda} \lambda^x}{x!} \text{ for } x = 0, 1, 2 \ldots$$

$$E(X) = \lambda$$

$$\text{Var}(X) = \lambda$$

This will appear in your formula book.

These results are not obvious, but their proof is beyond the scope of this course.

Notice that the values of mean and variance are equal for the Poisson distribution, and it follows that the standard deviation is the square root of this. This property is something you look out for when determining if data can be modelled by a Poisson distribution, although in itself it is not sufficient; there are other distributions with this feature.

A typical Poisson distribution – the Po(1.2) distribution – is shown as follows:

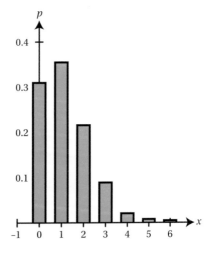

Notice that:

- the mean rate does not have to be a whole number
- the distribution is not symmetric
- the graph, in theory, should continue on to infinite values of X, but the probabilities of very large values of X get very small.

There are many situations in which events occur randomly, but you know the average rate of events within a given space or time.

WORKED EXAMPLE 3.1

Recordable accidents occur in a factory at an average rate of seven every year, independently of each other. Find the probability that in a given year exactly three recordable accidents occurred.

Let X be the number of recordable accidents in a year .... Define the random variable.

$X \sim Po(7)$ .... Give the probability distribution.

$P(X=3) = \dfrac{e^{-7}7^3}{3!}$ .... Write down the probability required, and calculate the answer.

$\qquad = 0.0521 \, (3 \text{ s.f.})$

The Poisson distribution is scalable. For example, if the number of butterflies seen on a flower in 10 minutes follows a Poisson distribution with mean λ, then the number of butterflies seen on a flower in 20 minutes follows a Poisson distribution with mean 2λ, and the number of butterflies seen on a flower in 5 minutes follows a Poisson distribution with mean $\dfrac{\lambda}{2}$.

 Tip

Learn how to use your calculator to find Poisson probabilities, $P(X = x)$, and cumulative probabilities, $P(X \leqslant x)$.

WORKED EXAMPLE 3.2

If there are, on average, twelve buses per hour arriving at a bus stop, find the probability that there are more than six buses in 30 minutes.

Let X be the number of buses in 30 minutes ...... Define the random variable.

$X \sim Po(6)$ .... Give the probability distribution.

$P(X>6) = 1 - P(X \leqslant 6)$ .... Write down the probability required. To use the calculator you must relate it to $P(X \leqslant k)$.

$\qquad = 0.394 \, (3 \text{ s.f.})$ from calculator.

The scalability of the Poisson distribution is a consequence of a more general result about the Poisson distribution. If two independent variables both follow a Poisson distribution then so does their sum.

Key point 3.2

If $X \sim \text{Po}(\lambda)$, $Y \sim \text{Po}(\mu)$ and $Z = X + Y$ then $Z \sim \text{Po}(\lambda + \mu)$

Although you do not need to know the proof of this fact, it does show an interesting link with the binomial expansion.

PROOF 3

$P(Z=z) = P(X=0)P(Y=z) + P(X=1)P(Y=z-1)$ $\quad\quad\quad\quad \dots + P(X=z)P(Y=0)$	Consider all the different ways in which Z can take the value z. If $X=0$ then $Y=z$. If $X=1$ then $Y=z-1$, etc.
$= \displaystyle\sum_{r=0}^{r=z} P(X=r)P(Y=z-r)$	Rewriting in sigma notation to keep the expression shorter.
$= \displaystyle\sum_{r=0}^{r=z} \frac{\lambda^r e^{-\lambda}}{r!} \times \frac{\mu^{z-r} e^{-\mu}}{(z-r)!}$	Using the formula for the Poisson distribution.
$= e^{-\lambda} e^{-\mu} \displaystyle\sum_{r=0}^{r=z} \frac{\lambda^r}{r!} \times \frac{\mu^{z-r}}{(z-r)!}$	Factors of $e^{-\lambda}$ and $e^{-\mu}$ can be taken out of the sum since they are constants.
$= \dfrac{e^{-(\lambda+\mu)}}{z!} \displaystyle\sum_{r=0}^{r=z} \frac{z!}{r!(z-r)!} \lambda^r \mu^{z-r}$	You are close to having a binomial coefficient. Multiply by $z!$ in the sum to get to this, but then you have to divide by $z!$ too.
$= \dfrac{e^{-(\lambda+\mu)}}{z!} \displaystyle\sum_{r=0}^{r=z} \binom{z}{r} \lambda^r \mu^{z-r}$	Replace the factorials with a binomial coefficient.
$= \dfrac{e^{-(\lambda+\mu)}(\lambda+\mu)^z}{z!}$	You can recognise the sum as a binomial expansion.

which is a Poisson distribution with mean $\lambda + \mu$.

WORKED EXAMPLE 3.3

Hywel receives an average of 4.2 emails and 3.1 texts each hour. These are the only types of messages he receives.

a Assuming that the number of emails and texts each follow independent Poisson distributions, find the probability that he receives more than four messages in an hour.

b Explain why the assumption that the emails and texts follow independent Poisson distributions is unlikely to be true.

a Z = 'Number of messages per hour'	
$Z \sim \text{Po}(7.3)$	You can use Key point 3.2 to combine the two Poisson distributions.

Continues on next page …

$P(Z > 4) = 1 - P(Z \leqslant 4)$

$= 0.853 \ (3 \text{ s.f.})$

You need to write the required probability in terms of a cumulative probability to use the calculator function.

b The rate of arrival of messages is unlikely to be constant – there will probably be more at some times of the day than others. Within each distribution messages are not likely to be independent as they might occur as part of a conversation. The two distributions are also probably not independent of each other, as times when more emails arrive might be similar to times when more texts might arrive.

WORK IT OUT 3.1

The number of errors in a computer code is believed to follow a Poisson distribution with a mean of 2.1 errors per 100 lines of code. Find the probability that there are more than 2 errors in 200 lines of code. Which is the correct solution? Can you identify the errors made in the incorrect solutions?

Solution 1	If X is the number of errors in 200 lines then $X \sim \text{Po}(4.2)$. $P(X > 2) = 1 - P(X \leqslant 2) = 1 - (P(X=0) + P(X=1) + P(X=2)) \approx 0.790$
Solution 2	If X is the number of errors in 100 lines then $X \sim \text{Po}(2.1)$. More than 2 errors in 200 lines is equivalent to more than 1 error in 100 lines, so you need $P(X > 1) = 1 - P(X \leqslant 1) = 1 - (P(X=0) + P(X=1)) = 0.620$
Solution 3	$X \sim \text{Po}(4.2)$. $P(X > 2) = 1 - P(X < 2) = 1 - (P(X=1) + P(X=0)) \approx 0.952$

EXERCISE 3A

1 State the distribution of the variable in each of the following situations.

a Cars pass under a motorway bridge at an average rate of six per 10 second period.

   i The number of cars passing under the bridge in one minute.

   ii The number of cars passing under the bridge in 15 seconds.

b Leaks occur in water pipes at an average rate of twelve per kilometre.

   i The number of leaks in 200 m.

   ii The number of leaks in 10 km.

c Twelve worms are found on average in a 1 m² area of a garden.

   i The number of worms found in a 0.3 m² area.

   ii The number of worms found in a 2 m by 2 m area of garden.

2 Calculate the following probabilities.

   a If $X \sim \text{Po}(2)$:   **i** $\text{P}(X=3)$ **ii** $\text{P}(X=1)$.

   b If $Y \sim \text{Po}(1.4)$:   **i** $\text{P}(Y \leqslant 3)$ **ii** $\text{P}(Y \leqslant 1)$.

   c If $Z \sim \text{Po}(7.9)$:   **i** $\text{P}(Z < 6)$ **ii** $\text{P}(Z < 10)$.

   d If $X \sim \text{Po}(5.9)$:   **i** $\text{P}(X \geqslant 3)$ **ii** $\text{P}(X > 1)$.

   e If $X \sim \text{Po}(11.4)$:   **i** $\text{P}(8 < X < 11)$ **ii** $\text{P}(8 \leqslant X \leqslant 12)$.

3 A random variable X follows a Poisson distribution with mean 1.7.
Copy and complete the following table of probabilities, giving results to three significant figures:

x	1	2	3	4	>4
$\text{P}(X=x)$					

4 From a particular observatory, shooting stars are observed in the night sky at an average rate of one every five minutes. Assuming that this rate is constant and that shooting stars occur (and are observed) independently of each other, what is the probability that more than 20 are seen over a period of one hour?

5 When examining blood from a healthy individual under a microscope, a haematologist knows they should see on average four white blood cells in each high-power field. Find the probability that blood from a healthy individual will show:

   a seven white blood cells in a single high-power field

   b a total of 28 white blood cells in 6 high-power fields, selected independently.

6 A wire manufacturer is looking for flaws. Experience suggests that there are on average 1.8 flaws per metre in the wire.

   a Determine the probability that there is exactly one flaw in one metre of the wire.

   b Determine the probability that there is at least one flaw in two metres of the wire.

A 7 The random variable X has a Poisson distribution with mean 5. Calculate:

   a $\text{P}(X \leqslant 5)$ **b** $\text{P}(3 < X \leqslant 5)$ **c** $\text{P}(X \neq 4)$ **d** $\text{P}(3 < X \leqslant 5 \mid X \leqslant 5)$.

A 8 The number of eagles observed in a forest in one day follows a Poisson distribution with mean 1.4.

   a Find the probability that more than three eagles will be observed on a given day.

   b Given that at least one eagle is observed on a particular day, find the probability that exactly two eagles are seen that day.

9 The random variable X follows a Poisson distribution. Given that $\text{P}(X \geqslant 1) = 0.6$, find:

   a the mean of the distribution   **b** $\text{P}(X > 2)$.

10 Let X be a random variable with a Poisson distribution, such that $\text{P}(X > 2) = 0.3$. Find $\text{P}(X < 2)$.

11 The number of emails you receive per day follows a Poisson distribution with mean 6. Let D be the number of emails received in one day and W the number of emails received in a seven-day week.

   a Calculate $\text{P}(D=6)$ and $\text{P}(W=42)$.

   b Find the probability that you receive six emails every day in a seven-day week.

   c Explain why this is not the same as $\text{P}(W=42)$.

12 The number of mistakes a teacher makes while marking homework has a Poisson distribution with a mean of 1.6 errors per piece of homework.

    a Find the probability that there are at least two marking errors in a randomly chosen piece of homework.

    b Find the most likely number of marking errors occurring in a piece of homework. Justify your answer.

    c Find the probability that in a class of twelve pupils fewer than half of them have errors in their marking.

A **13** A car company has two limousines that it hires out by the day. The number of requests per day has a Poisson distribution with mean 1.3 requests per day.

    a Find the probability that neither limousine is hired.

    b Find the probability that some requests have to be denied.

    c If each limousine is to be equally used, on how many days in a period of 365 days would you expect a particular limousine to be in use?

14 The random variable X follows a Poisson distribution with mean λ. If $P(X=2) = P(X=0) + P(X=1)$, find the exact value of λ.

15 The random variable Y follows a Poisson distribution with mean λ.

    a Show that $P(Y = y+2) = \dfrac{\lambda^2}{(y+1)(y+2)} P(Y = y)$.

    b Given that $\lambda = 6\sqrt{2}$, find the value of y such that $P(Y = y+2) = P(Y = y)$.

Checklist of learning and understanding

- To use the Poisson distribution you need the following conditions to hold:
  - the events must occur randomly
  - the events must be independent of each other
  - the average rate of the events must be constant (conventionally called λ).
- If $X \sim \text{Po}(\lambda)$ then:

  for $x = 0, 1, 2 \ldots$

  $E(X) = \lambda$

  $\text{Var}(X) = \lambda$.

- If $X \sim \text{Po}(\lambda)$, $Y \sim \text{Po}(\mu)$ and $Z = X + Y$ then $Z \sim \text{Po}(\lambda + \mu)$.

Mixed practice 3

1 The random variable R represents the number of robins who visit a bird table each hour. The random variable T represents the number of thrushes who visit the bird table each hour. These are the only types of birds who visit the table.

It is believed that $R \sim \text{Po}(1.5)$ and $T \sim \text{Po}(2.0)$.

B is the random variable 'Number of birds visiting the table each hour'.

a Stating a necessary assumption, write down the distribution of B.

b Find the probability that no birds visit the table in one hour.

c Find $P(1 < B \leqslant 6)$.

2 X is the random variable 'number of burgers ordered per hour in a restaurant'. It is thought that $X \sim \text{Po}(4.1)$.

a Write down two conditions required for the Poisson distribution to model data.

b Find $P(1 < X \leqslant 10)$.

3 Salah is sowing flower seeds in his garden. He scatters seeds randomly so that the number of seeds falling on any particular region is a random variable with a Poisson distribution, with mean value proportional to the area. He intends to sow 50 000 seeds over an area of 2 m².

a Calculate the expected number of seeds falling on a 1 cm² region.

b Calculate the probability that a given 1 cm² area receives no seeds.

4 **a** If $X \sim \text{Po}(10)$ write down $E(X)$ and $\text{Var}(X)$.

b Hence find $P(E(X) - \sigma < X < E(X) + \sigma)$ where σ is the standard deviation of X.

5 Seven observations of the random variable X, the number of power surges per day in a power cable, are shown as follows:

$$1, 1, 2, 2, 3, 4, 6$$

a Calculate the mean and standard deviation of this sample.

b Use your answer to part **a** to explain why the Poisson distribution could be a plausible model for X.

6 A receptionist at a hotel answers on average 35 phone calls a day.

a Find the probability that on a particular day she will answer more than 40 phone calls.

b Find the probability that she will answer more than 35 phone calls every day during a five-day week.

7 During the month of August in Bangalore, India, there are on average eleven rainy days.

a Find the probability that there are fewer than seven rainy days during the month of August in a particular year.

b Find the probability that in ten consecutive years, exactly five have fewer than seven rainy days in August.

8 The random variable X follows a Poisson distribution. Given that $P(X \geqslant 1) = 0.4$, find:

    a the mean of the distribution   **b** $P(2 < X < 6)$.

9 **a** Given that $X \sim \text{Po}(m)$ and $P(X = 0) = 0.305$ find the value of m.

    b $Y \sim \text{Po}(k)$. Find the possible values of k such that $P(Y = 1) = 0.2$.

    c If $W \sim \text{Po}(\lambda)$ and $P(W = w + 1) = P(W = w)$ express w in terms of λ.

10 A geyser erupts randomly. The eruptions at any given time are independent of one another and can be modelled using a Poisson distribution with mean 20 per day.

    a Determine the probability that there will be exactly one eruption between 10 a.m. and 11 a.m.

    b Determine the probability that there are more than 22 eruptions during one day.

    c Determine the probability that there are no eruptions in the 30 minutes Naomi spends watching the geyser.

    d Find the probability that the first eruption of a day occurs between 3 a.m. and 4 a.m.

    e If each eruption produces 12 000 l of water, find the expected volume of water produced in a week.

    f Determine the probability that there will be at least one eruption in at least six out of the eight hours the geyser is open for public viewing.

(A) **g** Given that there is at least one eruption in an hour, find the probability that there is exactly one eruption.

11 In a particular town, rainstorms occur at an average rate of two per week and can be modelled using a Poisson distribution.

    a What is the probability of at least eight rainstorms occurring during a particular four-week period?

    b Given that the probability of at least one rainstorm occurring in a period of n complete weeks is greater than 0.99, find the least possible value of n.

(A) 12 Patients arrive at random at an emergency room in a hospital at the rate of fourteen per hour throughout the day.

    a Find the probability that exactly four patients will arrive at the emergency room between 18:00 and 18:15.

    b Given that fewer than 15 patients arrive in 1 hour, find the probability that more than 12 arrive.

13 A shop has four copies of the magazine 'Ballroom Dancing Weekly' delivered each week. Any unsold copies are returned. The demand for the magazine follows a Poisson distribution with mean 3.2 requests per week.

    a Calculate the probability that the shop cannot meet the demand in a given week.

    b Find the most probable number of books sold in one week.

    c Find the expected number of books sold in one week.

    d Determine the smallest number of copies of the book that should be ordered each week to ensure that the demand is met with a probability of at least 98 per cent.

14 **i** The number of inhabitants of a village who are selected for jury service in the course of a 10-year period is a random variable with the distribution Po(4.2).

    a Find the probability that in the course of a 10-year period, at least 7 inhabitants are selected for jury service.

    b Find the probability that in 1 year, exactly 2 inhabitants are selected for jury service.

  ii Explain why the number of inhabitants of the village who contract influenza in 1 year can probably not be well modelled by a Poisson distribution.

© OCR, GCE Mathematics, Paper 4733, June 2010

  15 In a large city the number of traffic lights that fail in one day of 24 hours is denoted by Y. It may be assumed that failures occur randomly.

  i Explain what the statement 'failures occur randomly' means.

  ii State, in context, two different conditions that must be satisfied if Y is to be modelled by a Poisson distribution, and for each condition explain whether you think it is likely to be met in this context.

  iii For this part you may assume that Y is well modelled by the distribution Po(λ). It is given that $P(Y=7) = P(Y=8)$. Use an algebraic method to calculate the value of λ and hence calculate the corresponding value of $P(Y=7)$.

© OCR, GCE Mathematics, Paper 4733, January 2013

4 Non-parametric hypothesis tests

In this chapter you will learn:

- what is meant by a non-parametric hypothesis test and how to select an appropriate test
- how to perform a single-sample sign test and a single-sample Wilcoxon signed-rank test
- how to perform a paired-sample sign test, a Wilcoxon matched-pairs signed-rank test and a Wilcoxon rank-sum test
- how to perform the Wilcoxon signed-rank test and the rank-sum test using a normal approximation.

Before you start…

A Level Mathematics Student Book 1, Chapter 17	You should know how to calculate probabilities from a binomial distribution.	1 If $X \sim B(10, 0.2)$ find $P(X < 3)$.
A Level Mathematics Student Book 1, Chapter 18	You should know how to use the principles of hypothesis testing.	2 A dice is believed to be biased towards rolling '5's. Test at the 5 per cent significance level to see whether the dice is biased if it gets three '5's in six rolls.
A Level Mathematics Student Book 2, Chapter 17	You should know how to calculate probabilities from a normal distribution.	3 If $X \sim N(4, 25)$ find $P(X > 3)$.

What are non-parametric tests?

Hypothesis tests are designed to make decisions about a population based on a sample from that population. This often requires already having some knowledge about the population – particularly its distribution. For example, a binomial test requires the assumption that the underlying population follows a binomial distribution. If you have covered the hypothesis test for a mean (from A Level), that requires the assumption that the underlying distribution was normal. A non-parametric test makes far fewer assumptions about the distribution of the population, and does not need the data to be drawn from a specific distribution. This is usually done by replacing the original data with simpler information such as its rank within the sample.

Section 1: The single-sample sign test

This is a test that allows us to decide whether the median is different from a particular value. For example:

H_0: Median is 5.

H_1: Median is not 5.

Based on H_0 being true, you would expect half the data to be above five and half to be below five. You can therefore model the sample by just looking at the random variable 'number of values above five', excluding any values that equal the median. You would expect this to follow a binomial distribution.

Tip

You could also look at the 'number of values below five' – you would get the same result.

🔑 Key point 4.1

To conduct a single-sample sign test on a sample of size n:

- Count the number of observed values above the median according to the null hypothesis.
- Find the **p-value**. This is the probability of the observed value or more extreme using the $B(n, 0.5)$ distribution. Remember that for a two-tailed test 'more extreme' means further from the centre in either direction.

WORKED EXAMPLE 4.1

Test the following data at the 10% significance level to see if the median has changed from 120:

$$134, 123, 188, 149, 112$$

H_0: Median $= 120$
H_1: Median $\neq 120$

If X is the number of values above 120 then
$X \sim B(5, 0.5)$

You could also have chosen the number of values less than 120.

The distribution will always be $B(n, 0.5)$

You observe $X = 4$. This has a p-value of 0.375.

The p-value is the probability of this result or more extreme, i.e.
$P(X=4) + P(X=5) + P(X=0) + P(X=1)$.

You can visualise this graphically:

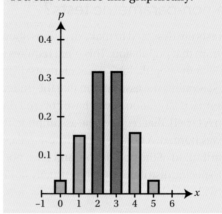

You therefore do not reject H_0. There is not significant evidence of a change in the median.

The p-value is greater than 10%, so the observed value is reasonably likely to be seen while H_0 is true.

If you want to use a one-tailed test, you must look at just those deviations in the direction of the alternative hypothesis.

WORKED EXAMPLE 4.2

Test the following data at the 10% significance level to see if the median is below 50:

$$44, 44, 48, 46, 41, 48, 52$$

H_0: Median $= 50$
H_1: Median < 50
If X is the number of values below 50 then
$X \sim B(7, 0.5)$
You observe $X = 6$. This has a p-value of 0.0625.

The p-value is the probability of this result or more extreme, i.e. $P(X = 6) + P(X = 7)$.

You therefore reject H_0. There is significant evidence that the median is below 50.

The p-value is less than 10%.

EXERCISE 4A

1 Test the following data at the 20% significance level to see if the median has changed from 80:
45, 60, 85, 100, 115, 130, 150.

2 Test the following data at the 10% significance level to see if the median has changed from 100:
40, 40, 40, 45, 75, 80, 95, 95, 102, 108.

3 Test the following data at the 10% significance level to see if the median has increased above 4.5:
1.3, 4.8, 4.9, 5.1, 5.5.

4 a What is the difference between a parametric and a non-parametric test?

b A teacher believes that the median score of her class in a test will be over 60 per cent. In a sample of 28 students, 19 score over 60 per cent. Test the teacher's belief at the 10 per cent significance level.

5 In a restaurant survey, people could give between zero and four stars to rate their service.
The following table shows the results of the survey:

Number of stars	1	2	3	4
Frequency	16	19	12	8

Use the single-sample sign test to determine at the 5% significance level whether the underlying median number of stars for the whole population is less than 2.5.

6 In a sample of 20 observations, n are less than 200. Find the smallest value of n so that in a two-tailed test the hypothesis 'the median is 200' is rejected at the 10% significance level.

Section 2: The single-sample Wilcoxon signed-rank test

The single-sample sign test is very simple, but in only looking at whether data is above or below the median it throws away a lot of information. You can improve this by looking at the **signed ranks**. This is the data ranked by distance away from the suggested median. A positive number is associated with the data above the suggested median and a negative number is associated with data below the suggested median. Key point 4.2 summarises how this can be used to create a test statistic.

> ### 🔑 Key point 4.2
>
> 1   Assign ranks to the differences from the median in order of increasing size.
> 2   Add a negative sign to ranks from data below the median.
> 3 W_+ is the sum of all the positive ranks.
> 4 W_- is the modulus of the sum of all the negative ranks.
> 5 T is the smaller of W_+ and W_-
> 6   Use the table in the formula book to determine the result of the test.
>
> Your formula book contains an abbreviated version of these instructions.

For each value of n, the table in the formula book gives the largest value of T that will lead to rejection of the null hypothesis at the level of significance indicated. The signed-rank test assumes that the population distribution is symmetrical.

WORKED EXAMPLE 4.3

Use the single-sample Wilcoxon signed-rank test at the 10% significance level to test for a difference from a median of ten in the following data:

$$3.1, 5.2, 7.7, 8.1, 9.2, 12.0, 15.9$$

H_0: Median $= 10$

H_1: Median $\neq 10$

Value	3.1	5.2	7.7	8.1	9.2	12.0	15.9
Difference	−6.9	−4.8	−2.3	−1.9	−0.8	2.0	5.9
|Difference|	6.9	4.8	2.3	1.9	0.8	2.0	5.9
Rank	7	5	4	2	1	3	6
Signed-rank	−7	−5	−4	−2	−1	3	6

Create a table of differences from the suggested median and ranks.

$W_+ = 3 + 6 = 9$ and

$W_- = |(-7) + (-5) + (-4) + (-2) + (-1)| = 19$

Assign each rank to the + or − group, and take the modulus of the W_- group so they can be compared.

So $T = 9$

The lowest value is the observed T-value.

Continues on next page …

From the table the critical value when $n = 7$ is 3. ·········· Two-tailed 0.10 value from the table of critical values for T.

The observed T-value is above this value, so you cannot reject H_0. ········· Anything above 3 means H_0 should not be rejected.

EXERCISE 4B

1 A single-sample Wilcoxon signed-rank test is conducted on a sample of size n. Test whether the following results are significant:

   a   **i** $n = 20$, $T = 44$, two-tailed 10% significance

        ii $n = 18$, $T = 32$, two-tailed 1% significance.

   b   **i** $n = 12$, $T = 10$, one-tailed 1% significance

        ii $n = 15$, $T = 28$, one-tailed 5% significance.

   c   **i** $n = 6$, $T = 2$, two-tailed 10% significance

        ii $n = 11$, $T = 10$, two-tailed 10% significance.

2 As part of a single-sample Wilcoxon signed-rank test, the difference from the median according to the null hypothesis was found and ranked:

    $1+ 2+ 3+ 4- 5- 6- 7- 8- 9- 10-$

   The sign after each rank denotes whether it was a positive or negative difference.

   Conduct a two-tailed test at the 5% significance level.

3 Test using the single-sample Wilcoxon signed-rank test at 5% significance to determine whether there is evidence that the following data is drawn from a population with a median above 100.

    90, 95, 103, 106, 108, 112, 125, 168

4 **a** When is it more appropriate to use a Wilcoxon signed-rank test rather than a test for the mean using a normal distribution?

Tip

In the real world you will often see masses colloquially referred to as weights.

   A random sample of weights, in kg, of eight children is:

    21.0, 23.0, 24.5, 26, 28.4, 29.6, 30.2, 31.4

   b Use the single-sample Wilcoxon signed-rank test to determine at the 5% significance level if the median is above 25 kg.

5 A single-sample Wilcoxon signed-rank test at 5% significance is used to test if a median is above 15 cm. A sample of 16 data items is found to have $W_+ = 116$. Determine if the null hypothesis can be rejected.

Section 3: Matched-pairs (or paired-sample) tests

A very common question statisticians ask is if there is a difference between two groups. If the data in the two groups are paired (for example, if each pair of values measures the same person at two different times) then you can find the difference between pairs and test the result using either a sign test or a Wilcoxon signed-rank test.

Technically the null hypothesis is that the two groups are drawn from populations with identical distributions. Rejecting the null hypothesis just means that the two populations are different in some way.

However, a common additional assumption is that the shapes of both distributions are the same. If this is the case then any difference between the two groups is due to a difference in the median, such as that shown in the following diagram.

Remember, that to use the Wilcoxon signed-rank test, the data (in this case the differences) must be drawn from a symmetric distribution. If the two distributions have the same shape then it turns out that the difference will follow a symmetric distribution.

Explore

If the Wilcoxon matched-pairs signed-rank test produces a significant result we can conclude that there is significant evidence that the distributions are different, but just because there is no significant result does not mean that the distributions really are identical. There are lots of ways in which the distributions might differ which are not picked up by this test. A more powerful test which can pick up more differences is called the Kolmogorov-Smirnov test. You might want to explore how this test works.

Key point 4.3

If the data occur in matched pairs find the differences between the pairs and test this difference using either the sign test or the Wilcoxon signed-rank test.

If the shapes of both distributions are the same then any difference can be attributed to a difference in medians.

WORKED EXAMPLE 4.4

Eight people tried to complete two Sudoku puzzles. The following table shows the time taken in minutes for each person to complete each puzzle.

a Use the matched-pairs Wilcoxon signed-rank test at 10% significance to determine if Puzzle 1 generally takes a different amount of time to complete than Puzzle 2.

b What further assumption would be required to test to see if the median time taken to complete the two puzzles was different?

Person	A	B	C	D	E	F	G	H
Puzzle 1	16	15	10	5	24	15	16	Could not complete
Puzzle 2	12	14	12	9.5	16	10	22	32

Continues on next page ...

a $d =$ Puzzle 1 time − Puzzle 2 time

> Define which difference you are using. Either would work, but you must be clear.

H_0: The distribution of time taken to solve the two puzzles is the same.

H_1: The distribution of time taken to solve the two puzzles is the difference.

Person	A	B	C	D	E	F	G	H
d	4	1	−2	−4.5	8	5	−6	??
Rank	3	1	2	4	7	5	6	8
Signed-rank	3	1	−2	−4	7	5	−6	8

> Construct the differences and rank them. For person H it is not possible to calculate d, but it is reasonable to interpret being unable to complete as 'taking a very long time' so you can give this result a rank of 8.

$W_+ = 3 + 1 + 7 + 5 + 8 = 24$

$W_- = |-2 + -4 + -6| = 12$

So $T = 12$.

The critical value when $n = 8$ is 5 so you cannot reject H_0. There is no significant evidence either puzzle is harder, based on their completion times.

> T is greater than the table value, so H_0 is retained.

b You would need to assume that the shape of the distribution of the two puzzles was the same and they only differed in location.

WORKED EXAMPLE 4.5

The heart rate of a group of six patients before and after taking a tablet was measured. The results, in beats per minute (bpm), are shown in the following table:

Patient	A	B	C	D	E	F
Heart rate before	48	88	66	72	72	66
Heart rate after	64	92	77	70	84	79

Assuming that the shape of the distribution of heart rates before and after differs only in its location, use a paired sign test at 10% significance to determine if the median heart rate after is more than 10 bpm more than the heart rate before.

$d =$ heart rate after - heart rate before.

H_0: median of $d = 10$

H_1: median of $d > 10$

> Since the shape of the distribution differs only in its location the null and alternative hypotheses can be written in terms of the median.

Patient	A	B	C	D	E	F
d	16	4	11	−2	12	13
Sign of $(d − 10)$	+	−	+	−	+	+

> Evaluate d for each patient and look at whether or not this difference is greater than 10.

Continues on next page ...

$p-\text{value} = P(2 \text{ or fewer} - \text{signs}) \approx 0.344 > 0.1$

If H_0 is true then the number of $-$ signs will follow a $B(6, 0.5)$ distribution. You can use your calculator to evaluate the probabilities from this distribution. We could also have worked out the probability of getting four or more $+$ signs; it would have given the same answer.

Therefore there is not significant evidence of a difference between the median heart rates.

EXERCISE 4C

1   Conduct a matched-pairs sign test on the following data to see if there is a difference between group A and group B at 10% significance.

A	10	14	17	16	14	12	6
B	21	16	20	35	18	10	−3

2   Conduct a matched-pairs sign test on the following data to see if there is an increase from A to B at 10% significance.

A	175	163	152	144	166	201	187
B	184	160	155	160	169	204	199

3   Conduct a matched-pairs Wilcoxon signed-rank test on the following data to see if there is a difference between group A and group B at 5% significance.

A	6	12	14	16	7	10	20
B	11	18	20	26	18	8	19

4   Conduct a matched-pairs Wilcoxon signed-rank test on the following data to see if there is an increase from A to B at 5% significance.

A	−3	1	10	7	12	16
B	2	0	15	6.5	15	20.5

5   A study is conducted to see if men tend to be older than their wives. A random sample of ten couples was conducted and the following data collected:

Couple	A	B	C	D	E	F	G	H	I	J
Husband's age	28	33	46	56	42	56	77	28	52	60
Wife's age	25	28	45	60	40	42	60	34	39	51

Conduct a matched-pairs Wilcoxon signed-rank test at the 5% significance level to see if this sample supports the idea that men tend to be older than their wives.

6 The time taken (in minutes) for six families to travel from Manchester to Leeds and back is recorded:

Family	A	B	C	D	E	F
Outward journey	56	84	71	60	74	56
Return Journey	58	80	76	55	80	Car broke down

Conduct an appropriate non-parametric test at the 5% significance level to determine if this sample supports the idea that return journeys tend to take longer than outward journeys.

7 The productivity in eight randomly sampled countries was measured in 2000 and 2010. The results, in dollars per day per person, are shown in the following table:

Country	A	B	C	D	E	F	G	H
Productivity (2000)	124	120	84	93	218	154	175	117
Productivity (2010)	158	158	112	117	253	184	190	146

Assume that the shape of the distribution of productivity before and after differs only in its location.

a Use a paired-sign test at 5% significance to determine if the median productivity in 2010 is more than 20 dollars per day per person more than the productivity in 2000.

b What would be the advantage of using a Wilcoxon matched-pairs signed-rank test instead of the test in part **a**?

Section 4: Wilcoxon rank-sum test

There are many situations when it is interesting to compare the medians of two groups that are not paired. If the two groups are independent you can use a Wilcoxon rank-sum test to test the null hypothesis that the two distributions are different. If you also assume that the distributions have the same shape then this can be used to test for a difference (one-tailed or two-tailed) between the medians of the two groups. Key point 4.4 shows how to do this.

> **i) Did you know?**
>
> An alternative version of the Wilcoxon rank-sum test is called the Mann-Whitney U test. Although the formula and tables are slightly different it turns out to be totally equivalent. If you read around this topic you might meet the alternative name.

> **Key point 4.4**
>
> To conduct a Wilcoxon rank-sum test:
>
> 1 The two samples have sizes m and n where $m \leqslant n$.
> 2 Rank all the values from both samples in order of increasing size (the lowest value getting a rank of one).
> 3 R_m is the sum of the ranks of the items in the sample of size m. W is the smaller of R_m and $m(m+n+1) - R_m$.
> 4 Use the tables of critical values of W to conduct the test.
>
> Your formula book contains an abbreviated version of these instructions.

For each pair of values of m and n, the table gives the largest value of W that will lead to rejection of the null hypothesis at the level of significance indicated.

The quantity $m(m+n+1) - R_m$ is the rank-sum that would have been obtained for the sample of size m if the values had been ranked in order of *decreasing* size (the other way round to R_m).

WORKED EXAMPLE 4.6

The following data shows the results in a test of a sample of students from two different countries. Test at the 5% significance level if there is a difference in the median test score of students in the two countries.

Country A: 48, 69, 53, 51   Country B: 46, 75, 49, 50, 55.

H_0: The median of the two countries is the same.

H_1: The median of the two countries is different.

Frequently the assumption that the distributions have the same shape is made implicitly, and the null and alternative hypotheses are written in terms of the median.

A	Rank	B	Rank
		46	1
48	2		
		49	3
		50	4
51	5		
53	6		
		55	7
69	8		
		75	9

Put the data for both countries in order and rank them, lowest at the top.

$m = 4, n = 5$

State m and n.

$R_m = 21$

$4 \times (4 + 5 + 1) - 21 = 19$

Find R_m as the sum of the ranks of country A. You also need to find $m(m + n + 1) - R_m$.

So $W = 19$.

W is the smaller of the R_m and $m(m + n + 1) - R_m$ values.

The critical value is eleven. The observed value is larger than this so you cannot reject H_0. There is insufficient evidence to conclude that the median score in the two countries is different.

Look up the value in the tables. Make a statement about the result.

💡 Tip

Notice that when using the normal approximation you do not need to calculate T (or W in the Wilcoxon rank-sum test). You can simply calculate how likely you were to see the observed statistic and compare it to the significance level.

EXERCISE 4D

 1   The number of eggs produced by chickens in two farms in a day is given as follows:

A	B
102	108
98	99
75	112
62	125
	146
	155

A Wilcoxon rank-sum test is used to test for a difference between the two farms.

a Write down the null and alternative hypotheses.

b Show that the test statistic, W, is eleven.

c Write down the critical value of the test statistic at the 10% significance level.

d Hence write down the conclusion of the test using a 10% significance level.

2 A Wilcoxon rank-sum test is carried out on a sample of twelve pupils split equally among girls and boys to see if there was a difference between genders in the time spent watching TV. The test statistic, W, was found to be 25. Is this result significant at the 2% level for a two-tailed test?

3 Use a Wilcoxon rank-sum test to determine if there is a difference between the median of the two following populations sampled using a 10% significance level. You may assume that the only difference between the two distributions is in its location.

A	B
2.4	3.0
2.9	2.5
3.1	2.1

4 Use a Wilcoxon rank-sum test to determine if the median value in population B is above the median value in population A, based on the sample shown. Use a 5% significance level. You may assume that the only difference between the two distributions is in its location.

A	B
51	59
60	75
58	80
44	114
55	96
	88

5 A class contains ten boys and ten girls. The number of books read by each pupil across a school year is recorded. The teacher decided to use a Wilcoxon rank-sum test to determine if there was a difference in the median number of books read by different genders across a school year.

a State two assumptions the teacher needs to make in conducting their test.

The teacher found that the sum of the ranks of the number of books for the girls was 124.

b What was the sum of the ranks of the number of books for the boys?

c Carry out the Wilcoxon test at the 10% significance level, stating your conclusion in context.

Section 5: Normal approximations

The tables for the Wilcoxon signed-rank test and the Wilcoxon rank-sum test can only be used for relatively small sample sizes. If your sample is larger than this you need to use the fact that the test statistics – T and W respectively – approximately follow a normal distribution. You can then use this normal distribution to calculate how likely you are to see the observed value (or more extreme) and use this value to conduct the test.

Key point 4.5

For the Wilcoxon signed-rank test, if H_0 is true then both W_+ and W_- can be approximated by the normal distribution with mean $\frac{1}{4}n(n+1)$ and variance $\frac{1}{24}n(n+1)(2n+1)$.

This result can be found in your formula book.

However, there is a slight correction that has to be made to take into account the fact that $W_{+/-}$ is an integer but the normal distribution is for continuous variables. You consider $W_{+/-}$ to cover the interval between $W_{+/-}-0.5$ and $W_{+/-}+0.5$. When calculating the p-value you choose the end that makes the tail as large as possible. Therefore, if $W_{+/-}$ is less than the mean of the normal distribution you choose $W_{+/-}+0.5$, but if it is above the mean of the normal distribution you choose $W_{+/-}-0.5$.

This process is called a **continuity correction**.

WORKED EXAMPLE 4.7

In a Wilcoxon signed-rank test on 32 items the sum of the positive ranks is 196.

Conduct a two-tailed test at the 20% significance level to determine if the median is different from the prior belief.

H_0: The median has not changed.

H_1: The median has changed.

$$W_+ \sim N\left(\frac{1}{4}\times 32 \times 33, \frac{1}{24}\times 32 \times 33 \times 65\right) = N(264, 2860)$$

Using $n = 32$ in Key point 4.5.

$P(W_+ \leqslant 196) \approx P(\text{normal approximation to } W_+ < 196.5) \approx 0.103$

You look at the probability of W_+ being equal or further from the mean than the observed value. Since the observed value is below the mean of the normal you also need a continuity correction adding on 0.5. You find the probability from your calculator...

So the p-value is approximately 0.207.

... then double it to get the p-value because it is just one-tailed and you need both tails. Remember that although you might write intermediate answers to three significant figures you should use the calculator to store answers to get better accuracy.

This is greater than the significance level, so do not reject H_0. There is not significant evidence of a change in the median.

You can also use a normal approximation when doing a Wilcoxon rank-sum test.

Key point 4.6

For the Wilcoxon rank-sum test, if H_0 is true then R_m can be approximated by the normal distribution with mean $\frac{1}{2}m(m+n+1)$ and variance $\frac{1}{12}mn(m+n+1)$.

This result can be found in your formula book.

Again, a continuity correction is needed. If R_m is below the mean, use $R_m + 0.5$. If R_m is above the mean, use $R_m - 0.5$.

WORKED EXAMPLE 4.8

A Wilcoxon rank-sum test is conducted on two sets of data of size 12 and 20. The null hypothesis 'median difference $= 0$' is tested against median difference > 0 at a 10% significance level. The value of R_m was found to be 240. What is the conclusion of the test?

H_0: The median difference $= 0$. H_1: The median difference > 0.	You do not yet know in which direction the difference has been calculated, but this does not matter for the null and alternative hypotheses.
$R_m \sim N = \left(\frac{1}{2} \times 12 \times 33, \frac{1}{12} \times 12 \times 20 \times 33\right) = N(198, 660)$	Put $m = 12$ and $n = 20$ into Key point 4.6.
$P(R_m \geqslant 240) \approx P(\text{normal approximation to}$ $R_m > 239.5) \approx 5.31\%$	It is clear that R_m is above the mean of this normal distribution, so to work out the p-value you need to find out the probability of the observed value or more extreme. Since the value is above the mean of the normal distribution the continuity correction requires subtracting 0.5. To find the probability use the normal distribution function on your calculator.
This is less than 10% so you can reject H_0. There is a significant evidence of an increase in the median between the two groups.	For a one-tailed test you can compare the calculated probability directly with the significance level.

EXERCISE 4E

1 In a Wilcoxon signed-rank test on 48 items the sum of the positive ranks is 456.

Conduct a two-tailed test at the 10% significance level to determine if the median is different from the prior belief.

2 In a Wilcoxon signed-rank test on 40 items the sum of the negative ranks is 406.

Conduct a one-tailed test at the 10% significance level to determine if the median is higher than the prior belief.

3 A Wilcoxon rank-sum test is conducted on two sets of data of size 15 and 25. The null hypothesis 'median difference = 0' is tested against median difference > 0 at a 5% significance level. The value of R_m was found to be 302. By using an appropriate normal approximation, find the conclusion of the test.

4 A Wilcoxon rank-sum test is conducted on two sets of data of size 16 and 18. The null hypothesis 'median difference = 0' is tested against median difference ≠ 0 at a 10% significance level. The value of R_m was found to be 265. What is the conclusion of the test?

Checklist of learning and understanding

- Non-parametric tests do not require detailed knowledge of the underlying distributions of the populations being investigated.
- A single-sample sign test is used to test if the median of a population is different from a prior belief. To conduct a single-sample sign test on a sample of size n:
  - Count the number of observed values above the median according to the null hypothesis.
  - Find the p-value as the probability of this value or more extreme using the B(n, 0.5) distribution.
- A single-sample Wilcoxon signed-rank test is used to test if the median of a population is different from a prior belief:
  - Assign ranks to the differences from the median in order of increasing size.
  - Add a negative sign to ranks from data below the median.
  - W_+ is the sum of all the positive ranks.
  - W_- is the modulus of the sum of all the negative ranks.
  - The test statistic, T, is the smaller of W_+ and W_-.
  - Use the table in the formula book to determine the outcome of the test.
- If the data occurs in matched pairs find the differences between the pairs and test this difference using either the sign test or the Wilcoxon signed-rank test. If the shapes of both distributions are the same then any difference can be attributed to a difference in medians.
- A Wilcoxon rank-sum test is used to look for a difference of the distributions for two unpaired groups. If the shapes of both distributions are the same then any difference can be attributed to a difference in medians.
  - The two samples have sizes m and n where $m \leqslant n$.
  - R_m is the sum of the ranks of the items in the sample of size m, with smaller values getting lower ranks.
  - The test statistic, W, is the smaller of R_m and $m(m+n+1) - R_m$.
  - Use the tables of critical values of W to conduct the test.
- For the Wilcoxon signed-rank test, if H$_0$ is true then both W_+ and W_- can be approximated by the normal distribution with mean $\frac{1}{4}n(n+1)$ and variance $\frac{1}{24}n(n+1)(2n+1)$.
- For the Wilcoxon rank-sum test, if H$_0$ is true then R_m can be approximated by the normal distribution with mean $\frac{1}{2}m(m+n+1)$ and variance $\frac{1}{12}mn(m+n+1)$.
- When using normal approximations a continuity correction is required.

Mixed practice 4

1. Use a single-sample sign test to test the following data at the 10% significance level to see if the median has increased above 3.6.

   1.2, 3.8, 4.9, 5.0, 6.5

2. Conduct a matched-pairs sign test on the following data to see if there is an increase from A to B at 10% significance.

A	7.5	1.6	15.0	4.4	6.8	2.2	8.7
B	9.4	1.0	16.6	6.0	6.9	3.4	9.4

3. A random sample of heights, in metres, of seven children is:

   1.12, 1.18, 1.19, 1.23, 1.30, 1.31, 1.35

   Use the single-sample Wilcoxon signed-rank test to determine at the 5% significance level if the median is above 1.2 m.

4. Conduct a matched-pairs Wilcoxon signed-rank test on the following data to see if there is an increase from A to B at 5% significance.

A	−4	20	12	18	10	9
B	1	2	15	14	17	21

5. **a** Determine if there is a difference between the median of the following two populations sampled, using a 10% significance level.

A	B
2.3	3.4
2.6	2.7
3.5	2.2
	4.8

   b Justify your choice of test.

6. Jack wants to find out if the savings of people in his community are higher at the end of the year compared to the beginning of the year. He records the savings of a random sample of six people from his community. The results are shown in the following table. All numbers are in pounds.

	Janet	Bart	Joachim	Kim	Lionel	Alice
Beginning of year	10 000	250	1000	1500	1450	7000
End of year	0	600	2000	1600	1700	5000

   a State appropriate null and alternative hypotheses for this test.

   b Conduct an appropriate non-parametric test to answer Jack's question. Use a 5% significance level.

7 In a Wilcoxon signed-rank test on 35 items the sum of the negative ranks is 306.

Conduct a one-tailed test at the 10% significance level to determine if the median is higher than the prior belief.

8 A Wilcoxon rank-sum test is conducted on two sets of data of size 20 and 30. The null hypothesis 'median difference = 0' is tested against median difference $\neq 0$ at a 5% significance level. The value of R_m was found to be 489. By using an appropriate normal approximation, find the conclusion of the test.

9 A botanist believes that some species of plants produce more flowers at high altitudes than at low altitudes. In order to investigate this belief the botanist randomly samples 11 species of plants each of which occurs at both altitudes. The numbers of flowers on the plants are shown in the table.

Species	1	2	3	4	5	6	7	8	9	10	11
Number of flowers at low altitude	5	3	4	7	2	9	6	5	4	11	2
Number of flowers at high altitude	1	6	10	8	14	16	20	21	15	2	12

i Use the Wilcoxon signed rank test at the 5% significance level to test the botanist's belief.

ii Explain why the Wilcoxon rank sum test should not be used for this test.

© OCR, GCE Mathematics, Paper 4735, June 2011

10 The effect of water salinity on the growth of a type of grass was studied by a biologist. A random sample of 22 seedlings was divided into two groups A and B, each of size 11.
Group A was treated with water of 0% salinity and group B was treated with water of 0.5% salinity. After three weeks the height (in cm) of each seedling was measured with the following results, which are ordered for convenience.

Group A	8.6	9.4	9.7	9.8	10.1	10.5	11.0	11.2	11.8	12.7	12.9
Group B	7.4	8.4	8.5	8.8	9.2	9.3	9.5	9.9	10.0	11.1	11.3

Jeffery was asked to test whether the two treatments resulted, on average, in a difference in growth. He chose the Wilcoxon rank sum test.

i Justify Jeffery's choice of test.

ii Carry out the test at the 5% significance level.

© OCR, GCE Mathematics, Paper 4735, June 2013

Proving the expectation and variance of the binomial distribution

In Chapter 2 you used the formulae for the mean and variance of the binomial distribution: if $X \sim \mathrm{B}(n,p)$ then $\mathrm{E}(X) = np$ and $\mathrm{Var}(X) = npq$. In this section you will prove these facts.

You need to know the formulae for binomial probabilities and the binomial expansion. One part of the proof also involves differentiation using the chain rule.

Questions

1 Expand $(p+q)^n$ where n is a positive integer.

2 Hence prove that if p is the probability of success and $q = 1 - p$ is the probability of failure then:

$$\sum_0^n \binom{n}{r} p^r q^{n-r} = 1$$

3 Explain why $\mathrm{E}(X) = \sum_0^n r \binom{n}{r} p^r q^{n-r}$.

A **4** By differentiating $(p + q)^n$ with respect to p (treating q as a constant) prove that $\mathrm{E}(X) = np$.

5 By writing the binomial coefficient in terms of factorials, explain why $r \binom{n}{r} = n \binom{n-1}{r-1}$.

Hence prove that $\mathrm{E}(X) = np$.

6 Show that $\mathrm{E}(X^2) = \mathrm{E}(X) + \sum_0^n r(r-1) \binom{n}{r} p^{n-r} q^r$. Hence prove that $\mathrm{Var}(X) = npq$.

FOCUS ON ... PROBLEM SOLVING 1

Getting the parameters of a distribution

Often you are not told directly the parameters of a distribution, but have to infer them from given information. If this is the case, sometimes the equations will be impossible to solve directly so you have to use technology to solve them.

WORKED EXAMPLE

In a Poisson distribution the probability of two events occurring is 0.1. Find the probability of one event occurring.

If $X \sim Po(m)$ then

$$P(X = 2) = \frac{m^2 e^{-m}}{2} = 0.1$$

Write the information given in terms of m, the parameter of the Poisson distribution.

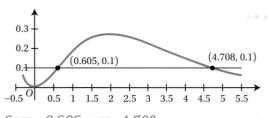

(0.605, 0.1)   (4.708, 0.1)

This equation is not solvable algebraically. You can use graphing software to solve it by finding the intersection of two graphs.

So $m \approx 0.605$ or $m \approx 4.708$.

$P(X = 1) = m e^{-m} \approx 0.330$ or 0.0425

You can read off the value of m from the graph. There are actually two different means which produce the given probability.

Questions

1 If $X \sim Po(m)$ and $P(X = 1) = 0.3$ find $P(X = 0)$.

2 If $X \sim B(10, p)$ and $P(X = 3) = 0.2$ find p.

3 If $X \sim B(n, 0.2)$ and $P(X = 2) = 0.294$ to three decimal places, find n.

4 If $X \sim Geo(p)$ and $P(X = 4) = 0.1$ find p.

5 The probability of a biased coin showing a head is p. In ten throws, one head is observed.

   a Show that the probability of this happening is $10p(1 - p)^9$.

   b In another 14 tosses 2 heads are observed. Show that the probability of this happening and the previous observation happening is $910p^3(1 - p)^{21}$.

   c By using technology or otherwise, find the value of p that maximises the probability of this happening.

🔍 Explore

This type of method is called 'maximum likelihood estimation' and is a very powerful tool in advanced statistics. Research and list the uses of this.

Situations for the Poisson distribution

The Poisson distribution is frequently used to model situations where there is a rate of 'events'. However, it can be misapplied because there are several conditions that must be met.

- The process must be random, so that it is not totally predictable.
- There must be a constant average rate, not something that changes in different areas or over time.
- The events must be independent of each other.

To help you to understand these in context, here are some examples of real-world situations. How appropriate would the Poisson distribution be to model each of the following situations?

Questions

1 The number of fish in a 10 m^3 volume of an ocean where fish occur at an average rate of 3 per m^3.

2 The number of signals received in an hour by a mobile phone from a communication mast when a signal is received on average every 30 seconds.

3 The number of beta particles emitted every minute by a radioactive substance that emits on average one beta particle every 10 seconds.

4 The waiting time for a bus when one arrives on average every 10 minutes.

5 The number of errors in ten pages of a textbook if there is an average of one error on every two pages.

6 The number of fish caught in ten hours in a small pond if an average of ten fish are caught every hour.

7 The number of girls in 100 randomly selected people if you expect 30 per cent of the population to be girls.

8 A binomial distribution $\mathrm{B}\left(n, \dfrac{\lambda}{n}\right)$ when n is very large.

In several of the situations where the Poisson conditions are not perfectly met, in reality, statisticians still use the Poisson model to make useful predictions. This is because all models are imperfect and the errors in estimating the average rate might well be larger than the errors caused by a weak dependency between the events. When interpreting models, it is vital to understand the sources and scales of uncertainty in the output.

▶▶) Fast forward

One sophisticated way to do this is to write the output as a confidence interval. You will learn more about this in Chapter 9.

1 The probability distribution of a discrete random variable, X, is shown below.

x	0	2
$P(X=x)$	a	$1-a$

i Find $E(X)$ in terms of a.   **ii** Show that $Var(X) = 4a(1-a)$

© OCR, AS GCE Mathematics, Paper 4732, January 2011

2 If $X \sim B(12, 0.2)$ find:

a $E(X)$ **b** $P(X < E(X))$.

3 The random variable Y represents the number of soft drinks Boris purchases while eating a burger. Boris models Y using the $U(4)$ distribution.

a Find the standard deviation in Y.

Z is the amount Boris spends on his meal in pounds. If the burger costs £6 and each drink costs £2 find:

b i $E(Z)$ **ii** $Var(Z)$.

4 The discrete random variable X follows the $U(n)$ distribution and satisfies $P(X \geqslant 10) = P(X \leqslant 3)$.

a Find $E(X)$.

b In three independent observations of X, find the probability that fewer than two have $X \leqslant 3$.

5 30% of people own a Talk-2 phone. People are selected at random, one at a time, and asked whether they own a Talk-2 phone. The number of people questioned, up to and including the first person who owns a Talk-2 phone, is denoted by X. Find:

i $P(X=4)$,   **ii** $P(X > 4)$,   **iii** $P(X < 6)$.

© OCR, AS GCE Mathematics, Paper 4732, June 2009

6 The random variable X is the number of minutes Cauchy spends on a mobile phone each month. The mean of X is 250 with standard deviation 50.

Cauchy is on a contract with a fixed charge of £5 each month, then 2p per minute.

a Find the mean and the variance in Y, the amount of money in pounds that Cauchy spends each month on his mobile phone.

b Cauchy has a budget of £25 per month for his phone. Anything that he does not spend on his phone he saves. Find the mean and variance in Z, the amount saved in pounds each month.

7 When a four-sided spinner is spun, the number on which it lands is denoted by X, where X is a random variable taking values 2, 4, 6 and 8. The spinner is biased so that $P(X=x) = kx$, where k is a constant.

i Show that $P(X=6) = \dfrac{3}{10}$.

ii Find $E(X)$ and $Var(X)$.

© OCR, AS GCE Mathematics, Paper 4732, January 2013

8 Find the value of p for which the distribution $B(10, p)$ has the largest possible variance.

9 Three letters are selected at random from the 8 letters of the word COMPUTER, without regard to order.

   i Find the number of possible selections of 3 letters.

   ii Find the probability that the letter P is included in the selection.

Three letters are now selected at random, one at a time, from the 8 letters of the word COMPUTER, and are placed in order in a line.

   iii Find the probability that the 3 letters form the word TOP.

© OCR, AS GCE Mathematics, Paper 4732, June 2009

10 The discrete random variable X follows the $U(n)$ distribution and satisfies $E(X) = Var(X)$.

   a Find the value of n.   **b** Show that $E(2X) \neq Var(2X)$.

11 In a large region of derelict land, bricks are found scattered in the earth.

   i State two conditions needed for the number of bricks per cubic metre to be modelled by a Poisson distribution.

Assume now that the number of bricks in 1 cubic metre of earth can be modelled by the distribution Po(3).

   ii Find the probability that the number of bricks in 4 cubic metres of earth is between 8 and 14 inclusive.

   iii Find the size of the largest volume of earth for which the probability that no bricks are found is at least 0.4.

© OCR, GCE Mathematics, Paper 4733, June 2009

12 In a Wilcoxon signed-rank test on 48 items the sum of the positive ranks is 484.

Conduct a two-tailed test at the 10% significance level to determine if the median is different from the prior belief.

13 An experiment to see the effect of caffeine on reaction times looks at reaction times to catch a dropping ruler when people take caffeine and reaction times when people do not take caffeine.

The following table shows the data. Times are measured in milliseconds.

With caffeine	110	215	136	188	201	214	139	145
Without caffeine	124	225	154	203	234	229	146	150

   a Assuming that the data is given in matched pairs, conduct an appropriate non-parametric hypothesis test at the 5% significance level.

   b Assuming that the data comes from two independent groups, conduct an appropriate non-parametric hypothesis test at the 5% significance level.

   c Explain why it is appropriate to use non-parametric tests rather than parametric tests for these data.

   d Which of the two experimental designs suggested in parts **a** and **b** is more suited to answering the question about whether caffeine has an effect on reaction times? Explain your answer.

14 A doctor's surgery has 4000 patients. On any given day there is a probability of 0.02 of any given patient wanting to see the doctor. It is assumed that this probability is independent of any other patient wanting to see the doctor.

    a According to this model find:

        i the expected number of people visiting the doctor on any given day

        ii the standard deviation in the number of people visiting the doctor on any given day

        iii the probability that more than 90 people want to visit the doctor in a day.

    b It is suggested that the assumption that the probability being independent is false. Suggest reasons why this is likely to be the case in this context.

15 Andy makes repeated attempts to thread a needle. The number of attempts up to and including his first success is denoted by X.

    i State two conditions necessary for X to have a geometric distribution.

    ii Assuming that X has the distribution Geo(0.3), find

        a $P(X = 5)$,   **b** $P(X > 5)$.

    iii Suggest a reason why one of the conditions you have given in part **i** might not be satisfied in this context.

© OCR, AS GCE Mathematics, Paper 4732, January 2010

16 Two drugs, I and II, for alleviating hay fever are trialled in a hospital on each of 12 volunteer patients. Each received drug I on one day and drug II on a different day. After receiving a drug, the number of times each patient sneezed over a period of one hour was noted. The results are given in the table.

Patient	1	2	3	4	5	6	7	8	9	10	11	12
Drug I	11	34	19	16	10	29	6	17	20	13	4	25
Drug II	12	20	10	18	3	21	9	13	10	19	9	12

The patients may be considered to be a random sample of all hay fever sufferers.

A researcher believes that patients taking drug II sneeze less than patients taking drug I.

Test this belief using the Wilcoxon signed rank test at the 5% significance level.

© OCR, GCE Mathematics, Paper 4735, June 2013

17 The five letters of the word NEVER are arranged in random order in a straight line.

    i How many different orders of the letters are possible?

    ii In how many of the possible orders are the two Es next to each other?

    iii Find the probability that the first two letters in the order include exactly one letter E.

© OCR, AS GCE Mathematics, Paper 4732, January 2010

18 Because of the large number of students enrolled for a university geography course and the limited accommodation in the lecture theatre, the department provides a filmed lecture. Students are randomly assigned to two groups, one to attend the lecture theatre and the other the film. At the end of term, the two groups are given the same examination. The geography professor wishes to test whether there is a difference in the performance of the two groups and selects the marks of two random samples of students, 6 from the group attending the lecture theatre and 7 from the group attending the films. The marks for the two samples, ordered for convenience, are shown below.

Lecture theatre	30	36	48	51	59	62	
Filmed lecture	40	49	52	56	63	64	68

Stating a necessary assumption, carry out a suitable non-parametric test, at the 10% significance level, for a difference between the median marks of the two groups.

© OCR, GCE Mathematics, Paper 4735, June 2012 [Abridged]

19 Given that $X \sim Po(m)$ with $m \neq 0$, and $P(X=7) = P(X=8) + P(X=9)$, find the value of m.

  20 R and S are independent random variables each having the distribution Geo(p).

i Find P($R=1$ and $S=1$) in terms of p.

ii Show that P($R=3$ and $S=3$) $= p^2q^4$, where $q = 1-p$.

iii Use the formula for the sum to infinity of a geometric series to show that

$$P(R=S) = \frac{p}{2-p}.$$

© OCR, AS GCE Mathematics, Paper 4732, January 2010

 21 The discrete random variable X satisfies the following distribution:

x	1	2	n
$P(X=x)$	0.25	0.5	0.25

a If $E(X) = 4E\left(\frac{1}{X}\right)$, find the possible values of n.

b For the larger value of n, find the value of $\dfrac{\text{Var}(X)}{\text{Var}\left(\frac{1}{X}\right)}$

  22 i How many different 3-digit numbers can be formed using the digits 1, 2 and 3 when

a no repetitions are allowed,

b any repetitions are allowed,

c each digit may be included at most twice?

ii How many different **4-digit** numbers can be formed using the digits 1, 2 and 3 when each digit may be included at most twice?

© OCR, AS GCE Mathematics, Paper 4732, January 2013

23 The number of bacteria in 1 ml of drug A has a Poisson distribution with mean 0.5. The number of the same bacteria in 1 ml of drug B has a Poisson distribution with mean 0.75. A mixture of these drugs used to treat a particular disease consists of 1.4 ml of drug A and 1.2 ml of drug B. Bacteria in the drugs will cause infection in a patient if 5 or more bacteria are injected.

  i Calculate the probability that, in a sample of 20 patients treated with the mixture, infection will occur in no more than one patient.

  ii State an assumption required for the validity of the calculation.

© OCR, GCE Mathematics, Paper 4734, June 2009

  24 A company wishes to buy a new lathe for making chair legs. Two models of lathe, 'Allegro' and 'Vivace', were trialled. The company asked 12 randomly selected employees to make a particular type of chair leg on each machine. The times, in seconds, for each employee are shown in the table.

Employee	1	2	3	4	5	6	7	8	9	10	11	12
Time on Allegro	162	111	194	159	202	210	183	168	165	150	185	160
Time on Vivace	182	130	193	181	192	205	186	184	192	180	178	189

The company wishes to test whether there is any difference in average times for the two machines.

  i State the circumstances under which a non-parametric test should be used.

  ii Use two different non-parametric tests and show that they lead to different conclusions at the 5% significance level.

  iii State, with a reason, which conclusion is to be preferred.

© OCR, GCE Mathematics, Paper 4735, June 2009

5 Correlation and regression

In this chapter you will learn how to:

- calculate the value of Pearson's product moment correlation coefficient
- calculate the value of Spearman's rank correlation coefficient and identify when it is appropriate to use it
- conduct hypothesis tests on correlation coefficients
- use linear regression to find the equation of a line of best fit.

Before you start…

A Level Mathematics Student Book 1, Chapter 16	You should know how to interpret correlation coefficients.	1	Describe the correlation of a data set with a correlation coefficient of 0.97.
GCSE	You should know how to work with the equations of straight lines.	2	What is the gradient of the line $x + 2y = 5$?
A Level Mathematics Student Book 1, Chapter 16	You should know how to find the variance of a data set.	3	Find the variance of 1, 1, 3, 5.
A Level Mathematics Student Book 1, Chapter 18	You should know how to use the principles of hypothesis testing.	4	Use a two-tailed binomial test at the 5% significance level to determine if a coin is biased if six tails are observed in eight tosses.

Formalising correlation

You have already met correlation coefficients as a way of quantifying the strength of correlation within a set of **bivariate data**. In this chapter you will see two ways of calculating correlation coefficients that measure slightly different things. You will also see how to use the correlation coefficient of the sample to conduct a hypothesis test to see if there is correlation in the population. If you know that there is linear correlation in the population, then it makes sense to try to find the equation of the line of best fit. You will see in this chapter that there is a formal way of finding the equation of this line.

Section 1: Pearson's product moment correlation coefficient

There are several different ways of measuring correlation. One popular correlation coefficient, which measures the strength of linear correlation (how well the data falls in a straight line), is called Pearson's product moment correlation coefficient (ppmcc) and given the symbol r. It is defined in Key point 5.1.

 Tip

You might also see this referred to as just Pearson's correlation coefficient. If you read about a correlation coefficient without any other name associated with it, it is probably Pearson's.

Key point 5.1

$$r = \frac{\sum x_i y_i - \dfrac{\sum x_i \sum y_i}{n}}{\sqrt{\left(\sum x_i^2 - \dfrac{(\sum x_i)^2}{n}\right)\left(\sum y_i^2 - \dfrac{(\sum y_i)^2}{n}\right)}}$$

This will appear in your formula book.

The formula in Key point 5.1 is justified in Focus on... Problem solving 2. The numerator is a measure of how much the points are spread along a diagonal. The brackets in the denominator might remind you of the formula for variance of x and variance of y. The denominator acts to 'standardise' the value of r, ensuring that it is between -1 and 1. This also removes the effect of changing units (also called a linear coding) on the correlation coefficient.

 Rewind

Remember from Chapter 2 that a linear coding is a change of the form $aX + b$.

 Key point 5.2

Any linear coding of either variable does not affect the correlation coefficient.

 Fast forward

Key point 5.2 applies to both the correlation coefficients (Pearson's and Spearman's) that you will meet in this chapter.

To make the calculation of r a little simpler, it can be broken down into parts, as shown in Key point 5.3.

 Key point 5.3

$$S_{xx} = \sum(x_i - \bar{x})^2 = \sum x_i^2 - \frac{(\sum x_i)^2}{n}$$

$$S_{yy} = \sum(y_i - \bar{y})^2 = \sum y_i^2 - \frac{(\sum y_i)^2}{n}$$

$$S_{xy} = \sum(x_i - \bar{x})(y_i - \bar{y}) = \sum x_i y_i - \frac{\sum x_i \sum y_i}{n}$$

$$r = \frac{S_{xy}}{\sqrt{S_{xx} S_{yy}}}$$

This will appear in your formula book.

 Tip

Make sure that you can use your calculator to find ppmcc if the original data is provided.

The information could be provided as raw data, or summarised using any of the sums from Key point 5.3.

WORKED EXAMPLE 5.1

The following data were collected:

Score in a Maths test (x)	42	50	67	71	92
Time spent revising (y)	1	1.2	2	2.3	3

Continues on next page ...

Show that the ppmcc for these data is approximately 0.995.

						Σ
x	42	50	67	71	92	322
x^2	1764	2500	4489	5041	8464	22 258
y	1	1.2	2	2.3	3	9.5
y^2	1	1.44	4	5.29	9	20.73
xy	42	60	134	163.3	276	675.3

If you had just been asked to find the ppmcc you would have used your calculator, but for a 'show that' you need to give the details. It is useful to create a table to find the sums required.

Using the formula with $n = 5$, $S_{xx} = 22\,258 - \dfrac{322^2}{5} = 1521.2$

There are five pairs of data so $n = 5$.

$$S_{yy} = 20.73 - \frac{9.5^2}{5} = 2.68$$

You should always check that both S_{xx} and S_{yy} are positive. S_{xy} is the only one that can be negative.

$$S_{xy} = 675.3 - \frac{322 \times 9.5}{5} = 63.5$$

$$r = \frac{63.5}{\sqrt{1521.2 \times 2.68}} \approx 0.9945 \approx 0.995$$

When showing an approximate value give your answer to one more significant figure first.

The ppmcc of the sample is a random variable that can vary from sample to sample. You can use it to test if there is correlation between the two populations. The symbol ρ (the Greek letter 'rho') is normally used for the population correlation coefficient. You test the null hypothesis that there is not really any correlation:

$$H_0: \rho = 0.$$

Your alternative hypothesis can be two-tailed if you have no prior belief about the direction of the correlation:

$$H_1: \rho \neq 0.$$

It can also be one-tailed if you have a prior belief about the direction of the correlation:

$$H_1: \rho > 0 \qquad \text{or} \qquad H_1: \rho < 0.$$

If both variables follow a normal distribution then the table of critical values can be used to conduct the hypothesis test. The null hypothesis is rejected if the sample correlation coefficient is more than the critical value associated with the sample size (n) and the significance level.

WORKED EXAMPLE 5.2

Phoebe is looking for evidence that the population of cod (c) and the population of tuna (t) (where population is assessed by kilograms of fish caught), in various seas are negatively correlated. She observes eleven pairs of values and summarises her results:

$$\Sigma c = 165, \; \Sigma c^2 = 2585, \; \Sigma t = 81, \; \Sigma t^2 = 757, \; \Sigma ct = 1184$$

a   Find the ppmcc for the data.

b   Conduct an appropriate test at the 5% significance level.

c   Phoebe realises that the numbers she recorded are actually in millions of tonnes. How does this change your answer in parts **a** and **b**?

a $S_{cc} = \Sigma c^2 - \dfrac{(\Sigma c)^2}{n} = 2585 - \dfrac{(165)^2}{11} = 110$

> The variables here are called c and t rather than x and y, but you can transform the standard formulae to write them in terms of c and t.

$S_{tt} = \Sigma t^2 - \dfrac{(\Sigma t)^2}{n} = 757 - \dfrac{(81)^2}{11} \approx 160.5$

> Notice that the values of S_{cc} and S_{tt} both have to be positive, which you can use to check for errors.

$S_{ct} = \Sigma ct - \dfrac{\Sigma c \, \Sigma t}{n} = -31$

> S_{ct} can take negative values.

$r = \dfrac{S_{ct}}{\sqrt{S_{cc} S_{tt}}} \approx \dfrac{-31}{\sqrt{110 \times 160.5}} \approx -0.233$

> r must take a value between -1 and 1.

b   If ρ is the population correlation coefficient:

$H_0 : \rho = 0$, $H_1 : \rho < 0$.

From the table of critical values, the critical value is 0.5214.

> You need to look at the highlighted figure from the formula book.

$|r| < 0.5214$ so you cannot reject H_0.
There is not significant evidence of negative correlation at the 5% significance level.

	5%	2½%	1%	½%	1-Tail Test	5
	10%	5%	2%	1%	2-Tail Test	1(
n					n	
1	-	-	-	-	31	0.3
2	-	-	-	-	32	0.2
3	0.9877	0.9969	0.9995	0.9999	33	0.2
4	0.9000	0.9500	0.9800	0.9900	34	0.2
5	0.8054	0.8783	0.9343	0.9587	35	0.2
6	0.7293	0.8114	0.8822	0.9172	36	0.2
7	0.6694	0.7545	0.8329	0.8745	37	0.2
8	0.6215	0.7067	0.7887	0.8343	38	0.2
9	0.5822	0.6664	0.7498	0.7977	39	0.2
10	0.5494	0.6319	0.7155	0.7646	40	0.2
11	0.5214	0.6021	0.6851	0.7348	41	0.2
12	0.4973	0.5760	0.6581	0.7079	42	0.2

c   Changing the units would just be a linear coding of the data. This will not change the correlation coefficient, so the conclusion is unchanged.

You might also be given a p-value for the observed correlation coefficient and use that to determine if there is significant evidence of correlation. You will see some examples of this in Exercise 5A.

EXERCISE 5A

1 Find the correlation coefficient for the following data:

a **i** (2, –5), (0, 3), (8, 12), (5, 19), (4, 10), (10, 24) **ii** (1,0), (1,3), (2,6), (2,2), (4,4), (5,9)

b **i** (3,15), (17,9), (22,10), (33,7) **ii** (22,50), (54,19), (100,0), (93,12)

c **i** (–2,3), (0,0), (2,1), (3,5), (4,2) **ii** (5,1), (9,3), (7,–2), (8,8)

d **i** (1,3), (2,5), (3,7), (5,11) **ii** (9,1), (4,6), (5,5), (11,–1).

2 Find the correlation coefficient for the following summary statistics:

a **i** $\Sigma x = 501$, $\Sigma x^2 = 33\,629$, $\Sigma y = 550$, $\Sigma y^2 = 43\,122$, $\Sigma xy = 31\,368$, $n = 10$

   ii $\Sigma x = 599$, $\Sigma x^2 = 45\,323$, $\Sigma y = 559$, $\Sigma y^2 = 38\,451$, $\Sigma xy = 28\,468$, $n = 11$

b **i** $\Sigma s = 719$, $\Sigma s^2 = 50\,493$, $\Sigma t = 688$, $\Sigma t^2 = 48\,438$, $\Sigma st = 41\,202$, $n = 12$

   ii $\Sigma a = 577$, $\Sigma a^2 = 43\,665$, $\Sigma b = 454$, $\Sigma b^2 = 26\,486$, $\Sigma ab = 14\,929$, $n = 12$

c **i** $\Sigma(x-\bar{x})^2 = 8904$, $\Sigma(y-\bar{y})^2 = 4604$, $\Sigma(x-\bar{x})(y-\bar{y}) = 3462$, $n = 10$

   ii $\Sigma(x-\bar{x})^2 = 9902$, $\Sigma(y-\bar{y})^2 = 6384$, $\Sigma(x-\bar{y})(y-\bar{y}) = -5130$, $n = 10$.

3 A research study looked at the correlation between the number of doctorates awarded in America and the sales of comic books. The sample ppmcc was found to be positive.

a Explain why this does not mean that there is positive correlation between the two variables being studied.

b A two-tailed test for correlation was conducted and the p-value was found to be 0.0666. What is the conclusion of the test at a 5% significance level?

c If the test had been one-tailed what would the p-value be? What would be the conclusion of the test at a 5% significance level?

4 Average life expectancy and processor speed of the CPU in PCs varied over 20 years as follows:

Year	Processor speed (Hz)	Life expectancy (years)
1990	6.6×10^7	74
1995	1.2×10^8	75
2000	1.0×10^9	77
2005	1.8×10^9	79
2010	2.4×10^9	80

a Calculate the correlation coefficient for the relationship between processor speed and life expectancy.

b Interpret this value.

c Conduct a hypothesis test at the 5% significance level to see if there is any correlation between processor speed and life expectancy.

d Does this result imply that CPU speed affects life expectancy?

5 A road safety group test the braking distance of cars of different ages.

Age in years	Braking distance in metres
3	31.3
6	38.6
7	40.1
7	35.1
9	48.4

   a Find the correlation coefficient between these two variables.

   b Interpret this value.

   c Conduct a two-tailed test for correlation on this data set at the 10% significance level.

   d Sai says that this provides evidence that older cars tend to have longer stopping distances. State with a reason whether you agree with her.

6 The time in education and the income of six different 45-year-olds is recorded:

Years in education	Income ($)
12	64 000
14	31 000
14	36 000
18	54 000
18	62 000
20	48 000

   a Find the correlation coefficient between these two variables.

   b The p-value of this correlation coefficient, for a two-tailed test, is approximately 0.759. Gavin says that this provides evidence that spending more time in education means you will be paid more. State with two reasons whether you agree with him.

7 A paper published in the *New England Journal of Medicine* in 2012 quoted a correlation coefficient of 0.791 between the amount of chocolate consumed in a country and the number of Nobel prize winners per million people in that country. The sample size was 22 countries.

   a Conduct a test at 5% significance to see if there is a correlation between chocolate consumption and Nobel prize winners in a country.

   b State two reasons why this does not mean that eating more chocolate makes you more likely to win a Nobel prize.

8 The following data show the time taken for a chemical reaction to complete at different temperatures. The temperatures were recorded in both degrees Celsius and degrees Fahrenheit:

Temperature in °C (c)	Temperature in °F (f)	Time in seconds (t)
10	50	43
15	59	39
20	68	34
25	77	29
30	86	22
35	95	18
40	104	15

a Find the correlation coefficient between c and t.

b Find the correlation coefficient between f and t.

c Comment on your answers.

9 A sample of size 50 of two random variables, X and Y, has a correlation coefficient of 0.74. A hypothesis test at 5% significance shows evidence of significant correlation. Does this mean that $Y = kX$?

Section 2: Spearman's rank correlation coefficient

When the samples are drawn from populations following a normal distribution, the ppmcc is a very good way to test for correlation. It has a relatively small probability of falsely accepting the null hypothesis (that there is no underlying correlation).

There is another measure of correlation, called Spearman's rank correlation coefficient. When using it to test for underlying correlation there is a slightly higher chance of falsely accepting the null hypothesis, but it has the very big advantage that it can be used when the samples do not come from normally distributed populations.

Spearman's rank correlation coefficient is the correlation coefficient of the **ranks** of each data value.

The formula for Spearman's rank correlation coefficient is given in Key point 5.4.

 Rewind

Because ranks are used instead of the original data values, testing for correlation using Spearman's rank correlation coefficient is an example of a non-parametric test, which you met in Chapter 4.

 Key point 5.4

$$r_s = 1 - \frac{6\Sigma d^2}{n(n^2 - 1)}$$

This will appear in your formula book.

 Focus on ...

This formula is proved in Focus on ... Proof 2.

In this formula d is the difference between the ranks of each item in the paired data and n is the number of data pairs.

The ppmcc is a measure of how linear the data are. Spearman's rank correlation coefficient is a measure of how much one variable increases or decreases with the other. Just knowing that r_s is close to one does not mean that there is a linear relationship. Spearman's rank correlation coefficient can be used to test for some kinds of non-linear association. It can test associations that are either

 Explore

Spearman's rank and ppmcc are probably the two most commonly used measures of correlation, but they are not the only ones. What are the advantages of Kendall's Tau?

increasing or decreasing, but not a mixture of the two. So for example it could test for this type of association:

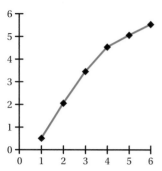

However, it would not pick up the association between these two variables:

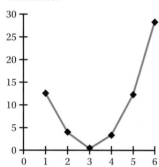

Once Spearman's correlation coefficient has been found it can be used to test for underlying correlation in the population. The process is similar to the process when testing the ppmcc, but the table for Spearman's rank is used instead.

In the null hypothesis for testing Spearman's rank correlation you should not say that you are testing $\rho = 0$ (or even worse $r_s = 0$). You are really testing for correlation among the ranked population, but it is easiest to simply have a null hypothesis stating that there is no association. The alternative hypothesis can then be for an association (two-tailed), or a positive association or a negative association (one-tailed).

WORKED EXAMPLE 5.3

Find the correlation coefficient of the following data set and test at the 10% significance level to see if there is correlation between the two variables.

x	21	56	89	53	47
y	15	40	93	7	78

The ranks are:

Rank x	5	2	1	3	4
Rank y	4	3	1	5	2

These are ranked from high to low. It doesn't matter which way you order the data as long as you choose the same order for both variables.

Continues on next page ...

d	1	−1	0	−2	2
d^2	1	1	0	4	4

You can work out the differences in either direction. The worked example here gives Rank x − Rank y.

$\Sigma d^2 = 10$ and $n = 5$ so:

$$r_s = 1 - \frac{6 \times 10}{5 \times 24} = 0.5$$

H_0: There is no association between x and y.
H_1: There is an association between x and y.

Notice that the tests are about association rather than any linear regression.

The critical value at 10% significance when $n = 5$ for a two-tailed test is 0.900. The calculated correlation coefficient is less than this, so you cannot reject the null hypothesis. There is no significant evidence of association between x and y.

Explore

Within the OCR specification you will not be asked about data with tied ranks, but how could you deal with this type of situation?

EXERCISE 5B

1 Find Spearman's rank correlation coefficient for each of the following sets of ranked data.

a i
Rank x	5	2	6	1	4	3
Rank y	4	1	6	5	3	2

ii
Rank x	2	1	4	3	6	5
Rank y	4	1	3	2	5	6

b i
Rank x	2	3	1	6	4	5
Rank y	5	3	6	1	2	4

ii
Rank x	4	1	3	6	2	5
Rank y	1	5	4	3	6	2

2 Find Spearman's rank correlation coefficient for each of the following data sets. Conduct a two-tailed test for association using a 10% significance level.

a i
x	46	32	22	53	73	31	37
y	75	38	98	70	36	92	26

ii
x	0	97	86	23	31	19	62
y	80	39	20	52	22	65	68

b **i**

x	71	76	50	26	94	62	15	70	27	24
y	25	29	52	14	58	22	2	97	92	17

ii

x	87	7	96	58	70	37	3	20	85	59
y	29	60	12	51	2	30	90	52	66	5

3 Two judges rank eight entrants in an art competition:

	A	**B**	**C**	**D**	**E**	**F**	**G**	**H**
Judge 1	5	6	2	1	8	4	3	7
Judge 2	6	3	1	5	7	4	2	8

   a Find Spearman's rank correlation coefficient for these data.

   b State the ppmcc for these data.

4 Rank the following data and hence calculate Spearman's correlation coefficient between 100 m times and 1500 m times of six athletes.

Athlete	100 m time	1500 m time
Usain	11.2 s	4 min 28 s
Mo	12.4 s	4 min 16 s
Jess	11.8 s	4 min 14 s
Greg	11.7 s	4 min 56 s
Tanni	12.3 s	4 min 05 s
David	12.2 s	3 min 58 s

What does this suggest about the relationship between 100 m times and 1500 m times for athletes?

5 Two judges provide the following results in a singing competition:

	Judge **A**	Judge **B**
1st	Alex	Alex
2nd	Beatrice	Fred
3rd	Chantelle	Emma
4th	Dhillon	Dhillon
5th	Emma	Beatrice
6th	Fred	Chantelle

Find the rank correlation coefficient between the two judges.

Test for association between the two judges' results at the 5% significance level.

6 The following table shows the top twelve countries in the medal tables in the 2012 and 2016 Olympics.

	2012	2016
1st	USA	USA
2nd	China	GB
3rd	GB	China
4th	Russia	Russia
5th	South Korea	Germany
6th	Germany	Japan
7th	France	France
8th	Australia	South Korea
9th	Italy	Italy
10th	Hungary	Australia
11th	Japan	Netherlands
12th	Netherlands	Hungary

Find Spearman's rank correlation coefficient between performance in the 2012 and 2016 Olympics for these countries.

Test at the 1% significance level whether this is evidence of positive association between the results of these countries in the two Olympics.

7 The following data show the results from burning six samples of coal.

Volume of CO_2 produced (l)	Volume of SO_2 produced (ml)
26	25
24	13
88	5
13	58
59	2
7	33

a Calculate the rank correlation coefficient between these data and interpret your value.

b Conduct a two-tailed test for association at the 5% significance level.

c Explain why it might be more appropriate to use Spearman's rank correlation coefficient for this test rather than the ppmcc.

8 a A scatter graph contains three points. Show that (assuming there are no tied ranks) there are four possible values that Spearman's rank can take.

b What is the probability that the modulus of Spearman's rank correlation coefficient of three points created at random is greater than 0.8?

c Find the expected value of the modulus of Spearman's rank correlation coefficient of three points created at random.

9 Sketch scatter diagrams to show data with the following properties:

a $r = 1$ and $r_s = 1$

b $r \approx 1$ and $r_s \neq 1$

c $r \neq 1$ and $r_s = 1$.

Section 3: Linear regression

Once you have established that there is a linear relationship (usually using ppmcc), you can then determine the form of that relationship. To do this you use a method called least squares regression.

Supposing that your x values are absolutely accurate, you can show how far the points are from the line:

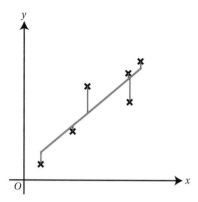

You could try to minimise this total distance by changing the gradient and axis intercept of the line. However, it turns out that it is easier to find the gradient and intercept which minimise the sum of the squares of the vertical distances to the line. This is represented by the squares in the following diagram.

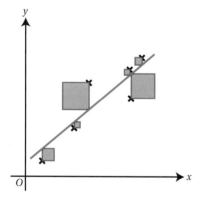

This leads to the formula in Key point 5.5, but it is often simpler to use your calculator to find the equation of this line of best fit. This is also referred to as a y-on-x **regression line**. The line of best fit always passes through the mean point – the point with coordinates $(\bar{x}, \bar{y})$.

In some situations the values of one of the variables can be pre-specified – for example, you might be able to fix the pH of a solution or the amount of time a person has to memorise a list of words. This variable is called the **controlled variable** and is conventionally plotted on the x-axis. The other variable (such as the reaction time or the numbers of words recalled) is referred to as the **response variable** and is conventionally plotted on the y-axis.

In some situations when collecting data you cannot pre-specify the values of one of the variables, but you might believe that one variable has an effect on the other. For example, if collecting data about revision time and exam results, you might identify revision time as an **independent variable** and exam results as a **dependent variable**. Conventionally independent variables are plotted on the x-axis and dependent variables are plotted on the y-axis.

There are also situations where there is not an obvious controlled or independent variable – for example, when finding the height and weight of a group of people. In this situation you can choose which axis to plot each variable on.

In all three situations described previously you can use the least squares regression line. However, you might find that there are other statistical processes (such as testing correlation) that have to be treated differently in the three situations.

Once you have the line of best fit you can use it to estimate unknown values. If you do this within the range of the data, you are **interpolating**. If you extend the model beyond the range of the data and use it to predict a value of the dependent variable, you are **extrapolating**, in which case it is important that you treat the result with caution – there is no reason to suppose that the pattern continues beyond your observations.

WORKED EXAMPLE 5.4

The following data were collected:

Score in a Maths test (m)	Time spent revising in hours (r)
42	1.0
50	1.25
67	2.0
71	2.3
92	3.0

a Which is the independent and which the dependent variable? Justify your answer.
b Find the equation of the regression line.
c Explain why it would not be appropriate to use the regression line to predict the score of someone who spent ten hours revising for the test.

a Time spent revising is the independent variable as it can be varied, whereas score in the test is probably dependent on the revision time.

b $m = 24.0r + 18.5$

> Because you have the original data, you should use a calculator to find the regression line.

c This would be an extrapolation from the data.

If the original data are not given, you can use the formula in Key point 5.5 to find the equation of the regression line.

 Key point 5.5

Least squares regression line of y on x is $y = a + bx$ where $a = \bar{y} - b\bar{x}$ and

$$b = \frac{S_{xy}}{S_{xx}} = \frac{\sum(x_i - \bar{x})(y_i - \bar{y})}{\sum(x_i - \bar{x})^2}$$

This will appear in your formula book.

S_{xy} and S_{xx} are defined in Key point 5.3.

WORKED EXAMPLE 5.5

Data summary values are given as follows:

$$\sum x = 21, \sum x^2 = 91, \sum y = 74, \sum y^2 = 994, \sum xy = 296, \ n = 6$$

a Find the equation of the y-on-x regression line.
b Predict the value of y when $x = 7$.
c The ppmcc is used in a two-tailed test for correlation. The p-value was found to be 5.54×10^{-4}. The original data covered x values between 0 and 10. Use this information to determine if the predicted value of y found in part **b** is valid.

a $S_{xx} = \sum x_i^2 - \dfrac{(\sum x_i)^2}{n}$

$= 91 - \dfrac{21^2}{6} = \dfrac{35}{2}$

> You first find b using Key point 5.5. This needs S_{xx} and S_{xy} from Key point 5.3.

$S_{xy} = \sum x_i y_i - \dfrac{\sum x_i \sum y_i}{n}$

$= 296 - \dfrac{21 \times 74}{6} = 37$

$b = \dfrac{S_{xy}}{S_{xx}} = \dfrac{74}{35} \approx 2.11$

$\bar{x} = \dfrac{\sum x}{n} = \dfrac{21}{6} = \dfrac{7}{2}$

$\bar{y} = \dfrac{\sum y}{n} = \dfrac{74}{6} = \dfrac{37}{3}$

> To find a using Key point 5.5 you need the mean of x and the mean of y.

So $a = \dfrac{37}{3} - \dfrac{74}{35} \times \dfrac{7}{2} = \dfrac{74}{15}$

> Use Key point 5.5.

So the equation is

$$y = \dfrac{74}{35}x + \dfrac{74}{15}$$

Continues on next page ...

b When $x = 7$,
$$y = \frac{74}{35} \times 7 + \frac{74}{15} = \frac{296}{15} \approx 19.7$$

c The p-value is very small - much less than the usual 5% significance level. This means that there is significant evidence of a linear relationship between the variables. Since the x value is within the values observed in the data the line is not to be used for extrapolation. This suggests that the prediction is valid.

🔍 Explore

In more sophisticated work with linear regression you will find that the formula you get by least squares regression actually gives the centre of a spread of possible values of y. Research a formula for finding the interval of plausible values of y.

A linear coding of either variable can be used to transform the equation of a regression line. To do this you use algebraic substitution.

WORKED EXAMPLE 5.6

A y-on-x regression line is found to be $y = 4x + 2$. If $p = 2y$ and $q = x - 1$ find the p-on-q regression line.

$y = \dfrac{p}{2}$ .... Rearrange the coding to make y and x the subjects.
$x = q + 1$

$\dfrac{p}{2} = 4(q + 1) + 2$ .... Substitute into the regression line.

$\phantom{\dfrac{p}{2}} = 4q + 4 + 2$
$\phantom{\dfrac{p}{2}} = 4q + 6$

$p = 8q + 12$

WORK IT OUT 5.1

It is assumed that the result in a final Maths exam (f) can be predicted from the result in the mock exam (m).

The results of a random sample of five students is given as follows.

Final result, f	66	58	88	92	44
Mock result, m	56	45	72	85	31

Continues on next page ...

What is the predicted final result of someone who scores 72 in the mock exam?

Which is the correct solution? Can you identify the errors made in the incorrect solutions?

Solution 1	From the table when someone scores 72 in the mock they score 88 in the final exam.
Solution 2	From the calculator, $y = 0.9369x + 15.445$ so when $x = 72$, predicted result is 82.9.
Solution 3	From the calculator, $m = 1.0416f - 14.697$. When $m = 72$, this means: $72 = 1.0416f - 14.697$ $86.697 = 1.0416f$ $f = 83.2$ So the predicted score is 83%.

EXERCISE 5C

1 Use a calculator to find the y-on-x regression line for the following data:

a i $(2,-5), (0,3), (8,12), (5,19), (4,10), (10,24)$ **ii** $(1,0), (1,3), (2,6), (2,2), (4,4), (5,9)$

b i $(3,15), (17,9), (22,10), (33,7)$ **ii** $(22,50), (54,19), (100,0), (93,12)$

c i $(-2,3), (0,0), (2,1), (3,5), (4,2)$ **ii** $(5,1), (9,3), (7,-2), (8,8)$

d i $(1,3), (2,5), (3,7), (5,11)$ **ii** $(9,1), (4,6), (5,5), (11,-1)$.

2 Find the y-on-x regression line for the following data:

a i $\Sigma x = 15, \Sigma x^2 = 55, \Sigma y = 21, \Sigma y^2 = 179, \Sigma xy = 93, n = 5$

   ii $\Sigma x = 53, \Sigma x^2 = 795, \Sigma y = 280, \Sigma y^2 = 21592, \Sigma xy = 4140, n = 6$

b i $\Sigma x = 26, \Sigma x^2 = 222, \Sigma y = -67, \Sigma y^2 = 1415, \Sigma xy = -560, n = 5$

   ii $\Sigma x = 38, \Sigma x^2 = 370, \Sigma y = -28, \Sigma y^2 = 288, \Sigma xy = -318, n = 6$

c i $n = 10, \Sigma x = 200, \Sigma y = 800, \Sigma(x-\bar{x})^2 = 2960, \Sigma(x-\bar{x})(y-\bar{y}) = -2845$

   ii $n = 8, \Sigma x = 151, \Sigma y = 756, \Sigma(x-\bar{x})^2 = 2844.875, \Sigma(x-\bar{x})(y-\bar{y}) = 13586.5$.

3 In a restaurant, the regression line connecting calories in a dessert (d) and the numbers of desserts sold (n) is given by $n = 0.14d - 20$. The mean number of desserts sold is 36 and the median number of desserts sold is 32.

a Find the value of the mean number of calories in a dessert, or state that it cannot be found.

b Find the value of the median number of calories in a dessert, or state that it cannot be found.

4 The following data show the average speeds of cars (v) passing points at 10 m intervals after a junction (d).

d (m)	v (km/h)
10	12.3
20	17.6
30	21.4
40	23.4
50	25.7
60	26.3

a Find the correlation coefficient, r.

b State, with a reason, which is the controlled variable.

c Using an appropriate regression line, find the value of v when $d = 45$.

d Explain why you cannot use your regression line to accurately estimate v when $d = 80$.

5 The following data show the height of a cake (h) when baked at different temperatures (T):

T (°F)	h (cm)
300	16.4
320	17.3
340	18.1
360	16.2
380	15.1
400	14.8

a Find the correlation coefficient.

b State which variable is the independent variable.

c Find the regression line for these data.

d State two reasons why it would be inappropriate to use the regression line found in part **b** to estimate the temperature required to get a cake of height 20 cm.

e Rebecca wants to have a regression line connecting H and T where H is the height measured in metres. Find the equation of this regression line.

6 The owner of a shop selling hats and gloves thinks that his sales are higher on colder days. Over a period of time he records the temperature and the value of the goods sold on a random sample of eight days:

Temperature (°C)	13	5	10	−2	10	7	−5	5
Sales (£)	345	450	370	812	683	380	662	412

a Calculate the ppmcc between the two sets of data.

b Suggest one other factor that might cause the sales to vary from day to day.

c Explain why temperature might be considered to be the independent variable.

d Find the equation of the regression line.

e Use this line to estimate the sales when the temperature is 0 °C. Explain why it was important to calculate the correlation coefficient before making this estimate.

f Explain why it would not be appropriate to estimate the sales when the temperature is −20 °C.

7 A y-on-x regression line is given by $y = a + bx$.

The variables x and y are coded using $p = ky$ and $q = kx$.

a Prove that the gradient of the coded regression line is the same as the original regression line.

b Find an expression for the y-axis intercept of the coded regression line.

8 Data from an experiment are given as follows:

x	−5	7	−6	−8	−4	−9	0	−6
y	25	52	35	62	13	89	−3	38

a Find the correlation coefficient between:

  i y and x **ii** y and x^2

b Use least squares regression to find a model for the data of the form $y = kx^2 + c$.

9. Which of the following statements are true for random variables X and Y?

a If $r = 0$ there is no relationship between the two variables.

b If $Y = kX$ then $r = 1$.

c If $r < 0$ then the gradient of the line of best fit is negative.

d As r increases then so does the gradient of the line of best fit.

Checklist of learning and understanding

- Pearson's product moment correlation coefficient (ppmcc), r, is a measure of the linear relationship between two random variables:

$$r = \frac{\sum x_i y_i - \frac{\sum x_i \sum y_i}{n}}{\sqrt{\left(\sum x_i^2 - \frac{(\sum x_i)^2}{n}\right)\left(\sum y_i^2 - \frac{(\sum y_i)^2}{n}\right)}}$$

- To make the calculation easier you can break it down:

$$S_{xx} = \sum(x_i - \bar{x})^2 = \sum x_i^2 - \frac{(\sum x_i)^2}{n}$$

$$S_{yy} = \sum(y_i - \bar{y})^2 = \sum y_i^2 - \frac{(\sum y_i)^2}{n}$$

$$S_{xy} = \sum(x_i - \bar{x})(y_i - \bar{y}) = \sum x_i y_i - \frac{\sum x_i \sum y_i}{n}$$

$$r = \frac{S_{xy}}{\sqrt{S_{xx} S_{yy}}}$$

- If you are given the original data you can find r on your calculator.
- Any linear coding of the data will not change r.
- You can use the calculated value of r to test if the underlying populations are correlated.
- Spearman's rank correlation coefficient, r_s, is a measure of an increasing or decreasing relationship between two random variables:

$$r_s = 1 - \frac{6\sum d^2}{n(n^2 - 1)}$$

- You can use the calculated value of r_s to do a non-parametric test to see if the underlying populations are associated.
- You can find a y-on-x regression line for data using a calculator or the formula:

$$y = a + bx$$

where:

$$a = \bar{y} - b\bar{x}$$

$$b = \frac{S_{xy}}{S_{xx}} = \frac{\sum(x_i - \bar{x})(y_i - \bar{y})}{\sum(x_i - \bar{x})^2}$$

- You can use regression lines to predict unknown values. This is only valid if there is significant linear correlation and you are not extrapolating from your data.
- A linear coding of either value will change the regression line. To find the new regression line, use algebraic substitution.

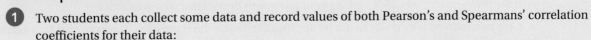

Mixed practice 5

1 Two students each collect some data and record values of both Pearson's and Spearmans' correlation coefficients for their data:

Alan: $r = 0.84$, $r_s = 1$

Bella: $r = 1$, $r_s = 0.96$.

Explain why Alan's results are possible but Bella's results are not.

2 Two judges rank six bottles of wine.

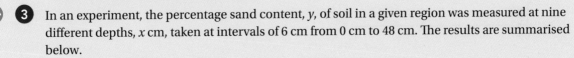

	A	B	C	D	E	F
Judge 1	5	6	2	1	3	4
Judge 2	6	3	1	5	2	4

a Calculate Spearman's rank correlation coefficient for these data.

b Test the association between Judge 1 and Judge 2 using a 5% significance level.

c State the ppmcc of the given data.

3 In an experiment, the percentage sand content, y, of soil in a given region was measured at nine different depths, x cm, taken at intervals of 6 cm from 0 cm to 48 cm. The results are summarised below.

$$n = 9 \quad \Sigma x = 216 \quad \Sigma x^2 = 7344 \quad \Sigma y = 512.4 \quad \Sigma y^2 = 30\,595 \quad \Sigma xy = 10\,674$$

i State, with a reason, which variable is the independent variable.

ii Calculate the product moment correlation coefficient between x and y.

iii a Calculate the equation of the appropriate regression line.

b This regression line is used to estimate the percentage sand content at depths of 25 cm and 100 cm. Comment on the reliability of each of these estimates. You are not asked to find the estimates.

© OCR, AS GCE Mathematics, Paper 4732, January 2012

4 A shopkeeper keeps a record of the amount of ice cream sold on a summer's day along with the temperature at noon. He repeats this for several days, and gets the following results:

Temperature (°C)	Ice creams sold
26	41
29	51
30	72
24	23
23	29
19	12

a Find the correlation coefficient.

b Stating an appropriate assumption, test at 5% significance the hypothesis that there is positive correlation between the number of ice creams sold and the temperature.

c Explain why changing the units of temperature to degrees Fahrenheit would not change the value of the correlation coefficient.

d By finding the equation of the regression line estimate the number of ice creams that would be sold if the temperature was 25 °C, giving your answer to the nearest whole number.

e Give two reasons why it would not be appropriate to use the regression line from part **b** to estimate the temperature on a day when no ice creams are sold.

5 The following data show the time taken to complete a race in minutes (y) against the amount of time spent preparing for the race in hours (x).

x	10	15	18	20	25	32
y	11	7	5	4	4.5	3

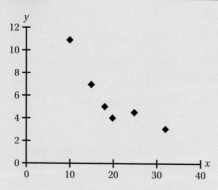

a Calculate the ppmcc for these data.

b Calculate Spearman's rank correlation coefficient for these data.

c Use the scatter graph to explain which measure is more appropriate to test for an association between these two variables.

6 **i** Two judges rank n competitors, where n is an even number. Judge 2 reverses each consecutive pair of ranks given by Judge 1, as shown.

Competitor	C_1	C_2	C_3	C_4	C_5	C_6	...	C_{n-1}	C_n
Judge 1 rank	1	2	3	4	5	6	...	$n-1$	n
Judge 2 rank	2	1	4	3	6	5	...	n	$n-1$

Given that the value of Spearman's coefficient of rank correlation is $\dfrac{63}{65}$, find n.

ii An experiment produced some data from a bivariate distribution. The product moment correlation coefficient is denoted by r, and Spearman's rank correlation coefficient is denoted by r_s.

a Explain whether the statement

$$r = 1 \Rightarrow r_s = 1$$

is true or false.

b Use a diagram to explain whether the statement

$$r \neq 1 \Rightarrow r_s \neq 1$$

is true or false.

© **OCR, AS GCE Mathematics, Paper 4732, January 2013**

7 Spearman's correlation coefficient between two judges in a dance competition for five dancers is found to be 0.68. A new dancer enters and is marked last by both judges. Is Spearman's correlation coefficient going to be larger than 0.68, less than 0.68, equal to 0.68 or is more information needed? Explain your answer.

8 A y-on-x regression line is given by $y = a + bx$.

The variables x and y are coded using $p = ky$ and $q = x + c$.

Find expressions for k and c in terms of a and b so that the p-on-q regression line is $p = q$.

9 The following data show the amount spent on quality control and the amount spent on customer services by six companies.

Quality control	Customer services
24	91
90	15
4	48
70	14
39	40
36	51

a Find the ppmcc between amount spent on quality control and the amount spent on customer services.

b Find Spearman's rank correlation coefficient between amount spent on quality control and the amount spent on customer services.

c The values given are actually in millions of dollars. State how this changes your answers to parts **a** and **b**.

d Conduct two-tailed tests for association at 10% significance using:

i the ppmcc

ii Spearman's rank correlation coefficient.

e Explain why it is possible that only one of the tests in part **d** gives a significant result.

f Find the equation of the regression line, assuming that the amount spent on customer services in millions (c) depends on the amount spent on quality control in millions (q).

g Explain whether it is valid to use this regression line to predict the value of c when:

i $q = 50$ **ii** $q = 150$

h Find the equation of the regression line connecting the amount spent on customer services in dollars (C), which depends on the amount spent on quality control in dollars (Q).

6 Chi-squared tests

In this chapter you will learn how to:

- check if two factors are independent
- use Yates' correction when required
- check if data come from a population with proportions.

(A) If you are following the A Level course, you will also learn how to:

- check if data come from a known distribution.

Before you start…

A Level Mathematics Student Book 1, Chapter 18	You should know how to conduct hypothesis tests.	1	A coin is tossed twelve times and ten heads are observed. Does this provide evidence (at a 5% significance level) that the coin is biased towards heads?
A Level Mathematics Student Book 1, Chapter 17	You should know how to calculate probabilities for independent events.	2	The probability of Andrew scoring a goal is 0.4 and the probability of Helen scoring a goal is 0.6. What is the probability that they both score a goal, if these outcomes are independent?
A Level Mathematics Student Book 2, Chapter 3	You should know how to evaluate expressions including the modulus function.	3	What is $|7 - 10| + 2$?

Independent?

One common question you can ask in a statistical situation is whether or not two variables are dependent – for example, do future earnings depend on A Level choices? In this chapter you will look at a statistical test to answer this type of question. You will also use a method to check if data follow any given distribution.

Did you know?

You might have already met a test to see if two variables are uncorrelated. This is related to independence, but it is not quite the same. For example, the scatter graph shows the results of a psychology experiment where people are asked to estimate the size of an angle, and the time taken for them to do so is measured.

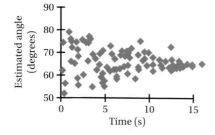

The two variables are not correlated (there is no linear trend) but they are not independent – people who spend longer making the estimate seem to have more tightly clustered estimates.

It turns out that if two variables are independent then they will definitely be uncorrelated, but the reverse is not true. You can write:

$$\text{independent} \Rightarrow \text{uncorrelated}$$

 Rewind

This $\Rightarrow$ notation was covered in A Level Mathematics Student Book 1, Chapter 1.

Section 1: Contingency tables

You can design a hypothesis test that decides whether the two variables are dependent:

H_0: The two variables are independent.
H_1: The two variables are dependent.

To describe the two variables you use **contingency tables** that list how often each combination of factors occurs. For example, the table illustrates the results of a survey of young families. The observed value in cell i is called O_i.

		Number of children			
		0	**1**	**2**	**3 or more**
Number of bedrooms	**2 or fewer**	12	18	6	4
	3	22	18	0	0
	4 or more	2	16	19	3

This table would be described as a 3×4 contingency table.

You are going to need a way of measuring how far this is away from the numbers you would expect if the two factors were independent. To do this you look at the totals:

Tip

You choose H_0 to be that the variables are independent because you can use that to calculate expected values. You cannot use the fact that two variables are dependent to calculate expected values unless you are given more information about what that dependence is.

Tip

A table with n rows and m columns is described as an $n \times m$ table, pronounced 'n by m'.

	Number of children				Total
	0	**1**	**2**	**3 or more**	
2 or fewer	12	18	6	4	40
3	22	18	0	0	40
4 or more	2	16	19	3	40
Total	36	52	25	7	120

(Row label: Number of bedrooms)

Based on your sample, the probability of having two bedrooms or fewer is $\frac{40}{120}$ and the probability of having two children is $\frac{25}{120}$. If the two factors are independent, the probability of both occurring is the product of each of these probabilities, so the probability of two children and two or fewer bedrooms is $\frac{40 \times 25}{120^2}$. In a sample of size 120 you would then expect there to be $\frac{40 \times 25}{120^2} \times 120 \approx 8.33$ families with two children and two or fewer bedrooms. You can denote the expected frequency in cell i by E_i.

This method is generalised in Key point 6.1.

Tip

Expected values do not have to be whole numbers.

Key point 6.1

$$E_i = \frac{\text{row total} \times \text{column total}}{\text{overall total}}$$

You can create another contingency table containing all the expected frequencies:

	Number of children			
	0	**1**	**2**	**3 or more**
2 or fewer	12	17.33	8.33	2.33
3	12	17.33	8.33	2.33
4 or more	12	17.33	8.33	2.33

(Row label: Number of bedrooms)

Tip

Notice that the rows, totals and the columns, totals are the same as the original data. This is a useful check.

There are several possible measures of the 'difference' between observed and expected values. The measure you need to know is called chi-squared (χ^2) (see Key point 6.2).

Key point 6.2

$$\chi^2_{\text{calc}} = \Sigma \frac{(O_i - E_i)^2}{E_i}$$

For your data, $\chi^2_{\text{calc}} = \frac{(12-12)^2}{12} + \frac{(18-17.33)^2}{17.33} + \ldots = 43.17$

Large values indicate a big difference between observed and expected data. Is this value large enough to conclude that number of bedrooms and number of children are not independent? To decide, you need to know the distribution of χ^2_{calc} to see how likely the observed value is. This distribution has a single parameter – the number of *degrees of freedom* – often given the symbol v (lowercase Greek letter 'nu') or df. The formula for the degrees of freedom is given in Key point 6.3.

 Key point 6.3

In an n by m contingency table:

$$v = (n-1)(m-1)$$

If the null hypothesis is true (that the variables are independent), χ^2_{calc} approximately follows the chi-squared distribution with the number of degrees of freedom, v – the χ^2_v distribution. However, this approximation is only valid if all the *expected* frequencies in the contingency table are at least five.

 Key point 6.4

If the null hypothesis is true and $E_i \geqslant 5$ for all i then

$$\chi^2_{calc} = \sum \frac{(O_i - E_i)^2}{E_i} \approx \chi^2_v$$

This will appear in your formula book.

> **Tip**
>
> It is only expected values that need to be at least 5. Observed values are irrelevant.

In the survey results, not all of the expected values are at least five. When this happens you need to combine some rows or columns in a way that is sensible in context. The most obvious way with the example given is to combine the '2 children' group with the '3 or more children' group:

		Number of children		
		0	**1**	**2 or more**
Number of bedrooms	**2 or fewer**	12	18	10
	3	22	18	0
	4 or more	2	16	22

You can then create the new contingency table of expected values:

		Number of children		
		0	**1**	**2 or more**
Number of bedrooms	**2 or fewer**	12	17.33	10.67
	3	12	17.33	10.67
	4 or more	12	17.33	10.67

> **Tip**
>
> Notice that the expected values can be found by adding up the corresponding expected values from the original table. You don't have to recalculate the frequencies using Key point 6.1.

You can find the contributions to each cell to the total chi-squared value.

		Number of children		
		0	**1**	**2 or more**
Number of bed rooms	**2 or fewer**	0	0.0256	0.0417
	3	8.33	0.0256	10.7
	4 or more	8.33	0.103	12.0

Totalling these contributions, $\chi^2_{calc} = 39.57$ and $v = (3-1) \times (3-1) = 4$. You can compare this value to critical values given in the formula book.

P	0.01	0.025	0.05	0.90	0.95	0.975	0.99	0.995	0.999
$v=1$	0.0^31571	0.0^39821	0.0^23932	2.706	3.841	5.024	6.635	7.879	10.83
2	0.02010	0.05064	0.1026	4.605	5.991	7.378	9.210	10.60	13.82
3	0.1148	0.2158	0.3518	6.251	7.815	9.348	11.34	12.84	16.27
4	0.2971	0.4844	0.7107	7.779	**9.488**	11.14	13.28	14.86	18.47
5	0.5543	0.8312	1.145	9.236	11.07	12.83	15.09	16.75	20.51
6	0.8721	1.237	1.635	10.64	12.59	14.45	16.81	18.55	22.46
7	1.239	1.690	2.167	12.02	14.07	16.01	18.48	20.28	24.32

The highlighted value gives the **critical value** for a test at the 5% significance level with four degrees of freedom. The column is headed 0.95 because 95 per cent of chi-squared values with four degrees of freedom are below this value, therefore 5 per cent are higher. The calculated value of 39.57 is higher than 9.488, so you reject the null hypothesis and conclude that the number of bedrooms and number of children are not independent.

The contingency table showing the contributions of each cell to the χ^2_{calc} sum shows some cells have a much larger value of $\dfrac{(O_i - E_i)^2}{E_i}$ than others. You can use this to analyse which combinations of the variables are very different from the expected frequencies. This can give us further insight into what is happening in the situation being investigated. In the example you can see that two or more children in three or more bedroom houses makes the largest contribution to the χ^2_{calc}. You could interpret this as meaning that large families preferring large houses is a big factor in why number of children and the number of bedrooms are dependent.

> **Tip**
>
> Some calculators allow you to do the chi-squared test automatically and provide you with the p-value, the expected frequencies and the contribution for each cell. This alternative approach is acceptable.

WORKED EXAMPLE 6.1

Determine at the 10% significance level whether or not the colour of a car sold by a dealership is independent of the gender of the purchaser:

		Gender		Total
		Male	**Female**	
Colour	**Blue**	18	20	38
	Red	14	12	26
	Green	19	14	33
	Silver	28	32	60
Total		79	78	157

Continues on next page ...

H_0: Gender and car colour are independent
H_1: Gender and car colour are not independent

Set up hypotheses.

The expected values are:

	Male	Female
Blue	19.1	18.9
Red	13.1	12.9
Green	16.6	16.4
Silver	30.2	29.8

Find expected values using Key point 6.1. Check that all the expected frequency values are at least five, which they are in this case.

$$\chi^2_{calc} \approx \frac{(18-19.1)^2}{19.1} + \frac{(20-18.9)^2}{18.9} + \dots$$
$$\approx 1.28$$

Find the chi-squared value using Key point 6.2. Although the working is written using three significant figures you should store the values on your calculator and use the full accuracy from the calculator to find the final answer.

$v = (4-1)(2-1) = 3$

Find the degrees of freedom using Key point 6.3.

The critical value is 6.251 which is more than χ^2_{calc}.

Use the formula book to find the critical value.

Therefore there is insufficient evidence to reject H_0; the data set is consistent with gender and car colour being independent.

Remember that χ^2_{calc} is a measure of distance between observed and expected values, so your calculated 'distance' is less than the critical distance.

The following example shows how to deal with combining groups.

WORKED EXAMPLE 6.2

The following contingency table shows the favourite sport played by different age groups in a sample at a sports centre.

		0–5	6–10	11–15	16–18
Sport	Soccer	3	18	21	20
	Basketball	0	12	16	26
	Swimming	8	16	11	8
	Tennis	8	11	13	18

(Age spans 0–5, 6–10, 11–15, 16–18 columns.)

a Test at the 5% significance level whether preferred sport and age are independent, showing the contributions of each cell.
b Interpret your results in context.

Continues on next page …

a H_0: Age and preferred sport are independent.

H_1: Age and preferred sport are not independent.

Set up hypotheses.

The expected values are:

	0–5	6–10	11–15	16–18
Soccer	5.64	16.9	18.1	21.4
Basketball	4.91	14.7	15.8	18.6
Swimming	3.91	11.7	12.6	14.8
Tennis	4.55	13.6	14.6	17.2

Find expected values. Check that all the expected values are at least five, which they are not in this case.

Several in the 0–5 range have a frequency less than 5, so combine this column with the 6–10 column giving:

	0–10	11–15	16–18
Soccer	22.5	18.1	21.4
Basketball	19.6	15.8	18.6
Swimming	15.6	12.6	14.8
Tennis	18.2	14.6	17.2

The most obvious choice is to combine the 0–5 and 6–10 groups.

And the corresponding observed values are:

	0–10	11–15	16–18
Soccer	21	21	20
Basketball	12	16	26
Swimming	24	11	8
Tennis	19	13	18

The contributions of each cell are:

	0–10	11–15	16–18
Soccer	0.106	0.466	0.0865
Basketball	2.97	0.00363	2.94
Swimming	4.47	0.191	3.13
Tennis	0.0368	0.174	0.0349

Use Key point 6.2.

$\nu = (4-1)(3-1) = 6$

$\chi^2_{calc} \approx 14.6$

The critical value is $12.59 < \chi^2_{calc}$

Compare χ^2_{calc} critical value from formula book and conclude.

Therefore reject H_0 – there is significant evidence that preferred sport and age are not independent.

b The main contributions to χ^2_{calc} come from basketball and swimming. It appears swimming is more popular than would be expected (if sport and age are independent) among younger students, while basketball is more popular than would be expected among older students. These are the combinations which have the largest contribution to the chi-squared statistic.

Use the contributions of each cell to find the most important factors. You also have to look at the expected frequencies compared to the observed frequencies to see which categories were over-represented and which ones were under-represented.

EXERCISE 6A

1 Test, at the 5% significant level, the following contingency tables to see if the two factors are independent. State carefully the number of degrees of freedom and the value of χ^2_{calc}. In part **b**, combine suitable columns to make all expected frequencies greater than five.

a i

		Exam grade		
		E or U	B, C or D	A or A*
Teacher	**Mr Archer**	13	15	18
	Ms Baker	26	28	30
	Mrs Chui	28	30	35

ii

		Time working		
		0–2 hours	2–6 hours	> 6 hours
Gender	**Male**	42	15	13
	Female	26	26	33

b i

		Age			
		0–15	16–25	26–40	41–50
Facebook friends	**0–199**	201	1236	341	18
	200–299	120	4254	945	4
	>300	340	1988	366	2

ii

		Cost		
		(1000, 5000)	(5000, 10 000)	(10 000, 20 000)
Colour	**Red**	28	36	3
	Green	24	14	1
	Blue	18	3	2

2 A Physics teacher wants to investigate whether or not there is any association between the Physics grade her students get and the Mathematics course they study. She collects the data for a random sample of 1000 students over several years. The results are given in the following table:

	D or lower	B or C	A or A*
Further Maths	30	280	104
Maths AS or A	49	154	210
No Maths	71	70	32

a State the null and alternative hypotheses.

b Calculate the expected frequencies.

c Calculate the value of χ^2 and write down the number of degrees of freedom.

d Test at the 5% significance level whether the Physics grade is independent of the Mathematics course studied. Show clearly how you arrived at your conclusion. Interpret your results in context.

3 The owner of a beauty salon wants to find out whether there is any association between the number of times in a year people visit the salon and the amount of money they spend on each visit. He collects the following data for a random sample of clients:

	Number of visits			
Amount spent per visit (£)	$\leqslant 5$	6–10	11–20	> 20
< 15	38	26	11	5
15–30	22	18	15	11
> 30	16	31	11	9

Is there evidence, at the 10% level of significance, of some association between the number of visits and the amount of money spent? Interpret your result in context.

4 A drugs manufacturer claims that the speed of recovery from a certain illness is higher for people who take a higher dose of their new drug. They provide the following data for a sample of 250 patients.

	No drug taken	Single dose	Double dose
$\leqslant 5$ days	2	12	6
6–10 days	43	56	61
11–14 days	8	21	11
> 14 days	14	11	5

Test whether there is evidence for the manufacturer's claim at the 1% level of significance. Interpret your results in context.

5 A company is investigating their gender equality policies. As a part of this investigation they collect data on salaries for a random sample of 170 employees, as shown in the following table.

	Male	Female
$< £20\,000$	10	5
$£20\,000–30\,000$	14	12
$£30\,000–40\,000$	52	33
$£40\,000–60\,000$	24	8
$\geqslant £60\,000$	6	6

a Assuming salary is independent of gender, calculate the corresponding expected frequencies.

b Carry out a suitable test to determine whether salary is independent of gender. State and justify your conclusion at the 10% level of significance.

6 **a** Prove that $\chi^2_{\text{calc}} = \left(\sum \dfrac{O_i^2}{E_i}\right) - n$ where $n = \sum O_i$.

b A 3 by 2 contingency table has $\sum \dfrac{O_i^2}{E_i} = 548.3$. Find the largest possible sample size.

c Find the largest sample size that will produce a significant result in the chi-squared test at the 5% significance level, assuming that all cells contain at least five expected objects.

7 A researcher believes that the following percentages are the true proportions of people voting for different political parties based on their gender:

	Male	Female
Party A	12%	18%
Party B	16%	14%
Party C	22%	18%

a Show that gender and voting intention are dependent.

b Show that if a sample of size 50 follows these proportions it will not provide a significant result in the chi-squared test at 5% significance.

c Calculate an estimate of the smallest sample size required to find significant evidence that gender and voting intention are dependent, using a 5% significance level.

d Explain why your answer to part **c** is only an estimate.

8 The following contingency table has some blank spaces.

		First factor				Total
		0	1	2	3	
Second factor	A	12	12	1		30
	B	10	1	4		20
	C					50
Total		25	15	30	30	100

a Copy the table and fill in the blanks.

b Hence explain why it can be said that this contingency table has six degrees of freedom.

9 Explain why the formula for chi-squared contains:

a squaring before summing **b** dividing by the expected value.

Section 2: Yates' correction

It turns out that when $v = 1$ (i.e. a 2 by 2 contingency table) then the approximation that $\chi^2_{\text{calc}} \sim \chi^2_v$ is not very good. To improve upon this you use an alternative formula, called Yates' corrected version of the chi-squared statistic.

⏮ Rewind

The modulus function, $|x|$, was covered in A Level Mathematics Student Book 2, Chapter 3.

🔑 Key point 6.5

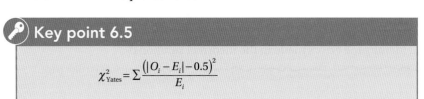

$$\chi^2_{\text{Yates}} = \sum \dfrac{\left(|O_i - E_i| - 0.5\right)^2}{E_i}$$

WORKED EXAMPLE 6.3

The following contingency table shows the results of 100 people in a driving test along with their gender.

		Gender	
		Male	Female
Result	Pass	34	24
	Fail	24	18

Test at the 10% significance level if the outcome of the test is independent of the gender.

H_0: Gender and result are independent

H_1: Gender and result are not independent

Set up hypotheses.

The expected values are:

Find the expected values using Key point 6.1.

		Gender	
		Male	Female
Result	Pass	33.64	24.36
	Fail	24.36	17.64

$$\chi^2_{Yates} = \frac{(|34-33.64|-0.5)^2}{33.64} + \frac{(|24-24.36|-0.5)^2}{24.36}$$
$$+ \frac{(|24-24.36|-0.5)^2}{24.36} + \frac{(|18-17.64|-0.5)^2}{17.64}$$
$$= 0.003\,30$$

Use Key point 6.5.

$v = 1$ so the critical value is $2.706 > \chi^2_{Yates}$

The null hypothesis cannot be rejected. There is no significant evidence of an association between gender and result.

WORK IT OUT 6.1

Test at the 10% significance level if there is any association between teacher and test result:

		Teacher		Total
		Mr A	Mrs B	
Result	Pass	14	11	25
	Fail	17	18	35
	Total	31	29	60

Which is the correct solution? Can you identify the errors made in the incorrect solutions?

Continues on next page ...

Solution 1

If there is no association then each cell will be the same, so the expected values are:

		Teacher	
		Mr A	Mrs B
Result	Pass	15	15
	Fail	15	15

So $\chi^2 = \dfrac{(14-15)^2}{15} + \dfrac{(11-15)^2}{15} + \dfrac{(17-15)^2}{15} + \dfrac{(18-15)^2}{15}$

$= 2$

The critical value when df $= 1$ is $0.016 < \chi^2$ so you can reject H_0: the result does not depend on the teacher.

Solution 2

H_0: The result depends on the teacher.

H_1: The result does not depend on the teacher.

The expected values are:

		Teacher	
		Mr A	Mrs B
Result	Pass	13	12
	Fail	18	17

Using Yates' correction,

$\chi^2_{\text{Yates}} = \dfrac{(1-0.5)^2}{14} + \dfrac{(1-0.5)^2}{11} + \dfrac{(1-0.5)^2}{17} + \dfrac{(1-0.5)^2}{18} = 0.069$

The critical value is 2.706 which is more than the calculated value, so accept H_0 – the result does depend on the teacher.

Solution 3

H_0: Teacher and result are independent.

H_1: Teacher and result are not independent.

The expected values are:

		Teacher	
		Mr A	Mrs B
Result	Pass	12.917	12.083
	Fail	18.083	16.917

Using Yates' correction:

$\chi^2_{\text{Yates}} = \dfrac{(1.083-0.5)^2}{12.917} + \dfrac{(1.083-0.5)^2}{12.083} + \dfrac{(1.083-0.5)^2}{18.083} + \dfrac{(1.083-0.5)^2}{16.917} = 0.0934$

The critical value is 2.706 which is more than the calculated value, so do not reject H_0 – the result and the teacher are independent.

EXERCISE 6B

1 Test the following contingency tables for evidence of association, using 5% significance, using Yates' correction.

a   i

	A	B
X	15	12
Y	21	26

ii

	A	B
X	24	30
Y	15	33

b   i

	A	B
X	150	120
Y	210	260

ii

	A	B
X	240	300
Y	150	330

2 Gregor Mendel, father of modern genetics, carefully observed peas and found the following results:

	Round	Wrinkled
Yellow	315	101
Green	108	32

Show that, at a 10% significance level, the round or wrinkled appearance of the pea is independent of the colour.

3 A scientist wanted to find out if a lady could tell whether tea or milk was put in the cup first, when tea was prepared for her. The results are shown as follows.

	Tea first	Milk first
Likes	14	18
Dislikes	21	15

Determine whether, at a 10% significance level, the lady's enjoyment is independent of whether tea or milk is added first.

4 The following table shows the number of books in libraries in rural and urban locations.

		Number of books	
	< 10 000	10 000 to 100 000	> 100 000
Rural	512	124	0
Urban	2613	612	19

Conduct a test at the 5% significance level to determine if the number of books differs between rural and urban libraries.

Explore

These results are actually suspiciously close to being perfect – some people believe Mendel faked his results. However, it is not possible to conduct a hypothesis test to check this. How is statistics used to check for authenticity in results? In particular, how is Benford's law used to check tax returns?

Did you know?

'The lady tasting tea' was one of the experiments reported by eminent statistician Ronald Fisher in his 1935 book *The Design of Experiments*. He used a variant on the chi-squared test called Fisher's exact test.

5 The following data show the number of murders each year and the amount spent on horror films in the cinema across the last 100 years in the UK:

		Amount spent on horror films in million £		
		< 1	1 to 10	> 10
Number of murders	< 500	32	21	1
	≥ 500	17	25	4

Test at the 5% significance level to see if there is an association between the amount spent on horror films and the number of murders each year. Does this provide evidence that watching horror films encourages people to commit murder?

6 In 1973 admissions to the six largest departments in Berkeley, a university in California, followed this pattern:

	Accepted	Rejected
Male	1158	1493
Female	557	1278

a Use the chi-squared test at 1% significance to show that acceptance patterns depend on gender. Is a higher percentage of men or women admitted? Is this evidence of bias?

b Data from the six departments are shown as follows:

Department	Men		Women		Total
	Admitted	Rejected	Admitted	Rejected	
A	512	313	89	19	933
B	313	207	17	8	545
C	120	205	202	391	918
D	138	279	131	244	792
E	53	138	94	299	584
F	22	351	24	317	714
Total	1158	1493	557	1278	4486

Conduct a test at the 1% significance level to determine if acceptance patterns are different in different departments. In how many departments is the proportion of men admitted higher than the proportion of women admitted?

7 Explain why the null hypothesis in a chi-squared test cannot be 'The two factors are dependent'.

> **i) Did you know?**
>
> This effect is called Simpson's Paradox. You have to be very careful when using statistics to support arguments!

Section 3: Goodness-of-fit tests

In Chapters 2 and 3 you met conditions that helped you decide if a situation could plausibly be modelled by a given distribution such as the geometric distribution or the Poisson distribution. Part of the modelling cycle is to then collect data and evaluate your model. This can be done in many different ways, such as by looking at graphs or calculating summary statistics. However, these methods rely on opinions about how close the model is to the observed data. The chi-squared statistic can be used to create a more formal hypothesis test to answer the question about whether the model is plausible.

The standard null and alternative hypotheses in this situation are:

H_0: The underlying population follows the given distribution.

H_1: The underlying population does not follow the given distribution.

You split all the possible values your variable can take into different ranges of values or categories called bins and note how many pieces of data are in each bin (these are the observed frequencies, O_i). You can then compare this to how often the model predicts that data should fall in each bin (these are the expected frequencies, E_i). You can use the same chi-squared statistic previously mentioned as a measure of 'distance' showing how far apart the observed and expected data are. You will also need to find the degrees of freedom using the formula in Key point 6.6.

Key point 6.6

v = number of bins − number of constraints

A constraint is a parameter in the model which is found from the data and then fixed to take the same value in the model. One constraint that is always required is the total frequency: you always want the total expected frequency to be the same as the total observed frequency, otherwise you are not comparing the results fairly. If you have to find a mean, standard deviation or proportion from the data and use that value in predicting the expected values, these all add to the number of constraints.

Tests for given ratios or proportions

One simple way of describing the distribution is to provide proportions or ratios. The expected values are then found by taking the total observed frequency and splitting it into those ratios or proportions.

WORKED EXAMPLE 6.4

Eggs are sold in four categories: small, medium, large and extra large. A supermarket model predicts that these will be sold in the ratio $1:2:3:1$. To check this model the supermarket looks at sales in a store in one day.

Size of eggs	Small	Medium	Large	Extra large
Number sold	16	17	24	13
Expected	10	20	30	10

Continues on next page ...

a Calculate the expected values if the model is correct.

b Use an appropriate statistical test to determine if the model fits this data, using a 5% significance level.

a $n = 16 + 17 + 24 + 13 = 70$

Find the total frequency.

Size of Eggs	Small	Medium	Large	Extra large
Expected	10	20	30	10

Split in the given ratio. There are seven 'parts' in total so each 'part' corresponds to ten sales.

b H_0: The underlying population is in the ratio $1:2:3:1$

H_1: The underlying population is not in the ratio $1:2:3:1$

The chi-squared test is the appropriate test for this question. First write hypotheses.

$$\chi^2 = \frac{(16-10)^2}{10} + \frac{(17-20)^2}{20} + \dots$$

$$= 6.15$$

$$v = 4 - 1 = 3$$

Since all expected frequencies are above five, no bins need to be combined. The chi-squared statistic can be calculated.

There are four bins and one constraint (the total must be 70) so there are three degrees of freedom.

The critical value is 7.815.

Look up the appropriate value from the tables. Your calculator might also be able to find a p-value.

This is greater than the observed value so we do not reject H_0. There is no significant evidence that the eggs are sold in a ratio different from $1:2:3:1$.

WORKED EXAMPLE 6.5

A random number generator claims to produce random numbers from the U(4) distribution. A sample of 100 random numbers produced by this generator shows the following results.

Value	1	2	3	4
Frequency	20	22	28	30

Test at the 10% significance level to see if the random number generator is working as expected.

H_0: data is taken from U(4)

H_1: data is not taken from U(4)

The expected values are:

Since the numbers are generated from a uniform distribution they should all have the same frequency.

Value	1	2	3	4
Frequency	25	25	25	25

$$\chi^2_{calc} = \frac{(25-20)^2}{25} + \dots$$

$$= 2.72$$

Find χ^2_{calc} using the formula.

Continues on next page ...

There are 3 degrees of freedom. .... There are four groups and the only constraint is the total.

The critical value is 6.251. .... Look this up in the table.

Since $\chi^2_{calc} < 6.251$ you cannot reject the null hypothesis. There is not significant evidence that the random numbers are not drawn from U(4). .... Compare to χ^2_{calc} and conclude in context.

A Tests for other known distributions

In questions on the χ^2 test you might be given a distribution and you need to use this to find the expected frequencies. You can do this by finding the probabilities of being in each bin and then using the formula in Key point 6.7.

 Key point 6.7

Expected frequency in bin A = probability of being in bin A × total observed frequency

Tip

 You can use some calculators to generate a list of expected probabilities for normal, Poisson and binomial distributions. Your calculator might also work out the χ^2 value and the p-value. You should show all those values in your working.

There might be some occasions when the model predicts that the results could extend beyond what has been observed. When you find the predicted values, you might have to rename the bins to take this into account. This is what you have to do in Worked example 6.6.

WORKED EXAMPLE 6.6

It is thought that the time taken to complete a puzzle follows a normal distribution with mean 10 minutes and standard deviation 2 minutes. Is this consistent, at the 10% significance level, with the following data?

Time, T (min)	$5 < t \leqslant 8$	$8 < t \leqslant 10$	$10 < t \leqslant 12$	$12 < t \leqslant 15$
Frequency	10	35	36	7

H_0: $T \sim N(10, 2^2)$
H_1: T does not follow this distribution .... Set up hypotheses.

$n = 88$ .... Find the total frequency.

Time	$t \leqslant 8$	$8 < t \leqslant 10$	$10 < t \leqslant 12$	$t > 12$
Prob	0.159	0.341	0.341	0.159
Freq.	13.96	30.04	30.04	13.96

Find the probabilities for each group, and the associated expected frequencies. To make the probabilities add up to one, you need to allow the time to go from $-\infty$ to ∞, even though negative times are not possible.

Continues on next page ...

$\chi^2_{calc} = 6.60$ (from calculator) .... Find χ^2_{calc} using a calculator.

4 bins, 1 constraint (total) so $v = 3$ .... Find the number of degrees of freedom.

Critical value of χ^2 at 10% significance is 6.25 .... Find the critical value.

$\chi^2_{calc} > 6.25$ therefore reject H_o at the 10% significance level. There is sufficient evidence to say that the data has not been drawn from the given model. .... Compare to χ^2_{calc} and conclude.

In Worked example 6.6 you tested whether the data could plausibly have come from a specified normal distribution. You can contrast this with Worked example 6.7, where you test whether the data could plausibly have come from *any* normal distribution.

WORKED EXAMPLE 6.7

It is thought that the time taken to complete a puzzle follows a normal distribution. Is this consistent, at the 10% significance level, with the following data?

Time, T (min)	$5 < t \leqslant 8$	$8 < t \leqslant 10$	$10 < t \leqslant 12$	$12 < t \leqslant 15$
Frequency	10	35	36	7

H_0: $T \sim N(\mu, \sigma^2)$
H_1: T does not follow this distribution .... Set up hypotheses.

$n = 88$ .... Find the total frequency.

Time	$5 < t \leqslant 8$	$8 < t \leqslant 10$	$10 < t \leqslant 12$	$12 < t \leqslant 15$
Midpoint	6.5	9	11	13.5

From calculator: $\bar{x} \approx 9.8920$, $s \approx 1.7883$

You are not given μ and σ, so estimate them from the data. You should input the midpoints of each group into the calculator.

Time	$t < 8$	$8 < t \leqslant 10$	$10 < t \leqslant 12$	$t > 12$
Probability	0.1450	0.3790	0.3567	0.1192
Frequency	12.76	33.35	31.39	10.49

Find the probabilities for each group, using a N(9.8920, 1.7883²) distribution. Then find the associated expected frequencies by multiplying by the total (88).

4 bins, 3 constraints (total, mean, standard deviation) so $v = 1$. .... Find the number of degrees of freedom.

Continues on next page ...

$$\chi^2_{calc} = \frac{(10-12.76)^2}{12.76} + \frac{(35-33.35)^2}{33.35} + \ldots \approx 2.52$$

Even though the working here has been written to 4 significant figures, ideally you should use the storage facilities on your calculator to use the most precise values you have.

Critical value of χ^2_1 at 10% significance is 2.71

Find the critical value.

$\chi^2_{calc} < 2.71$, therefore do not reject H_0 at the 10% significance level – there is no significant evidence that a normal distribution does not fit the data.

Compare to χ^2_{calc} and conclude.

As in Worked example 6.6, this calculation needs to cover all possible values so the groups need to be relabelled.

As the parameters of the normal distribution were not specified in the second example, you might as well try the best possible normal distribution, which you get by estimating the parameters from the data. This produces a lower value of χ^2_{calc} but it must also be compared to a lower critical value since the number of degrees of freedom has decreased.

As with contingency tables, the expected frequency in every bin must be at least five. If there is a bin that has an expected frequency of less than five it must be combined with an adjacent bin.

▶▶ **Fast forward**

You will see in Chapter 8 that the best way to estimate the standard deviation is to use the value described as 's' in most calculators rather than 'σ'.

WORKED EXAMPLE 6.8

The following data give the number of chocolates picked from a box until a toffee-centred chocolate is found. Test at the 10% level whether the data fit a geometric distribution.

Number of chocolates (c)	1	2	3	4	5 or more
Frequency	28	20	12	8	0

H_0: $C \sim Geo(p)$
H_1: C does not follow this distribution

Set up hypotheses (this should be done before data is collected).

$n = 68$

Find the total frequency.

$$\bar{c} = \frac{136}{68} = 2$$
$$p = \frac{1}{\bar{c}} = 0.5$$

Estimate p from the data.

c	1	2	3	4	$\geqslant 5$
$P(C = c)$	0.5	0.25	0.125	0.0625	0.0625
Frequency	34.0	17.0	8.5	4.25	4.25

Find the probabilities for each group, and the associated expected frequencies (use calculator).

Continues on next page ...

Combine the last two groups:

c	1	2	3	$\geqslant 4$
Frequency	34.0	17.0	8.5	8.5

Check that all expected values are above five.

4 bins, 2 constraints (total, p) so $\nu = 2$

Find the number of degrees of freedom. The total and the value of p have been estimated from the data so act as constraints.

$\chi^2_{calc} = 3.06$

Critical value is 4.605

$\chi^2_{calc} < 4.605$ Therefore do not reject H_o at the 10% significance level – there is significant evidence that a geometric distribution fits the data.

Compare χ^2_{calc} to the critical value and conclude.

Tip

Although there is only one degree of freedom, Yates' correction is only used for contingency tables.

EXERCISE 6C

1 For each table do the following: find the χ^2 value, state the number of degrees of freedom (you can assume that only the total has been fixed by the data) and test at the 5% significance level whether the observed values fit the expected values.

a i

Value	5–10	11–20	21–30	31–40	41–50	51–55
Observed frequency	21	63	28	54	43	24
Expected frequency	17.1	60.2	40.5	40.2	58.8	16.2

ii

Value	$2 < x \leqslant 8$	$8 < x \leqslant 15$	$15 < x \leqslant 20$	$20 < x \leqslant 25$	$25 < x \leqslant 30$
Observed frequency	19	45	60	42	12
Expected frequency	14.8	49.5	52.5	42.2	19.0

b i

Value	$4 < x \leqslant 16$	$16 < x \leqslant 30$	$30 < x \leqslant 50$	$50 < x \leqslant 80$	$80 < x \leqslant 100$
Observed frequency	3	5	12	14	6
Expected frequency	6.4	7.6	13.6	9.5	2.9

ii

Value	50–70	71–100	101–150	151–200	201–250	251–300
Observed frequency	2	6	8	15	12	7
Expected frequency	6.9	7.1	7.8	12.2	11.6	4.4

2 A flower can have three genotypes, labelled AA, Aa and aa. A genetic theory predicts that these should occur in the ratio 1 : 2 : 1. The following data are collected.

Genotype	AA	Aa	aa
Frequency	70	80	50

Test at the 5% significance level if there is evidence that the genetic theory is incorrect.

3 A population is thought to follow the U(4) distribution. 1000 data items are collected and summarised as follows.

x	1	2	3	4
Proportion	0.2	0.2	0.3	0.3

Test at the 5% significance level if there is evidence that the population does not follow the U(4) distribution.

4 Josh believes that the number (X) of passengers (including the driver) in a car can be modelled by a probability distribution given by $P(X = x) = k(30 - x^2)$ for $x = 1, 2, 3, 4, 5$.

a Find the value of k.

Josh collects the following data from a random sample of 100 cars:

number of passengers	1	2	3	4	5
observed frequency	29	34	17	12	8

b Use an appropriate test, with a 5% significance level, to test Josh's belief.

A 5 Jessie knows that the heights of students at her college follow a normal distribution with mean 167 cm and standard deviation 7 cm. Michael wants to know whether the heights of students at his college follow the same normal distribution. He records the heights of 50 students as follows:

Height (cm)	Observed frequency	Expected frequency
< 160	9	7.93
$160 \leqslant x < 165$	11	
$165 \leqslant x < 170$	13	13.9
$170 \leqslant x < 175$	12	10.4
$\geqslant 175$	5	

a State suitable hypotheses for Michael's test.

b Fill in the missing expected frequencies, showing clearly how you arrived at your answers.

c Calculate the χ^2 value and the number of degrees of freedom.

d Hence decide, using the 10% level of significance, whether Michael's data could plausibly follow the normal distribution N(167, 7^2).

A **6** A road planner believes that the number of accidents on a 50 km section of road follows a Poisson distribution. He collects data for 100 such sections of roads.

Number of accidents	Frequency
0	6
1	17
2	40
3	20
4	11
5	6

a Calculate the mean number of accidents per 50 km section of road.

b i Write down suitable hypotheses to decide if these data do follow a Poisson distribution.

ii Carry out a test at the 5% significance level and state your conclusion.

7 A six-sided dice has faces labelled 1, 1, 2, 2, 3 and 4. Hanna claims that this dice is fair. To check the claim, she throws the dice 260 times.

Outcome on dice	Frequency
1	95
2	75
3	46
4	44

State suitable hypotheses and, using an appropriate test, determine whether or not Hanna's claim can be accepted at the 10% significance level.

A **8** A teacher thinks that the number of mistakes in a five-question multiple choice test follows a binomial distribution. In her class of 30 students she records the following results:

Number of mistakes	Frequency
0	2
1	6
2	13
3	6
4	3
5	0

a i Calculate the mean number of mistakes per student.

ii Hence estimate p, the probability that a randomly chosen question is answered incorrectly.

b By calculating an appropriate χ^2 statistic, determine at the 5% significance level whether these data fit a binomial distribution.

A **9** All students at a college take a computer-based Mathematics entrance test every year. In order to test whether the times taken by students to complete the test follow a normal distribution, a sample of 50 students is taken and the following data are recorded:

Time (to the nearest minute)	Observed frequency	Expected frequency
15–19	6	5.01
20–24	10	
25–29	15	15.5
30–34	11	12.2
35–39	8	
Total	50	

a Find the estimates of the mean and standard deviation of the times based on the data in the table.

b Calculate the missing expected frequencies.

c Test at the 5% significance level whether the observed times could have been drawn from a population following a normal distribution. You must state your hypotheses clearly and show how you arrived at your conclusion.

A **10** Five coins are tossed simultaneously 200 times with the following results:

0 heads	6 times
1 head	21 times
2 heads	59 times
3 heads	68 times
4 heads	34 times
5 heads	12 times

Test whether all the coins are fair using:

a 5% significance level

b 10% significance level.

11 The grades in an exam are supposed to follow a prescribed distribution, defined by the following rule:

$P(G \leqslant g) = \dfrac{1}{49} g(14 - g)$ for $g = 3, 4, 5, 6, 7$.

In a certain year, a random sample of 200 candidates achieved the following grades:

grade	3	4	5	6	7
number of candidates	126	35	18	15	6

a Find the expected frequencies. Hence determine whether any columns need to be combined.

b Test at the 5% significance level whether the grades in this year followed the prescribed distribution.

12 In order to test whether collected data fit a proposed model, the observed and expected frequencies are recorded in the following table:

Bin	1	2	3	4	5
Observed	16	18	35	x	y
Expected	12	21	32	25	10

    a Write an expression for y in terms of x.

    b Find the χ^2 value in terms of x.

    c The following hypotheses are tested at the 5% significance level:

        H_0: the model fits the data. H_1: the model does not fit the data.

    Given that the critical value of χ^2 is 9.49 and that the null hypothesis was accepted, find the range of possible values of x.

13 Consider the following table of observed and expected data, where x and y are integers:

Bin	1	2	3	4	5
Observed	21	30	47	x	20
Expected	24	30	41	y	25

    a Explain why $y = x - 2$.

    b Given that the value of the χ^2 statistic is 2.378 (4 s.f.), find the values of x and y.

Checklist of learning and understanding

- The χ^2 distribution provides a very important method for deciding whether two factors are independent or not.

- If the factors are independent you use the formula:

$$E_i = \frac{\text{row total} \times \text{column total}}{\text{overall total}}$$

  to find the expected values in each cell.

- The test statistic used is:

$$\chi^2_{\text{calc}} = \Sigma \frac{\left(O_i - E_i\right)^2}{E_i}$$

- v is the number of degrees of freedom, calculated as (number of rows – 1) × (number of columns – 1).
- If $E_i > 5$ then $\chi^2_{\text{calc}} \sim \chi^2_v$.
- If the contingency table reduces to a 2×2 table then you use an alternative formula, called Yates' corrected chi-squared statistic:

$$\chi^2_{\text{Yates}} = \Sigma \frac{\left(|O_i - E_i| - 0.5\right)^2}{E_i}$$

- You can also use the chi-squared test to to see if your model fits observed data:

        v = number of bins – number of constraints

A   Expected frequency in bin A = probability of being in bin A × total observed frequency

Mixed practice 6

1 The following contingency table shows data from a sample measuring a person's location and economic status, as measured by salary purchasing power (SPP).

	Europe	Asia	Africa
High SPP	17	14	12
Low SPP	8	16	16

Test at the 5% significance level if the location and economic status are dependent.

2 For families with two children, it is believed that the gender mixes 2 girls, 2 boys or 1 of each should be split in the ratio 1 : 1 : 2.

To test this, the following data were collected:

2 girls	2 boys	1 of each
66	59	115

Test the claim that the population ratio is 1 : 1 : 2 at the 5% significance level.

3 The following contingency table shows the data on hair colour and eye colour for a sample of 200 children.

		Eye colour		
		blue	green	brown
Hair colour	brown	51	35	15
	blonde	62	30	7

a Assuming the hair colour and eye colour are independent, calculate the expected frequencies.

b Calculate the value of the χ^2 statistic for this data and state the number of degrees of freedom.

c Perform a suitable hypothesis test at the 10% level of significance to decide whether hair colour and eye colour are independent. State your hypotheses and your conclusion clearly.

4 A nurse thinks that she has noticed that more boys are born at certain times of the year. She records the data for babies born in her hospital in one year:

	Boy	Girl
Spring	32	18
Summer	21	26
Autumn	30	35
Winter	14	18

Test at the 5% significance level whether her data give evidence for any association between the gender of the baby and the time of the year. You must show all your working clearly.

5 A teacher wants to find out whether the distribution of grades in an exam has changed since last year. She collects data for a random sample of 80 students, shown as the observed frequencies in the table. She also calculates that if the distribution of the grades is the same as last year, the frequencies are expected to be as shown in the third row of the table:

Grade	D	C	B	A	A*
Observed frequencies	3	21	27	18	11
Expected frequencies	7	16	38	11	8

The teacher wants to perform a χ^2 test at the 5% level of significance.

a State suitable hypotheses.

b Carry out the test to decide whether the model fits the observed data. Show clearly how you arrived at your conclusion.

6 Find the value of the appropriate chi-squared test statistic (to three significant figures) for the following contingency table:

	A	B
C	25	18
D	15	42

A 9.06   **B** 10.3

C 16.2   **D** 17.5

7 The director of a large company wants to know whether there is any association between the age of his staff and the department they work in. The following table shows the data for a sample of 480 employees:

	16–18	19–21	22–25	26–40	> 40
Accounts	2	17	22	38	61
Personnel	5	12	22	31	22
Marketing	2	31	18	58	16
Communications	12	22	26	42	21

Perform a suitable test at the 5% level of significance to decide whether there is any association between the age and the department.

8 The crew of the fishing boat 'Flipper' record the number of dolphins they observe per day during a tourist season. The data is shown in the table as follows:

Number of dolphins observed	8–11	12–14	15–18	19–21	22–25
Number of days	6	10	14	26	7

a i Calculate the mean and the variance of the observed data.

   ii Explain why your results from part **i** suggest that a Poisson distribution might be a suitable model for the data.

b Stating your hypotheses and conclusion clearly, test at the 5% level of significance whether the data can be modelled by a Poisson distribution.

9 A dice is thrown 240 times with the following results.

Score	1	2	3	4	5	6
Frequency	37	25	50	51	31	46

a Showing all steps clearly, test whether the dice is fair:

   i at the 5% level of significance

   ii at the 1% level of significance.

b Explain what is meant by 'level of significance' in part **a**.

10 In a study of the inheritance of skin colouration in corn snakes, a researcher found 865 snakes with black and orange bodies, 320 snakes with black bodies, 335 snakes with orange bodies and 112 snakes with bodies of other colours. Theory predicts that snakes of these colours should occur in the ratios 9 : 3 : 3 : 1. Test, at the 5% significance level, whether these experimental results are compatible with theory.

© OCR, GCE Mathematics, Paper 4734, June 2014

11 A random sample of 80 students who had all studied Biology, Chemistry and Art at a college was each asked which they enjoyed most. The results, classified according to gender, are given in the table.

		Subject		
		Biology	Chemistry	Art
Gender	Male	13	4	11
	Female	37	8	7

It is required to carry out a test of independence between subject most enjoyed and gender at the $2\frac{1}{2}\%$ significance level.

i Calculate the expected values for the cells.

ii Explain why it is necessary to combine cells, and choose a suitable combination.

iii Carry out the test.

© OCR, GCE Mathematics, Paper 4734, June 2013

12 The following table shows the experience of a bank over a long period of the types of loan that they give and whether they are repaid or defaulted (i.e. not repaid).

	Repaid	Defaulted
Personal	16%	4%
Mortgage	40%	10%
Business	25%	5%

a Show that the probability a loan gets repaid depends on the type of loan.

A statistician samples N loans at random and performs a chi-squared test for independence using a 5% significance level.

b Show that when $N = 200$, even if the sample proportions were identical to the population proportions, the test would not show dependence between the two factors.

c Find the smallest whole number N for which a sample with the same proportions as the population would provide significant evidence in **a**. You can assume that all expected values are above five.

13 A bag contains a large number of black and white balls. Balls are drawn out of the bag until a white ball is found. Let X be a random variable representing the number of balls drawn.

a Assuming that the balls are drawn independently of each other and that the probability, p, of selecting a white ball is constant,

i state the probability distribution of X.

ii Find the expected value of X in terms of p.

b The experiment is repeated 100 times and the values of X are recorded in the table as follows.

Number of balls drawn	1	2	3	4	5	6	7	8
Frequency	34	30	15	10	7	3	0	1

i Find the mean of the data in the table.

ii Hence estimate the value of p.

iii Test using the 5% level of significance whether the number of balls drawn can be modelled using a geometric distribution.

7 Continuous distributions

In this chapter you will learn how to:

- describe probabilities of continuous variables
- calculate expected statistics of continuous variables
- calculate expected statistics of functions of continuous variables
- convert between the probability density function f(x) and the cumulative distribution function F(x) = P($X \leqslant x$)
- find the median and quartiles
- use two new probability distributions – the continuous uniform and the exponential
- use the cumulative distribution function to find the distribution of the function of a random variable.

Before you start...

Chapter 2	You should know how to calculate expectations and variances for discrete distributions.	1 Find Var(X) if X has the distribution:

x	1	3	6
P($X = x$)	0.25	0.25	0.5

A Level Mathematics Student Book 2, Chapters 9 and 11	You should know how to integrate all functions from A level Mathematics.	2 Find $\int \sin 3x \, dx$.
A Level Mathematics Student Book 2, Chapter 16	You should know how to use the rules of probability including conditional probability.	3 If P($A \cap B$) = 0.4 and P(B) = 0.8 find P($A \mid B$).
A Level Mathematics Student Book 1, Chapter 16	You should know the meaning of the statistical measures covered in A Level Mathematics.	4 Find the interquartile range of the following data: 1, 1, 4, 5, 7, 9

From discrete to continuous

In Chapter 2 you saw that the ability to describe random variables allowed you to make predictions about their properties. However, a major limitation was that the methods in Chapter 2 only applied to discrete variables. In reality, many variables you are interested in, such as height, weight and time, are continuous variables. In this chapter you will extend the methods of Chapter 2 to work with continuous variables.

Section 1: Continuous random variables

Consider the following data for the masses of several 5 kg bags of rice, recorded to the nearest 100 g.

Mass (kg)	Frequency
4.9	12
5.0	16
5.1	20
5.2	14

A bag with mass 5.1358 kg or 5.087 954 6 kg would be counted in the 5.1 kg category. It is impossible to list all the different possible actual masses, and it is impossible to measure the mass absolutely accurately. When you collect continuous data, you have to put it into groups. This means that you cannot talk about the probability of a single value of a **continuous random variable** (crv). You can only talk about the probability of the crv being in a specified interval.

A useful way of representing probabilities of a crv is as an area under a graph. The probability of a single value would correspond to the 'area' of a vertical line, which would be zero. However, you can find the area of the crv in any interval by integration.

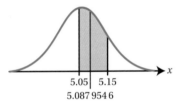

The function that you have to integrate is called the **probability density function** (pdf), and it is often denoted $f(x)$. The defining feature of $f(x)$ is that the area between two x values is the probability of the crv falling between those two values (see Key point 7.1).

Rewind

In Chapter 2 you saw the convention that capital letters were used for the names of random variables and lower case letters for the values they can take.

Key point 7.1

$$P(a < X < b) = \int_a^b f(x)\,dx$$

Tip

For a continuous variable, it does not matter whether you use strict inequalities ($a < x < b$) or inclusive inequalities ($a \leqslant x \leqslant b$).

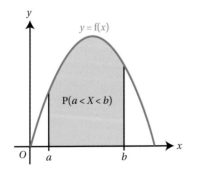

Rewind

You saw an example of a crv when you studied the normal distribution in A Level Mathematics Student Book 2.

As with discrete probabilities, the total probability must equal 1. Also, no probability can ever be negative. This provides two requirements for a function to be a pdf, listed in Key point 7.2.

Tip

The limits $-\infty$ and ∞ represent the fact that a crv could take any real value. In practice, the limits of the integral are set to the lowest and the highest value the variable can take.

Key point 7.2

For $f(x)$ to be a probability density function, it must satisfy:

$$\int_{-\infty}^{\infty} f(x)\, dx = 1$$

$$f(x) \geqslant 0$$

WORKED EXAMPLE 7.1

A crv has a pdf:

$$f(x) = \begin{cases} kx^2 & 0 \leqslant x < 1 \\ 0 & \text{otherwise} \end{cases}$$

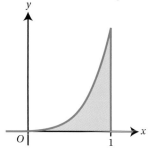

a Find the value of k.

b Find the probability of x being between 0.2 and 0.6.

a $\quad 1 = \int_0^1 kx^2\, dx$ . . . . Total area is 1. Area is only found between 0 and 1.

$$= \left[\frac{kx^3}{3} \right]_0^1$$

$$= \frac{k}{3}$$

$$\Leftrightarrow k = 3$$

b $\quad P(0.2 < X < 0.6) = \int_{0.2}^{0.6} 3x^2\, dx$

$$= \left[x^3 \right]_{0.2}^{0.6}$$

$$= 0.208$$

EXERCISE 7A

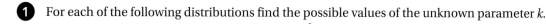

1 For each of the following distributions find the possible values of the unknown parameter k.

a **i** $\quad f(x) = \begin{cases} kx^3 & 2 < x < 3 \\ 0 & \text{otherwise} \end{cases}$
 $\qquad$ **ii** $\quad f(x) = \begin{cases} k\sqrt{x} & 1 < x < 4 \\ 0 & \text{otherwise} \end{cases}$

b **i** $\quad f(x) = \begin{cases} x^2 + k & -1 < x \leqslant 2 \\ 0 & \text{otherwise} \end{cases}$
 $\qquad$ **ii** $\quad f(x) = \begin{cases} 3x + k & -2 \leqslant x < 3 \\ 0 & \text{otherwise} \end{cases}$

c **i** $f(x)=\begin{cases} x^3 & 0<x<k \\ 0 & \text{otherwise} \end{cases}$
    ii $f(x)=\begin{cases} 2x-1 & 1<x<k \\ 0 & \text{otherwise} \end{cases}$

d **i** $f(x)=\begin{cases} x & k<x<k+1 \\ 0 & \text{otherwise} \end{cases}$
    ii $f(x)=\begin{cases} x^2 & k<x<2k \\ 0 & \text{otherwise} \end{cases}$

e **i** $f(x)=\begin{cases} kx^2 & 0<x<k \\ 0 & \text{otherwise} \end{cases}$
    ii $f(x)=\begin{cases} x+k & 0<x<k \\ 0 & \text{otherwise} \end{cases}$

f **i** $f(x)=\begin{cases} \dfrac{1}{x^2} & 1<x<k \\ 0 & \text{otherwise} \end{cases}$
    ii $f(x)=\begin{cases} \dfrac{1}{2\sqrt{x}} & k<x<1 \\ 0 & \text{otherwise} \end{cases}$

g **i** $f(x)=\begin{cases} e^{kx} & 0<x<2 \\ 0 & \text{otherwise} \end{cases}$
    ii $f(x)=\begin{cases} \sin kx & 0<x<\pi \\ 0 & \text{otherwise} \end{cases}$

h **i** $f(x)=\begin{cases} \dfrac{1}{(x+k)^2} & 0\leqslant x\leqslant 1 \\ 0 & \text{otherwise} \end{cases}$
    ii $f(x)=\begin{cases} \dfrac{1}{x+k} & 0\leqslant x\leqslant 1 \\ 0 & \text{otherwise} \end{cases}$

i **i** $f(x)=\begin{cases} ke^{-x^2} & 3<x<8 \\ 0 & \text{otherwise} \end{cases}$
    ii $f(x)=\begin{cases} k\sin\sqrt{x} & \pi<x<\pi^2 \\ 0 & \text{otherwise.} \end{cases}$

2 **a** $f(x)=\begin{cases} 2-2x & 0<x<1 \\ 0 & \text{otherwise} \end{cases}$

    i Find $P(0.3<X<0.9)$.
    ii Find $P(0<X<0.5)$.

  b $f(x)=\begin{cases} \cos x & 0<x<\dfrac{\pi}{2} \\ 0 & \text{otherwise} \end{cases}$

    i Find $P\left(\dfrac{\pi}{4}<X\leqslant\dfrac{\pi}{3}\right)$.
    ii Find $P\left(0\leqslant X<\dfrac{\pi}{6}\right)$.

  c $f(x)=\begin{cases} \dfrac{1}{x\ln 10} & 1<x<10 \\ 0 & \text{otherwise} \end{cases}$

    i Find $P(X>5)$.
    ii Find $P(X\leqslant 3)$.

3 **a** $f(x)=\begin{cases} 2x & 0<x<1 \\ 0 & \text{otherwise} \end{cases}$

    i Find a if $P(X<a)=0.4$.
    ii Find b if $P(X<b)=0.9$.

  b $f(x)=\begin{cases} \dfrac{x}{8} & 0<x<8 \\ 0 & \text{otherwise} \end{cases}$

    i Find a if $P(X>a)=0.9$.
    ii Find b if $P(X>b)=0.5$.

  c $f(x)=\begin{cases} \dfrac{x}{16} & 2<x<6 \\ 0 & \text{otherwise} \end{cases}$

    i Find a if $P(2+a<X<6-a)=0.8$.
    ii Find b if $P(b<X<b+1)=0.25$.

4 A model predicts that the angle, G, an alpha particle is deflected by a nucleus is modelled by

$$f(g)=\begin{cases}kg^2 & 0<g<\pi \\ 0 & \text{otherwise.}\end{cases}$$

 a Find the value of the constant k.

 b 10 000 alpha particles are fired at a nucleus. If the model is correct, estimate the number of alpha particles deflected by an angle of less than $\dfrac{\pi}{3}$ radians.

5 D is the random variable 'distance a seed is found from a tree'. The pdf of D, $f(d)$, is proportional to $\dfrac{1}{d^2}$. The minimum distance that a seed is from the tree is 0.5 m. Find the probability of a seed being found more than 1 m from the tree.

6 A random variable Y has distribution $f(y)=\begin{cases}3e^{-3y} & y>0 \\ 0 & \text{otherwise.}\end{cases}$
Find the exact value of $P(Y>2)$.

7 If $f(x)=\begin{cases}\dfrac{1}{x} & 1<x<e \\ 0 & \text{otherwise.}\end{cases}$

 a Find b in terms of k if $P(b<X<b^2)=k$.

 b Find a in terms of k if $P(2-a<X\leqslant 2+a)=k$.

8 The crv X has the pdf $f(x)=ax$ for $0<x<b$ and 0 otherwise. The probability of two independent observations of x both being less than 0.5 is $\dfrac{1}{256}$. Find the values of a and of b.

9 If $f(x)=\begin{cases}e^x & k<x<2k \\ 0 & \text{otherwise}\end{cases}$, find $P\left(X>\dfrac{3k}{2}\right)$.

10 The crv T has pdf given by $f(t)=16t^3+6t$ for $0<t<k$ and 0 otherwise. Prove that there is only one possible value of k, and state that value.

Section 2: Averages and measures of spread of continuous random variables

The expressions for expectation and variance of crvs both involve integration (see Key point 7.3).

Key point 7.3

$$\mu=E(X)=\int_{-\infty}^{\infty}x\,f(x)\,dx$$

$$\sigma^2=\text{Var}(X)=\int_{-\infty}^{\infty}(x-\mu)^2\,f(x)\,dx\int_{-\infty}^{\infty}x^2\,f(x)\,dx-\mu^2$$

These formulae will appear in your formula book.

These integrals need to be evaluated over the whole **domain** of the pdf.

Tip

You might have notice that the expressions for E(X) and Var(X) look similar to those for discrete random variables, but with integration instead of summation signs. This is because there is a link between sums and integrals.

If you use the fact that $E(X^2) = \int_{-\infty}^{\infty} x^2 f(x)dx$ then you can see that Var(X) is still $E(X^2) - E(X)^2$.

WORKED EXAMPLE 7.2

A crv has pdf:

$$f(x) = \begin{cases} \dfrac{3}{4}x(2-x) & 0 < x < 2 \\ 0 & \text{otherwise,} \end{cases}$$

find E(X) and the standard deviation of X.

$E(X) = \int_0^2 x \times \dfrac{3}{4}x(2-x)dx$ ..... You can do the definite integration on the calculator.

$= \dfrac{3}{4}\int_0^2 x^2(2-x)\,dx$

$= 1$

$E(X^2) = \int_0^2 x^2 \times \dfrac{3}{4}x(2-x)\,dx$ ..... To find standard deviation you must first find Var(X) which requires you to find $E(X^2)$.

$= \dfrac{3}{4}\int_0^2 x^3(2-x)\,dx$

$= 1.2$

$Var(X) = E(X^2) - E(X)^2$

$= 1.2 - 1^2$

$= 0.2$

Standard deviation $= \sqrt{0.2} = 0.447$

It is also possible to find the median and mode for a continuous distribution.

The defining feature of the median is that half of the data should be below this value and half above. The mode is the most likely value. You can interpret this in terms of probability, as shown in Key point 7.4.

 Key point 7.4

If you represent the median by m then it satisfies

$$\int_{-\infty}^{m} f(x)\,dx = \dfrac{1}{2}$$

The mode is the value of x at the maximum value of f(x).

You can use similar ideas to find the quartiles (or any other percentile). For example if Q_1 is the lower quartile and Q_3 is the upper quartile then

$$\int_{-\infty}^{Q_1} f(x)\,dx = \frac{1}{4} \qquad\qquad \int_{-\infty}^{Q_3} f(x)\,dx = \frac{3}{4}$$

Although the lower limit is written as minus infinity, in practice it starts from the lowest value where the pdf is non-zero.

WORKED EXAMPLE 7.3

Find the median and mode of a random variable X with the pdf

$$f(x) = \begin{cases} \dfrac{3}{50}(x^2 - 4x + 5) & 0 \leqslant x \leqslant 5 \\ 0 & \text{otherwise.} \end{cases}$$

$\displaystyle\int_0^m \frac{3}{50}(x^2 - 4x + 5)\,dx = \frac{1}{2}$ .... Probability of being below the median is $\dfrac{1}{2}$.

$\dfrac{x^3}{50} - \dfrac{3x^2}{25} + \dfrac{3x}{10} = \dfrac{1}{2}$

$m = 3.78$ (from calculator) .... This is a cubic equation. Solve it using a calculator.

$f'(x) = \dfrac{3}{25}x - \dfrac{6}{25} = 0$ .... For the mode check for a maximum point. This could be where the derivative is zero or

$\Rightarrow x = 2$ at an end point.

$f(2) = \dfrac{3}{50}$

$f(0) = \dfrac{3}{10}$

$f(5) = \dfrac{3}{5}$

Hence the mode is 5. .... The largest of these three numbers is $f(5)$.

💡 **Tip**

Students often forget to look at the endpoints when finding the mode.

EXERCISE 7B

1 Find $E(X)$, the median of X, the mode of X and $Var(X)$ if X has the given pdf.

a i $f(x) = \begin{cases} 2 - 2x & 0 \leqslant x \leqslant 1 \\ 0 & \text{otherwise} \end{cases}$ **ii** $f(x) = \begin{cases} \dfrac{x}{32} & 0 \leqslant x \leqslant 8 \\ 0 & \text{otherwise} \end{cases}$

b i $f(x) = \begin{cases} \dfrac{1}{x\ln 10} & 1 \leqslant x \leqslant 10 \\ 0 & \text{otherwise} \end{cases}$ **ii** $f(x) = \begin{cases} \dfrac{2}{x^2} & 1 \leqslant x \leqslant 2 \\ 0 & \text{otherwise} \end{cases}$

c i $f(x) = \begin{cases} \cos x & 0 \leqslant x \leqslant \dfrac{\pi}{2} \\ 0 & \text{otherwise} \end{cases}$ 　　**ii** $f(x) = \begin{cases} e^x & 0 \leqslant x \leqslant \ln 2 \\ 0 & \text{otherwise} \end{cases}$

d i $f(x) = \begin{cases} \dfrac{3}{x^4} & x \geqslant 1 \\ 0 & \text{otherwise} \end{cases}$ 　　**ii** $f(x) = \begin{cases} \dfrac{4}{x^5} & x \geqslant 1 \\ 0 & \text{otherwise} \end{cases}$

2　a Given that $E(X) = 1.1$ find k if:

i $f(x) = \begin{cases} \dfrac{1}{x \ln k} & 1 < x < k \\ 0 & \text{otherwise} \end{cases}$ 　　**ii** $f(x) = \begin{cases} \dfrac{k-1}{x^k} & 1 < x < \infty \\ 0 & \text{otherwise} \end{cases}$

b Given that $E(X) = 3$ find k if:

i $f(x) = \begin{cases} k & k < x < k + \dfrac{1}{k} \\ 0 & \text{otherwise} \end{cases}$ 　　**ii** $f(x) = \begin{cases} \dfrac{1}{x+k} & 0 < x < (e-1)k \\ 0 & \text{otherwise} \end{cases}$

3 The crv X has pdf $f(x) = \begin{cases} \dfrac{3}{20}\left(4x^2 - x^3\right) & 0 \leqslant x \leqslant 2 \\ 0 & \text{otherwise.} \end{cases}$

a Find the mean of X.

b Find the mode of X.

4 A crv B has pdf $f(b) = \begin{cases} ab^2 & 3 < b < 10 \\ 0 & \text{otherwise.} \end{cases}$

a Find the value of the constant a.

b Find $E(B)$.

5 Consider the function $f(y) = \begin{cases} ke^{-ky} & y > 0 \\ 0 & \text{otherwise.} \end{cases}$

a Show that, for all values of k, the function f satisfies the conditions to be a pdf.

b A random variable Y has a pdf $f(y)$. Find $E(Y)$ in terms of k.

6 Y is a crv with pdf $f(y) = \begin{cases} ay^2 & -k < y < k \\ 0 & \text{otherwise.} \end{cases}$

a Show that $a = \dfrac{3}{2k^3}$.

b Given that $\text{Var}(Y) = 5$ find the exact value of k.

7 If the crv X has a pdf $f(x) = \begin{cases} \sec^2 x & 0 < x < \dfrac{\pi}{4} \\ 0 & \text{otherwise} \end{cases}$, find the interquartile range of X.

8 Given that $f(x) = \dfrac{1}{\sqrt{2\pi}} e^{-\frac{x^2}{2}}$, $x \in \mathbb{R}$ is a probability distribution, find $E(X)$ and prove that $\text{Var}(X) = 1$.

Section 3: Expectation and variance of functions of a random variable

Linear transformations

Suppose the average height of people in a class was 1.75 m and their standard deviation was 0.1 m. If they were all to stand on their 0.5 m high chairs then the new average height would be 2.25 m, but the standard deviation would remain 0.1 m. If you add a constant on to a variable, you add the same constant on to the expectation, but the variance does not change:

$$E(X+c)=E(X)+c, \text{Var}(X+c)=\text{Var}(X)$$

If, instead, each pupil were given a magical growing potion that doubled their heights, the new average height would be 3.5 m. However, the range would have doubled along with any other linear measure of variability, so the new standard deviation would be 0.2 m. This means that their variance would change from 0.01 m^2 to 0.04 m^2. If you multiply a variable by a constant, you multiply the expectation by the constant and multiply the variance by the constant squared:

$$E(aX)=aE(X), \text{Var}(aX)=a^2\text{Var}(X)$$

These ideas can be combined together to form the equations in Key point 7.5.

 Key point 7.5

$$E(aX+c)=aE(X)+c, \text{Var}(aX+c)=a^2\text{Var}(X)$$

WORKED EXAMPLE 7.4

A 100 cm long pipe is to be cut into two pieces. The cut is placed at random so that the length of the longer piece has mean 80 cm and standard deviation 2 cm. Find the mean and standard deviation of the length of the shorter piece.

$L =$ 'Length of longer piece'
$S =$ 'Length of shorter piece'

> Define your variables.

$S = 100 - L$

> Connect your variables.

$E(S) = E(100 - L)$
$\quad = 100\,cm - E(L)$
$\quad = 100\,cm - 80\,cm$
$\quad = 20\,cm$

> Apply expectation algebra.

$\text{Var}(S) = \text{Var}(100 - L)$
$\quad = (-1)^2\text{Var}(L)$
$\quad = \text{Var}(L)$
$\quad = 4\,cm^2$

So the standard deviation of S is also 2 cm.

General transformations

When finding the variance you used the fact that $E(X^2)=\int x^2\text{f}(x)\,dx$. This is generalised to any function of X in Key point 7.6.

 Rewind

You have already met this idea for discrete random variables in Key point 2.5. In this chapter you extend it to crvs, which is very similar.

 Tip

It is important to know that this only works for the structure $aX + c$, which is called a linear function. So, for example, $E(X^2)$ cannot be simplified to $[E(X)]^2$. Nor is $E(|X|) \equiv |E(X)|$.

Tip

You should always get a positive variance.

Key point 7.6

If X is a crv with pdf f(x) then
$$E\big(g(X)\big)=\int_{-\infty}^{\infty} g(x)f(x)\,dx$$

WORKED EXAMPLE 7.5

If the random variable X has probability density $\dfrac{1}{21}x^2$ for $1 < x < 4$ and 0 otherwise,

find $E\left(\dfrac{7}{X}\right)$.

$E\left(\dfrac{7}{X}\right)=\displaystyle\int_1^4 \dfrac{7}{x}\times\dfrac{1}{21}x^2 dx$ · · · · · · · · · · · · Identify $f(x)=\dfrac{1}{21}x^2$ and $g(x)=\dfrac{7}{x}$. The limits are between 1 and 4 because that is where f(x) is not zero.

$\quad=\displaystyle\int_1^4 \dfrac{1}{3}x\,dx$

$\quad=\left[\dfrac{x^2}{6}\right]_1^4 = 2.5$

EXERCISE 7C

1 If $E(X)=4$ find:

  a **i** $E(3X)$ **b** **i** $E\left(\dfrac{X}{2}\right)$ **c** **i** $E(-X)$

      ii $E(6X)$ **ii** $E\left(\dfrac{3X}{4}\right)$ **ii** $E(-4X)$

  d **i** $E(X+5)$ **e** **i** $E(5-2X)$

      ii $E(X-3)$ **ii** $E(3X+1)$.

2 If $Var(X)=6$ find:

  a **i** $Var(3X)$ **b** **i** $Var\left(\dfrac{X}{2}\right)$ **c** **i** $Var(-X)$

      ii $Var(6X)$ **ii** $Var\left(\dfrac{3X}{4}\right)$ **ii** $Var(-4X)$

  d **i** $Var(X+5)$ **e** **i** $Var(5-2X)$

      ii $Var(X-3)$ **ii** $Var(3X+1)$.

3 If X is a discrete random variable with pdf $f(x)=2x$ for $0 < x < 1$, find:

  a **i** $E(X^2)$ **ii** $E(X^3)$

  b **i** $E\left(\dfrac{5}{X}\right)$ **ii** $E\left(\dfrac{6}{\sqrt{X}}\right)$

  c **i** $E(\sin X)$ **ii** $E(e^X)$

  d **i** $E(\ln(X)-1)$ **ii** $E\big(\sqrt{X}\big(\sqrt{X}+1\big)\big)$.

4 The expectation of the distance of a random taxi journey is 3.2 miles with standard deviation 0.8 miles. The charge for a taxi journey is £4 plus £2 per mile (so that for example a 6.2 mile journey would cost £16.40). Find:

    a the expectation of the charge

    b the standard deviation in the charge for a taxi journey.

5 The random variable X has $E(X) = 6$ and $\text{Var}(X) = 2$. If $Y = aX$ and $E(Y) = \text{Var}(Y)$ find a.

6 Daniel has 6 hours of playtime each Sunday afternoon. In that time he either reads or plays games. If the expected amount of time reading is 2 hours with a standard deviation of 0.5 hours find:

    a the expected amount of time playing games

    b the standard deviation of the amount of time spent playing a game.

7 The side of a cube, S, is a crv with pdf $f(s) = \dfrac{1}{9}s^2$ for $0 < s < 3$ and zero otherwise.

    a Find $E(S)$.

    b Find the expected volume of the cube.

 Tip

Notice that the answer to **b** is not the cube of the answer to **a**.

8 The random variable X has a pdf $f(x) = \cos 2x$ for $-\dfrac{\pi}{4} < x < \dfrac{\pi}{4}$ and 0 otherwise. Find:

    a $E(X)$ b $E(2X - 1)$ c $E(|X|)$.

9 The random variable X has a pdf $f(x) = 1.5x^2$ for $-1 < x < 1$ and 0 otherwise.

    a Find $E(X^n)$ where n is a positive whole number.

    b Find $\text{Var}(X^2)$.

Section 4: Cumulative distribution functions

A **cumulative distribution function** (cdf) measures the probability of being less than or equal to a particular value. Normally, if the pdf is called $f(x)$, the cdf is called $F(x)$, as in Key point 7.7.

Tip

The t in the integral is a 'dummy variable'. It could be replaced by any other symbol. The only real variable in this expression is the x in the upper limit, which corresponds to the x in the left-hand expression.

Key point 7.7

For a continuous distribution

$$P(X \leqslant x) = F(x) = \int_{-\infty}^{x} f(t)\,dt$$

Notice that you have already used this: when finding the median you solve the equation $P(X \leqslant m) = \dfrac{1}{2}$, which can be written as $F(X) = \dfrac{1}{2}$. However, cdfs have many other, sometimes surprising, uses. This is because, unlike a pdf, the cdf gives actual probabilities, so you can apply probability laws to it.

Since integration can be 'undone' by differentiation, this allows us to recover the pdf from F(x).

 Key point 7.8

$$f(x) = \frac{d}{dx}F(x)$$

WORKED EXAMPLE 7.6

Find the cdf if a crv X has a pdf $f(x) = e^x$ for $0 < x < \ln 2$ and 0 otherwise.

If $x \leqslant 0 : F(x) = 0$

If $x \geqslant \ln 2 : F(x) = 1$. | State F($x$) when x is below and above the range in which f(x) is defined. When x is above ln 2 the probability of being below x is 1, because all observed x values are between 0 and ln 2.

If $0 < x < \ln 2$:

$$F(x) = \int_0^x e(x)\,dx$$ | Since there is no probability of being below $x = 0$, the integral starts at $x = 0$.

$$= [e(x)]_0^x$$
$$= e^x - 1$$

Once you have the cdf you can use it to find the median, quartiles and any other percentiles, since the pth percentile is defined as the value x such that $P(X \leqslant x) = p\%$. i.e. $F(x) = \dfrac{p}{100}$.

 Rewind

You saw that you could do this without explicitly referring to a cdf in Exercise 7B.

WORKED EXAMPLE 7.7

The crv X has a cdf

$$F(x) = \begin{cases} 0 & x \leqslant 0 \\ x^2 & 0 < x < 1 \\ 1 & x \geqslant 1. \end{cases}$$

a Find the pdf of X.
b Find the lower quartile of X.

a $f(x) = \dfrac{d}{dx}F(x)$ | pdf is the derivative of cdf.

$= 2x$ if $0 < x < 1$

And zero otherwise

b At the lower quartile: | Lower quartile is 25th percentile.

$$F(x) = 0.25$$
$$x^2 = 0.25$$
$$x = \pm 0.5$$

f(x) is non-zero only if $0 < x < 1$ | Decide which solution to choose.

Therefore $x = 0.5$.

EXERCISE 7D

1 Find the cdf for each of the following pdfs, and hence find the median of the distribution:

a **i** $f(x)=\begin{cases}2-2x & 0<x<1 \\ 0 & \text{otherwise}\end{cases}$ **ii** $f(x)=\begin{cases}\dfrac{x}{16} & 2<x<6 \\ 0 & \text{otherwise}\end{cases}$

b **i** $f(x)=\begin{cases}\sin x & 0<x<\dfrac{\pi}{2} \\ 0 & \text{otherwise}\end{cases}$ **ii** $f(x)=\begin{cases}\dfrac{1}{x\ln 10} & 1<x<10 \\ 0 & \text{otherwise}\end{cases}$

2 Given the following continuous cdfs, find the pdf and the median.

a **i** $F(x)=\begin{cases}0 & x<1 \\ x-1 & 1\leqslant x<2 \\ 1 & x\geqslant 2\end{cases}$ **ii** $F(x)=\begin{cases}0 & x<0 \\ 3x & 0\leqslant x<\dfrac{1}{3} \\ 1 & x\geqslant\dfrac{1}{3}\end{cases}$

b **i** $F(x)=\begin{cases}0 & x<1 \\ x^2-x & 1\leqslant x<\dfrac{1+\sqrt5}{2} \\ 1 & x\geqslant\dfrac{1+\sqrt5}{2}\end{cases}$ **ii** $F(x)=\begin{cases}0 & x<0 \\ \sin x & 0\leqslant x<\dfrac{\pi}{2} \\ 1 & x\geqslant\dfrac{\pi}{2}\end{cases}$

3 Find the exact value of the 80th percentile of the crv Y that has pdf $f(y)=\dfrac{1}{y}$ for $1<y<e$ and zero otherwise.

4 A continuous variable has cdf

$$F(x)=\begin{cases}0 & x<0 \\ e^{2x}-1 & 0\leqslant x<k \\ 1 & x\geqslant k.\end{cases}$$

a Find the value of k.

b Find the pdf.

c Find the median of the distribution.

Section 5: Piecewise-defined probability density functions

A pdf can have different function rules on different parts of its domain. Such a function is said to be **defined piecewise**. All the techniques from the previous sections still apply. However, when evaluating definite integrals you need to split them into several parts.

 Rewind

You already met this idea in the context of kinematics, in A Level Mathematics Student Book 1, Chapter 19.

WORKED EXAMPLE 7.8

A crv X has the pdf given by

$$f(x) = \begin{cases} k \sin x & \text{for } 0 \leqslant x \leqslant \dfrac{\pi}{2} \\[2mm] k \cos 4x & \text{for } \dfrac{\pi}{2} < x \leqslant \dfrac{5\pi}{8} \\[2mm] 0 & \text{otherwise.} \end{cases}$$

a Sketch $f(x)$.

b Show that $k = \dfrac{4}{5}$.

c Find $P\left(X \leqslant \dfrac{11\pi}{20}\right)$.

d Find the exact value of $E(X)$.

a

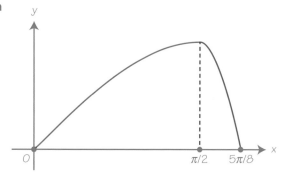

b $\displaystyle\int_{0}^{\frac{\pi}{2}} k \sin x \, dx + \int_{\frac{\pi}{2}}^{\frac{5\pi}{8}} k \cos 4x \, dx = 1$

As before, the total area under the graph of $f(x)$ must be 1. However, the area is now made up of two separate parts.

$\Leftrightarrow \left[-k \cos x\right]_{0}^{\frac{\pi}{2}} + \left[\dfrac{k}{4} \sin 4x\right]_{\frac{\pi}{2}}^{\frac{5\pi}{8}} = 1$

$\Leftrightarrow k + \dfrac{k}{4} = 1$

$\Leftrightarrow k = \dfrac{4}{5}$

c $P\left(X \leqslant \dfrac{11\pi}{20}\right) = P\left(X \leqslant \dfrac{\pi}{2}\right) + P\left(\dfrac{\pi}{2} < X \leqslant \dfrac{11\pi}{20}\right)$

$\dfrac{11\pi}{20} > \dfrac{\pi}{2}$ so the probability needs to be calculated in two parts.

$\qquad = k + \left[\dfrac{k}{4} \sin 4x\right]_{\frac{\pi}{2}}^{\frac{11\pi}{20}}$

You have already done the integration in part **b**.

$\qquad = 0.918 \, (3 \text{ s.f.})$

Continues on next page ...

d $E(X) = \int_0^{\frac{\pi}{2}} \frac{4}{5} x \sin x \, dx + \int_{\frac{\pi}{2}}^{\frac{5\pi}{8}} \frac{4}{5} x \cos 4x \, dx$

> The integral for $E(X)$ also needs to be split into two.

$= \left[-\frac{4}{5} x \cos x \right]_0^{\frac{\pi}{2}} + \int_0^{\frac{\pi}{2}} \frac{4}{5} \cos x \, dx + \left[\frac{1}{5} x \sin 4x \right]_{\frac{\pi}{2}}^{\frac{5\pi}{8}}$

$\qquad - \int_{\frac{\pi}{2}}^{\frac{5\pi}{8}} \frac{1}{5} \sin 4x \, dx$

> You are asked for the exact value, so you can't use a calculator to evaluate the integral. Use integration by parts for each integral, taking $u = \frac{4}{5} x$ in both.

$= 0 + \frac{4}{5} \sin \frac{\pi}{2} + \frac{1}{5} \frac{5\pi}{8} \sin \frac{5\pi}{2} - \frac{1}{20} \cos 2\pi$

$= \frac{6 + \pi}{8}$

WORKED EXAMPLE 7.9

A random variable Y has the pdf

$$f(y) = \begin{cases} \dfrac{1}{6} y, & 0 \leqslant y \leqslant 2 \\[2mm] \dfrac{1}{2} - \dfrac{1}{12} y, & 2 < y \leqslant 6 \\[2mm] 0 & \text{otherwise.} \end{cases}$$

a Find the cdf of Y.
b Find the median of Y.

a When $0 \leqslant y \leqslant 2$:

$F(y) = P(Y \leqslant y)$

> You need to look at the two parts of the domain separately.

$\qquad = \int_0^y \frac{1}{6} t \, dt = \frac{1}{12} y^2$

When $2 < y \leqslant 6$:

$F(y) = P(Y \leqslant y)$

$\qquad = P(Y \leqslant 2) + P(2 < Y \leqslant y)$

> You need to split the probability into two parts to use the different expressions.

$\qquad = \frac{1}{12}(2^2) + \int_2^y \frac{1}{2} - \frac{1}{12} t \, dt$

> Use $P(Y \leqslant 2) = F(2)$, which you found previously.

$\qquad = \frac{1}{3} + \left[\frac{1}{2} t - \frac{1}{24} t^2 \right]_2^y$

$\qquad = \frac{1}{2} y - \frac{1}{24} y^2 - \frac{1}{2}$

Continues on next page ...

Hence,

$$F(y) = \begin{cases} 0, & y < 0 \\ \dfrac{1}{12}y^2, & 0 \leqslant y \leqslant 2 \\ \dfrac{1}{2}y - \dfrac{1}{24}y^2 - \dfrac{1}{2}, & 2 < y \leqslant 6 \\ 1, & y > 6 \end{cases}$$

> Remember to write out the full expression for F(y).

b If the median is m, then $F(m) = \dfrac{1}{2}$.

If $0 \leqslant m \leqslant 2$:

$$\frac{1}{12}m^2 = \frac{1}{2} \Rightarrow m^2 = 6$$

$$\Rightarrow m = \pm\sqrt{6} \notin [0, 2]$$

> Remember to check that any solution you found is in the correct interval; in this case, neither of these values can be the median.

If $2 \leqslant m \leqslant 6$:

$$\frac{1}{2}y - \frac{1}{24}y^2 - \frac{1}{2} = \frac{1}{2}$$
$$\Rightarrow y^2 - 12y + 24 = 0$$
$$\Rightarrow y = 2.54 \text{ or } 9.46$$

Hence the median is 2.54.

> The median must be between two and six.

EXERCISE 7E

1 A crv X has pdf

$$f(x) = \begin{cases} kx, & 0 \leqslant x < 5 \\ k(10 - x), & 5 \leqslant x < 10 \\ 0 & \text{otherwise.} \end{cases}$$

a Sketch the graph of $f(x)$.

b Find the value of k.

c Find the value of a such that $P(X < a) = 0.68$.

2 A random variable Y has cdf

$$F(y) = \begin{cases} 0 & \text{for } y < 0 \\ \dfrac{1}{2}y & \text{for } 0 \leqslant y < 1 \\ \dfrac{1}{3}y + \dfrac{1}{6} & \text{for } 1 \leqslant y < 2 \\ \dfrac{1}{6}y + \dfrac{1}{2} & \text{for } 2 \leqslant y \leqslant 3 \\ 1 & \text{for } y > 3. \end{cases}$$

a Find the median of Y.

b Find the mean and the variance of Y.

3 A crv X has pdf

$$f(x) = \begin{cases} cx, & 0 \leqslant x \leqslant 2 \\ \dfrac{2c}{9}(x-5)^2, & 2 < x \leqslant 5 \\ 0, & \text{otherwise.} \end{cases}$$

a Show that $c = \dfrac{1}{4}$.

b Find the cdf of X.

c Write down the value of $P(X \leqslant 2)$.

d Find the upper quartile of X.

4 The crv W is defined by the pdf $f(w)$, where

$$f(w) = \begin{cases} \dfrac{w^2}{27} & 0 \leqslant w < 3 \\ \dfrac{7}{12} - \dfrac{w}{12} & 3 \leqslant w < k \\ 0 & \text{otherwise.} \end{cases}$$

a Sketch the pdf.

b Find the value of k.

c Find $E(W)$.

d Find the median of W.

e Find the mode of W.

5 **In this question you must show detailed reasoning.**

Function f is defined by

$$f(x) = \begin{cases} e^x & \text{for } -\ln 2 < x < 0 \\ e^{-x} & \text{for } 0 \leqslant x < \ln 2 \\ 0 & \text{otherwise.} \end{cases}$$

a Show that f is a valid pdf.

b Find the variance of a random variable X whose pdf is f.

6 The crv X has the pdf

$$f(x) = \begin{cases} ax^3 & 0 \leqslant x < 1 \\ \dfrac{a}{x} & 1 \leqslant x < 2 \\ 0 & \text{otherwise.} \end{cases}$$

a Find the value of a.

b Find the expectation of X.

c Find the cdf of X.

d Find the median of X.

e Find the lower quartile of X.

Section 6: Continuous uniform distribution

The continuous uniform distribution is related to the discrete uniform distribution. It is a distribution where any equally sized part of the domain has an equal probability of occurring. It is defined by the endpoints of the domain, a and b. The pdf is a constant, and this constant must be chosen so that the total area under the graph is 1.

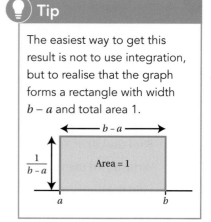

> **Tip**
>
> The easiest way to get this result is not to use integration, but to realise that the graph forms a rectangle with width $b - a$ and total area 1.

> 🔑 **Key point 7.9**
>
> If X follows a uniform distribution between a and b, then $f(x) = \dfrac{1}{b-a}$ for $a < x < b$
>
> **This will appear in your formula book.**

The mean and variance of this distribution can be found using integration:

WORKED EXAMPLE 7.10

Prove that if X is a random variable following a continuous uniform distribution over $[a, b]$ with $b > a$ then $E(X) = \dfrac{a+b}{2}$.

$E(X) = \displaystyle\int_{-\infty}^{\infty} x f(x)\,dx$ · · · · · · · · · Use the definition of expectation for a continuous variable.

$= \displaystyle\int_{a}^{b} x \dfrac{1}{b-a}\,dx$

$= \dfrac{1}{b-a} \displaystyle\int_{a}^{b} x\,dx$ · · · · · · · · Use the laws of integration.

$= \dfrac{1}{b-a} \left[\dfrac{x^2}{2} \right]_{a}^{b}$

$= \dfrac{b^2 - a^2}{2(b-a)}$

$= \dfrac{(b-a)(b+a)}{2(b-a)}$ · · · · · · · · · Use the difference of two squares.

$= \dfrac{b+a}{2}$

Since $b - a \neq 0$

You can use a similar method to find the variance (see Key point 7.10).

> ⏭️ **Fast forward**
>
> You are asked to do this in Exercise 7F, question 6.

> 🔑 **Key point 7.10**
>
> If X is a random variable following continuous uniform distribution over $[a, b]$:
>
> $$E(X) = \dfrac{a+b}{2}$$
>
> $$\mathrm{Var}(X) = \dfrac{(b-a)^2}{12}$$

WORKED EXAMPLE 7.11

When a measurement is quoted to the nearest kg it is equally likely to be anywhere within 0.5 kg of the stated value. A large number of measurements of different objects, all of which round to 42 kg, are made and their accurate values noted.

a Find the probability that an object quoted as being 42 kg to the nearest kg is actually more than 0.3 kg away from 42 kg.

b Find the standard deviation of the difference between the quoted value and the true value (with quoted values below the true value giving a negative difference).

a X = 'true mass of an object quoted as 42 kg'

Define variables.

X follows a continuous uniform distribution over $[41.5, 42.5]$

Identify the distribution.

Required probability is $P(X > 42.3) + P(X < 41.7)$

Write the requirement in mathematical terms.

$= 0.2 \times \dfrac{1}{42.5 - 41.5} + 0.2 \times \dfrac{1}{42.5 - 41.5}$

Use areas of rectangles rather than integration.

$= 0.4$

b $Var(42 - X) = Var(X)$

Use expectation algebra.

$= \dfrac{(42.5 - 41.5)^2}{12}$

Use the formula for $Var(X)$.

$= \dfrac{1}{12}$

EXERCISE 7F

1 Find the following probabilities; in parts **a** to **d**, X follows a continuous uniform distribution over $[a, b]$:

a **i** $P(2 < X \leqslant 4)$, $a = -1$, $b = 6$ **ii** $P(-3 < X < 10)$ $a = -10$, $b = 10$

b **i** $P(3.2 < X < 6.4)$ $a = 4.1$, $b = 8.9$ **ii** $P(2.5 \leqslant X < 7.1)$ $a = 5$, $b = 10.5$

c **i** $P(X > 3)$ $a = 2$, $b = 5$ **ii** $P(X \leqslant 5.2)$ $a = 0$, $b = 12$

d **i** $P(|X - 5| > 2)$ $a = 1$, $b = 10$ **ii** $P(|X - 6.8| > 1.2)$ $a = 4$, $b = 12$.

e **i** When a measurement is quoted to the nearest centimetre it is equally likely to be anywhere within 0.5 cm of the stated value. Find the probability that a measurement quoted as being 23 cm to the nearest cm is actually above 23.4 cm.

   ii A car's odometer shows the number of completed miles it has done. Jerry's car shows 9999 miles. What is the probability that it will show 10 000 miles in the next 0.3 miles?

2 Find the expected mean and standard deviation of the following:

a **i** X follows a continuous uniform distribution over $[-1, 6]$

   ii X follows a continuous uniform distribution over $[4.2, 7.9]$

b i The true value of a result quoted as being 17 m to the nearest m.

   ii The true age of a boy who (honestly) describes himself as eighteen years old.

3 A piece is cut off one end of a log of length 8 m. If the cut is equally likely to be made anywhere along the log:

   a find the probability that the length of the piece is less than 2.5 m.

   b Find the expected mean and standard deviation of the length of the piece.

4 A string of length 3 m is randomly cut into two pieces. Find the probability that the length of the shorter piece is less than 1 m.

5 Five random numbers are selected from the interval $[3,7]$. Find the probability that they are all smaller than 4.5.

6 **a** Prove using integration that the variance of the continuous uniform distribution between a and b is $\operatorname{Var}(X)=\dfrac{(b-a)^2}{12}$.

   b Hence prove that the ratio $\dfrac{\text{range}}{\text{standard deviation}}$ is independent of a and b, stating its value.

7 A rod of length 3 m is cut into two parts. The position of the cut is uniformly distributed along the length of the rod. Find the mean and standard deviation of the length of the *shorter* part.

Section 7: Exponential distribution

The geometric distribution modelled the number of trials until the first success in a binomial-type situation. There is an analogous distribution for modelling the waiting interval until an event in a Poisson-type situation called the **exponential distribution**. It has one parameter – the number of events in a unit interval of time, λ, and it is written as $\operatorname{Exp}(\lambda)$. Since the waiting interval is a continuous variable the probability distribution is described using a pdf (Key point 7.11).

 Rewind

The Poisson distribution was covered in Chapter 3.

 **Key point 7.11**

If $X \sim \operatorname{Exp}(\lambda)$ then:

$$f(x)=\lambda e^{-\lambda x}\text{ for }x\geqslant 0$$

This will appear in your formula book.

 Tip

For a proof of the result in Key point 7.11, see question 11 in Exercise 7G.

The mean and the variance of the exponential distribution can be found using integration (Key point 7.12).

Key point 7.12

$$E(X)=\frac{1}{\lambda}$$
$$\operatorname{Var}(X)=\frac{1}{\lambda^2}$$

This will appear in your formula book.

PROOF 4

Prove that if $X \sim \text{Exp}(\lambda)$ then $E(X) = \dfrac{1}{\lambda}$.

$E(X) = \displaystyle\int_{-\infty}^{\infty} x f(x)\, dx$	Start from the definition of expectation (Key point 7.3).
$ = \displaystyle\int_{0}^{\infty} x \times \lambda e^{-\lambda x}\, dx$	The integral starts from 0 as this is the lower limit of the probability distribution.
Identify: $u = x,\ \dfrac{dv}{dx} = \lambda e^{-\lambda x}$	Integration by parts is required. As usual when doing integration by parts, start by identifying u and $\dfrac{dv}{dx}$ ...
So $\dfrac{du}{dx} = 1,\ v = -e^{-\lambda x}$	... then find $\dfrac{du}{dx}$ and v.
So $E(X) = \left[-xe^{-\lambda x} \right]_{0}^{\infty} - \displaystyle\int_{0}^{\infty} -e^{-\lambda x} \times 1\, dx$	Use $\displaystyle\int u\frac{dv}{dx}\, dx = uv - \int v\frac{du}{dx}\, dx$
$ = 0 + \displaystyle\int_{0}^{\infty} e^{-\lambda x}\, dx$	When $x = 0$ the square bracket term is 0. It is less obvious what happens at the upper limit but it turns out that as x tends to infinity, $xe^{-\lambda x}$ tends to zero.
$ = \left[-\dfrac{1}{\lambda} e^{-\lambda x} \right]_{0}^{\infty}$	
$ = 0 - \left(\dfrac{-1}{\lambda} \right)$	
$ = \dfrac{1}{\lambda}$	

The exponential distribution models the waiting interval in a Poisson-type process. Somewhat surprisingly, it turns out that it does not matter when the waiting starts – the exponential distribution is memory-less. In Worked example 7.12 the waiting starts from one event occurring – i.e. the exponential distribution can also be thought of as modelling the interval *between* events occurring.

 Rewind

The conditions for using an exponential distribution are the same as for using a Poisson distribution. See Chapter 3.

WORKED EXAMPLE 7.12

A sewer pipe has on average three leaks per 2 miles distributed independently of each other. An inspector enters the pipe at a manhole and then walks along it looking for leaks.

a Find the probability that the first leak will be found in the first half mile.
b Find the variance of the distance until the first leak is found.

a $X = $ 'Distance in miles until first leak'	Define variables, including units.

Continues on next page ...

$X \sim \text{Exp}(1.5)$ .... Identify the distribution. Notice that the parameter has to be in leaks per mile.

$P(0 < X < 0.5) = \int_0^{0.5} 1.5e^{-1.5x} dx$ .... Write the requirement in mathematical terms and use probability density.

$$= \left[-e^{-1.5x} \right]_0^{0.5}$$

$$= 1 - e^{-0.75}$$

$$= 0.528 \text{ (3 s.f.)}$$

b $\text{Var}(X) = \dfrac{1}{1.5^2} = 0.444 \text{ (3 s.f.)}$ .... Use the formula for $\text{Var}(X)$.

You might also be asked to find a probability of a variable with an exponential distribution being greater than a particular value. You can do this by integration, but it is useful to know the cdf. You can find this using integration. If $X \sim \text{Exp}(\lambda)$ then

$$P(X < x) = \int_0^x \lambda e^{-\lambda t} dt = \left[-e^{-\lambda t} \right]_0^x = -e^{-\lambda x} - (-1)$$

Neatening this up you get the formula in Key point 7.13.

 Tip

Remember the variable in the integral is a dummy variable – you can call it anything. It is called t here to avoid confusion with the x in the limits.

 Key point 7.13

If $X \sim \text{Exp}(\lambda)$ then

$$F(x) = \begin{cases} 0, & x < 0 \\ 1 - e^{-\lambda x}, & x \geqslant 0 \end{cases}$$

WORKED EXAMPLE 7.13

During the summer Tanis sneezes on average two times every hour.

a State an assumption that must be made to model the time between consecutive sneezes by an exponential distribution.

b Assuming that the time between consecutive sneezes can be modelled by an exponential distribution find the exact probability that Tanis goes more than ninety minutes without sneezing.

a You must assume that sneezes occur independently of each other. .... Any of the assumptions used for a Poisson distribution could be used here.

b T = 'time after waking until first sneeze (hours)' .... Define variables, including units.

$T \sim \text{Exp}(2)$ .... Identify the distribution. The exponential can be used with any starting point, so the fact that it is time after waking is not important.

$P(T > 1.5) = 1 - F(1.5)$ .... Write the requirement in mathematical terms and use the cdf. Remember that units are hours.

$$= 1 - (1 - e^{-2 \times 1.5})$$

$$= e^{-3}$$

EXERCISE 7G

1 Find the following probabilities.

a **i** $P(4 < X < 8)$ if $X \sim \text{Exp}(0.4)$

ii $P(5.2 < X < 6.1)$ if $X \sim \text{Exp}(0.15)$

b **i** $P(X > 0.2)$ if $X \sim \text{Exp}(4.2)$

ii $P(X \geqslant 4)$ if $X \sim \text{Exp}(1)$

c **i** Waiting more than 30 seconds for an emission from a radioactive substance that emits three alpha particles per minute on average.

ii Waiting less than fifteen minutes for a bus that comes three times per hour on average.

2 Find the mean and standard deviation of the following:

a **i** $\text{Exp}(0.8)$

ii $\text{Exp}(3.2)$

b **i** The distance travelled in a car before reaching the first pothole, if potholes along a certain road are spread independently at an average rate of four per kilometre.

ii The time from the beginning of the day until the first phone call at a call centre that receives an average of 20 calls per hour.

3 The number of emails I receive in an hour follows a Poisson distribution with mean seven. What is the probability that the next email arrives in less than five minutes?

4 Birds arrive at a feeding table independently, at an average rate of six per hour.

a Find the probability that two birds will arrive in the next ten minutes.

b Find the probability that I have to wait more than ten minutes before the next bird arrives.

c Find the expected mean and standard deviation of the time (in minutes) I have to wait for a bird.

5 When I walk down the street, I meet people I know at an average rate of three every five minutes. Different meetings are independent of each other. What is the probability that I have to walk for more than two minutes before I meet a person I know?

6 The probability of waiting less than two minutes for a bus is 0.2. If the waiting time is modelled by an exponential distribution find the probability of waiting more than three minutes.

7 The probability of waiting more than k minutes for a phone call is p. Find an expression for the mean waiting time for a phone call in terms of k and p, assuming the waiting time can be modelled by the exponential distribution.

8   Show that the probability of a variable with an exponential distribution $\text{Exp}(\lambda)$ taking a value larger than its mean is independent of λ.

9   The number of buses arriving at a bus stop in an hour follows a Poisson distribution with mean five.

    a   Name the distribution that models the time, *in minutes*, I have to wait until the next bus arrives. State any necessary parameters.

    b   Given that I have already been waiting for 10 minutes, find the probability that I have to wait at least 18 minutes.

    c   Show that the answer in **b** is the same as the probability that I have to wait at least eight minutes.

10   Prove that if $X \sim \text{Exp}(\lambda)$ then $\text{Var}(X) = \dfrac{1}{\lambda^2}$.

11   X is the number of successes that occur in one unit of time, so that $X \sim \text{Po}(\lambda)$. Y is the number of successes that occur in t units of time.

    a   Write down the distribution of Y.

    b   Find $P(Y = 0)$, giving your answer in terms of λ and t.

    T is the exponential distribution $\text{Exp}(\lambda)$.

    c   Explain why $P(T > t) = P(Y = 0)$.

    d   Hence prove that the pdf of T is $\lambda e^{-\lambda t}$ for $t > 0$

Explore

The property illustrated in question 9 is often described by saying that the exponential distribution is 'memoryless'. Because of this, it is used to model situations where the probability of future events does not depend of what has happened before. It is the basis of a famous problem called 'The Gambler's Ruin'. What is this?

Section 8: Distributions of functions of a continuous random variable

Suppose you had the following discrete distribution:

x	-1	0	1
$P(X = x)$	$\dfrac{3}{11}$	$\dfrac{1}{11}$	$\dfrac{7}{11}$

If you wanted to find the distribution of a random variable Y that was related to X by the formula $Y = X^2 + 3$ you could do this by listing all the possible values of Y and their probabilities (remembering that $y = 4$ when $x = 1$ or -1):

y	3	4
$P(Y = y)$	$\dfrac{1}{11}$	$\dfrac{10}{11}$

There are many situations where you might like to do the same thing with a crv but this is much more difficult as you cannot access probabilities directly with the pdf. You must use the cumulative function instead and differentiate it to find the pdf.

WORKED EXAMPLE 7.14

X is the random variable 'length of the side of a square'. It is equally likely to take any value between 1 and 3. Find the pdf of Y, the area of the square.

The pdf of X is $f(x) = \dfrac{1}{2}$, $1 < x < 3$ and 0 otherwise

> Define functions.

The cdf of X where $f(x)$ is non-zero is therefore

$F(x) = \dfrac{x}{2} - \dfrac{1}{2}$, $1 < x < 3$

The cdf of Y is $G(y)$.

$G(y) = P(Y < y)$

> Use the fact that $Y = X^2$.

$\quad\ = P(X^2 < y)$

$\quad\ = P(-\sqrt{y} < X < \sqrt{y})$

> Solve the inequality.

$\quad\ = P(X < \sqrt{y}) - P(X < -\sqrt{y})$

> Write in terms of cumulative probabilities.

$\quad\ = F(\sqrt{y}) - F(-\sqrt{y})$

> Write in terms of the cdf of X.

$\quad\ = \dfrac{\sqrt{y}}{2} - \dfrac{1}{2} - 0$

> Remember that $F(x) = 0$ when $x < 1$.

This is only true if $1 < \sqrt{y} < 3$

> Consider the domain of $F(x)$.

i.e. $1 < y < 9$

$g(y) = \dfrac{d}{dy}\left(\dfrac{\sqrt{y}}{2} - \dfrac{1}{2}\right) = \dfrac{1}{4\sqrt{y}}$, $1 < y < 9$

> pdf is the derivative of cdf.

and zero otherwise.

EXERCISE 7H

1 A crv T has pdf $f(t) = 0.5$ for $1 < t < 3$ and 0 otherwise.

   a Find the cdf of T.

   b Two independent observations of T are made. Show that the probability that both are less than 2.5 is $\dfrac{9}{16}$.

   c S is the larger of the two independent observations of T. By considering the cdf of S show that S has pdf $g(s) = \dfrac{s-1}{2}$, $1 < s < 3$ and 0 otherwise.

2 X is a crv with cdf $F(x) = 1 - \dfrac{1}{x^4}$, $x > 1$ and zero otherwise. If $Y = \dfrac{1}{X^2}$ show that Y has pdf $g(y) = 2y$, $0 < y < 1$ and zero otherwise.

3 The volume of a spherical soap bubble (V) follows a continuous uniform distribution between 0 and 10.

   a Find the cdf of V.

   b Hence find the pdf of R, the radius of the bubble.

4 X is a crv with pdf $f(x) = \dfrac{3}{26} x^2$, for $1 < x < 3$ and zero otherwise.

  a Find the cdf of X.

  b If $Y = \dfrac{1}{X}$ find the probability that $Y > \dfrac{3}{4}$.

5 X is a crv with continuous uniform distribution between 0 and 1.

  a Write down the pdf of X.

  b Three independent observations of X are made. Find the pdf of Y, where Y is the maximum of the three observations.

  c Find $E(Y)$.

Section 9: Goodness-of-fit test with continuous distributions

You can now extend the χ^2 goodness-of-fit test to continuous distributions. The bins are now intervals on the real number line. As before, the expected frequency for each bin is its probability times the total frequency. The number of degrees of freedom is one less than the number of bins, minus any parameters you needed to estimate from the data.

 Rewind

You already used goodness-of-fit tests with normal distributions in Chapter 6, Section 3.

WORKED EXAMPLE 7.15

The length of time, in minutes, that a customer has to wait at the till in a shop is thought to have the pdf

$$f(x) = \begin{cases} \dfrac{1}{2}\sin x & \text{for } 0 \leqslant x \leqslant \pi \\ 0 & \text{otherwise} \end{cases}$$

The manager samples 40 customers, and finds the following observed frequencies:

waiting time (t)	$0 \leqslant t < \dfrac{\pi}{4}$	$\dfrac{\pi}{4} \leqslant t < \dfrac{\pi}{2}$	$\dfrac{\pi}{2} \leqslant t < \dfrac{3\pi}{4}$	$\dfrac{3\pi}{4} \leqslant t \leqslant \pi$
Frequency	7	12	11	10

Test, at the 10% significance level, whether the waiting times follow the assumed distribution.

H_0: The waiting times come from a population with the assumed distribution

H_1: The waiting times do not come from such a population.

State the hypotheses.

Expected frequencies:

To find expected frequencies, find the probability for each group and then multiply by 40.

$e.g.\ 40 \times \displaystyle\int_0^{\frac{\pi}{4}} \dfrac{1}{2}\sin x \, dx = 5.858$

Show at least one full example in your working.

Continues on next page ...

observed	7	12	11	10
expected	5.858	14.14	14.14	5.858
contribution	0.223	0.324	0.697	2.93

All expected frequencies are at least five, so no columns need to be combined.

Calculate the contribution for each group:

$$\frac{(\text{obs} - \text{exp})^2}{\text{exp}}$$

Your calculator may be able to find the contributions and the x^2 value.

$x^2_{\text{calc}} = 4.17$

Add the contributions to find the x^2 statistic.

$v = 4 - 1 = 3$

As no parameters were estimated from the data, the number of degrees of freedom is one fewer than the number of bins.

Critical x^2_3 value at the 10% significance level is 6.25.

Find the critical value from the tables.

$4.17 < 6.25$ so there is not sufficient evidence to reject H_0.

There is no evidence that the waiting times do not follow the given distribution.

Remember that x^2 measures the difference between the observed and expected frequencies. To reject H_0 this difference needs to be large.

EXERCISE 7I

1 A manufacturer of light bulbs claims that their lifetimes, in hundreds of hours, follow a distribution with the pdf

$$f(x) = \begin{cases} \dfrac{3}{4}x(2-x) & \text{for } 0 \leqslant x \leqslant 2 \\ 0 & \text{otherwise.} \end{cases}$$

A sample of 70 light bulbs was tested, with the following results:

lifetime (100 hours)	0–0.5	0.5–1	1–1.5	1.5–2
frequency	8	21	22	19

Test the manufacturer's claim at the 5% significance level.

2 Pieces of string, each of length 3 m, are supposed to be cut in two by a single cut made at a randomly chosen point along the string. A sample of 50 such pieces is found to have the following lengths:

length (m)	0–0.6	0.6–1.2	1.2–1.8	1.8–2.4	2.4–3.0
frequency	9	7	12	15	7

Test at a 5% significance level whether the lengths of string follow the continuous uniform distribution over [0, 3].

3 The time Nina has to wait for the bus is supposed to follow an exponential distribution with parameter $\frac{1}{7}$. The actual waiting times for a random sample of 40 days were as follows:

time (min)	0–3	3–6	6–9	9–12	12–15
frequency	17	12	6	4	1

a Show that there is evidence, at the 10% significance level, that the waiting times do not follow the exponential distribution with parameter $\frac{1}{7}$.

b Test, at the 10% significance level, whether the waiting times follow any exponential distribution.

4 A sample of 50 flowers from a certain meadow is measured and the heights are summarised in the following table:

height (h, cm)	$12 \leqslant h < 20$	$20 \leqslant h < 25$	$25 \leqslant h < 30$	$30 \leqslant h < 37$	$37 \leqslant h \leqslant 45$
frequency	7	11	14	9	9

Test, at the 5% significance level, whether the heights of the flowers in this meadow follow a normal distribution with mean 28 cm.

5 The sales department in a large firm found that the length of phone calls (in minutes) answered by their staff follow a probability distribution with the pdf

$$f(x) = \begin{cases} \dfrac{kx}{1+x^2} & \text{for } 0 \leqslant x \leqslant 15 \\ 0 & \text{otherwise} \end{cases}$$

a Find the exact value of k.

b The legal department in the same firm investigated the length of phone calls answered by their staff. A random sample of 70 phone calls was found to have the following distribution of lengths:

length of a phone call (to the nearest minute)	0–4	5–6	7–8	9–10	>10
number of phone calls	30	13	10	9	8

You may assume that no phone call was longer than 15 minutes. Test, at the 5% significance level, whether the lengths of phone calls answered by the legal department follow the same distribution as the length of calls answered by the sales department.

✎ Checklist of learning and understanding

- The probability of a crv taking any single value is a meaningless concept, but it is possible to work with the probability of it being in a given range. To do this you use a pdf such that the area under the curve represents probability.
  - The total area is therefore 1, and the function is never negative.
- The summation formulae for expectation of discrete variables become integrals for continuous variables:

$$E(X) = \int_{-\infty}^{\infty} x\,f(x)\,dx$$

$$E(X^2) = \int_{-\infty}^{\infty} x^2 f(x)\,dx$$

- Var(X) for a crv is still $E(X^2) - E(X)^2$
- The expectation and variance of a linear transformation are given by:

$$E(aX + b) = aE(X) + b$$

$$\mathrm{Var}(aX + b) = a^2\mathrm{Var}(X)$$

- The expectation of a function of a random variable is given by:

$$E(g(X)) = \int_{-\infty}^{\infty} g(x)f(x)\,dx$$

- The cdf, F(x), gives the probability of the random variable taking a value less than or equal to x.
- For a continuous distribution with pdf $f(x)$

$$P(X \leqslant x) = F(x) = \int_{-\infty}^{x} f(t)\,dt$$

$$f(x) = \frac{d}{dx}F(x)$$

- The main uses of cdfs are to find percentiles of a distribution and to convert from a distribution of one continuous variable to a distribution of a function of that variable.

- If X follows a uniform distribution between a and b then:

$$f(x) = \frac{1}{b-a} \text{ for } a \leqslant x \leqslant b, E(X) = \frac{a+b}{2}, \mathrm{Var}(X) = \frac{(b-a)^2}{12}, F(x) = \frac{(x-a)}{(b-a)}.$$

- If $X \sim \mathrm{Exp}(\lambda)$ then:

$$f(x) = \lambda e^{-\lambda x} \text{ for } x \geqslant 0, E(X) = \frac{1}{\lambda}, \mathrm{Var}(X) = \frac{1}{\lambda^2}, F(x) = 1 - e^{-\lambda x}.$$

Mixed practice 7

1 The crv Y has probability density $g(y) = ky(1-y)$, $0 < y < 1$ and zero otherwise.

   a Find the cdf of Y.   **b** Find $E(Y)$.   **c** Find $E(20Y-1)$.

2 If X is a crv with pdf $f(x) = \begin{cases} k - 0.5x & 0 < x < 1 \\ 0 & \text{otherwise,} \end{cases}$

   a find the value of k **b** find the expectation of X **c** find the variance of X.

3 The Jones' expected spend on their garden is £600 with a variance of £^{2}10 000. This is paid for out of a bank account containing £1500.

   a What is the standard deviation of the amount remaining in the bank account after the garden has been paid for?

   However much the Jones spend on their garden, the Smiths will spend twice as much plus £100.

   b What is the expected amount that the Smiths will spend?

   c What is the standard deviation of the amount that the Smiths will spend?

4 **a** If X is a crv with pdf $f(x) = \begin{cases} ax + b & 1 < x < 5 \\ 0 & \text{otherwise} \end{cases}$ and $E(X) = 3.5$

      find the value of the constants a and b.

   b Evaluate:

      i $E(2X+4)$ **ii** $E\left(\dfrac{1}{X}\right)$

5 The crv X has the pdf

$$f(x) = x + k - 5, \quad 5 \leqslant x \leqslant 6 \text{ and } 0 \text{ otherwise.}$$

   a Find the cdf of X.   **b** Find the exact value of the median of X.

6 The crv X has pdf $f(x) = \dfrac{3}{4}(1 - x^2)$, $-1 < x < 1$ and zero otherwise. Find the interquartile range of X.

7 The pdf for the crv Z is kz for $1 < z < 3$ and zero otherwise.

   a Find the value of k.   **b** Find $E(Z)$.

   c Find $E(6Z + 5)$.   **d** Find the exact value of $E\left(\dfrac{1}{1 + Z^2}\right)$.

8 The number of beta particles emitted by a radioactive substance follows a Poisson distribution. The probability of observing no particles in 2 hours is 0.4.

   a Find the expected waiting time until the first beta particle is observed.

   b Find the probability of waiting more than 90 minutes to observe a beta particle.

   c Given that no particles have been observed in the first 90 minutes, find the probability that it takes more than 3 hours to observe a beta particle.

9 X is a random variable following a continuous uniform distribution between a and b with $a < b$.

   a Prove that $\text{Var}(x) = \dfrac{(b-a)^2}{12}$

   b Find the cumulative distribution function of X.

   c Two independent observations of X are made. Find an expression for the probability that the maximum of these two observations is less than c where $a < c < b$

10 The crv X can only take values between 1 and 3. Within this range X has a cdf $F(x) = \frac{1}{8}(8x - x^2 - 7)$, $1 < x < 3$. Find the probability that in four observations of X more than two observations take a value of less than 2.

11 The crv X can only take values between a and b. In this range X has cdf $F(x) = cx^3$, $a < x < b$. The median of X is $\sqrt[3]{4}$. Find the values of a, b and c.

12 The crv X has a pdf $f(x)$ where

$$f(x) = \begin{cases} e - ke^{kx} & 0 \leqslant x \leqslant 1 \\ 0 & \text{otherwise.} \end{cases}$$

a Show that $k = 1$.

b What is the probability that the random variable X has a value that lies between $\frac{1}{4}$ and $\frac{1}{2}$? Give your answer in terms of e.

c Find the mean and variance of the distribution. Give your answers in terms of e.

This random variable X represents the lifetime, in years, of a certain type of battery.

d Find the probability that a battery lasts more than six months.

A calculator is fitted with three of these batteries. Each battery fails independently of the other two. Find the probability that at the end of six months

e i none of the batteries has failed

ii exactly one of the batteries has failed.

13 i The continuous random variable X has the probability density function

$$f(x) = \begin{cases} \dfrac{1}{2\sqrt{x}} & 1 \leqslant x \leqslant 4, \\ 0 & \text{otherwise.} \end{cases}$$

Find

a $E(X)$, **b** the median of X.

ii The continuous random variable Y has the probability density function

$$g(y) = \begin{cases} \dfrac{1.5}{y^{2.5}} & y \geqslant 1, \\ 0 & \text{otherwise.} \end{cases}$$

Given that $E(Y) = 3$, show that $\text{Var}(Y)$ is not finite.

© OCR, GCE Mathematics, Paper 4733, January 2012

14 The continuous random variable X has probability density function

$$f(x) = \begin{cases} kx^2 & 0 \leqslant x \leqslant a \\ 0 & \text{otherwise,} \end{cases}$$

where a and k are constants.

i Sketch the graph of $y = f(x)$ and explain in non-technical language what this tells you about X.

ii Given that $E(X) = 4.5$, find:

a the value of a, **b** $\text{Var}(X)$.

© OCR, GCE Mathematics, Paper 4733, June 2012

In this chapter you will learn:

- how to find the mean and variance of the sum of two independent random variables
- how to apply these ideas to making predictions about the average or the sum of a sample
- about the distribution of linear combinations of normal variables
- about the distribution of the sum or average of many observations from any distribution.

Before you start…

A Level Mathematics Student Book 1, Chapter 16	You should know how to calculate standard deviation from data.	1	Find the standard deviation of 1, 3, 8, 12.
A Level Mathematics Student Book 1, Chapter 17	You should know how to use the basic rules of probability.	2	A and B are independent events with $P(A) = 0.4$ and $P(B) = 0.5$. Find the probability of A and B both occurring.
A Level Mathematics Student Book 2, Chapter 17	You should know how to calculate probabilities from a normal distribution.	3	If $X \sim N(3, 49)$ find $P(X < 4)$.
Chapter 2	You should know how to find the expectation or variance of linear functions of a variable.	4	If $\text{Var}(X) = 6$ find $\text{Var}(10 - 2X)$.

A different algebra for statistics?

If you know the average height of a brick, it is fairly easy to guess the average height of two bricks, or the average height of half of a brick. What turns out to be less obvious is the variation of these heights.

Even if you can predict the mean and the variance of a random variable, this is not sufficient to find the probability of it taking a particular value. To do that, you also need to know the distribution of the random variable. There are some special cases where it is possible to calculate directly, but it is here that you meet the enormous significance of the normal distribution – if the sample is large enough, the sample average will almost always follow a normal distribution (exceptions are covered later in the chapter).

Section 1: Adding independent random variables

A tennis racquet is formed by adding together two components – the handle and the head. If both components have their own distribution of length and they are combined together randomly then you have formed a new random variable – the length of the racquet. It is not surprising that the average length of the racquet is the sum of the average lengths of the parts, but with a little thought you can reason that the standard deviation will be less than the sum of the standard deviation of the parts. To get extremely long or extremely short tennis racquets you must have extremes in the same direction for both the handle and the head. This is not very likely if the two parts vary independently. It is more likely that both are close to the average. Although standard deviations do not add, it turns out that variances do. This can be written as $\mathrm{Var}(X+Y) = \mathrm{Var}(X) + \mathrm{Var}(Y)$. You met in Chapter 7 the idea that $\mathrm{Var}(aX+c) = a^2\mathrm{Var}(X)$. These ideas together lead to the formula in Key Point 8.1.

🔑 Key point 8.1

If X and Y are independent random variables:

$$\mathrm{E}(aX + bY + c) = a\mathrm{E}(X) + b\mathrm{E}(Y) + c$$

$$\mathrm{Var}(aX + bY + c) = a^2\mathrm{Var}(X) + b^2\mathrm{Var}(Y)$$

💡 Tip

Notice in particular from Key point 8.1 that

$\mathrm{Var}(X - Y)$
$\quad = (1)^2 \times \mathrm{Var}(X) + (-1)^2 \times \mathrm{Var}(Y)$

$\quad = \mathrm{Var}(X) + \mathrm{Var}(Y)$

It turns out that the result for the expectation of the sum of random variables is also true if the random variables are not independent.

The result extends to more than two variables.

WORKED EXAMPLE 8.1

The mean thickness of the base of a burger bun is 1.4 cm with variance 0.02 cm^2.

The mean thickness of a burger is 3.0 cm with variance 0.14 cm^2.

The mean thickness of the top of the burger bun is 2.2 cm with variance 0.2 cm^2.

Find the mean and standard deviation of the total height of the whole burger in the bun, assuming that the thickness of each part is independent.

$X =$ 'Thickness of base (cm)'	Define your variables, including units.
$Y =$ 'Thickness of burger (cm)'	
$Z =$ 'Thickness of top (cm)'	
$T =$ 'Total thickness (cm)'	
$T = X + Y + Z$	Connect your variables.
$\mathrm{E}(T) = \mathrm{E}(X + Y + Z)$	Apply expectation algebra.
$\quad = \mathrm{E}(X) + \mathrm{E}(Y) + \mathrm{E}(Z)$	
$\quad = 6.6\ cm$	
$\mathrm{Var}(T) = \mathrm{Var}(X + Y + Z)$	
$\quad = \mathrm{Var}(X) + \mathrm{Var}(Y) + \mathrm{Var}(Z)$	
$\quad = 0.36\ cm^2$	
So the standard deviation of T is 0.6 cm.	

Key point 8.1 stresses that X and Y have to be independent, but this does not mean that they have to be drawn from different populations. They could be two different observations of the same population, e.g. the heights of two different people added together. This is a different variable from the height of one person doubled. Use a subscript to emphasise when there are repeated observations from the same population:

$X_1 + X_2$: adding together two different observations of X

$2X$: observing X once and doubling the result.

The expectation of both of these combinations is the same: $2E(X)$. However, the variance is different.

From Key point 8.1:

$$\text{Var}(X_1 + X_2) = \text{Var}(X_1) + \text{Var}(X_2)$$
$$= 2\text{Var}(X)$$

From Key point 8.1:

$$\text{Var}(2X) = 4\text{Var}(X)$$

So the variability of a single observation doubled is greater than the variability of two independent observations added together. This is consistent with the earlier argument about the possibility of independent observations 'cancelling out' extreme values.

WORKED EXAMPLE 8.2

In a shop the mean mass of the oranges is 84 g and the standard deviation is 11 g. The mean mass of lemons in the shop is 64 g and the standard deviation is 6 g. The shopkeeper thinks that if four lemons are picked at random their total mass will be more than three times the mass of a randomly selected orange. Let D be the random variable, the amount by which four lemons are heavier than three times the mass of a single orange, assuming that all these fruit are chosen independently. Find the mean and standard deviation of D. Comment on your answer.

$X = $ 'Mass of an orange (g)'

$Y = $ 'Mass of an lemon (g)'

Define your variables, including units.

$D = Y_1 + Y_2 + Y_3 + Y_4 - 3X$

Connect your variables.

$E(D) = E(Y_1) + E(Y_2) + E(Y_3) + E(Y_4) - 3E(X)$

$\quad = 64 + 64 + 64 + 64 - 3 \times 84 = 4g$

Apply expectation algebra.

$\text{Var}(D) = \text{Var}(Y_1) + \text{Var}(Y_2) + \text{Var}(Y_3) + \text{Var}(Y_4) + (-3)^2 \times \text{Var}(X)$

$\quad = 6^2 + 6^2 + 6^2 + 6^2 + 9 \times 11^2$

$\quad = 1233\,g^2$

So the standard deviation of D is 35.1 g

Continues on next page ...

So on average the mass of four lemons is greater than three times the mass of a single orange.

However, the large standard deviation shows that there is a significant possibility that D is negative – i.e. that the mass of the four lemons is smaller than the mass of a single orange.

Interpret your results in context.

The calculations do not tell you how likely it is that D is negative. In certain circumstances it is possible to find the exact distribution of linear combinations of random variables. You can then go on to calculate probabilities of different values of D.

 **Fast forward**

This will be covererd in Section 4.

EXERCISE 8A

1 Let X and Y be two independent variables with $E(X) = -1$, $\text{Var}(X) = 2$, $E(Y) = 4$ and $\text{Var}(Y) = 4$. Find the expectation and variance of:

a **i** $X - Y$ **ii** $X + Y$

b **i** $3X + 2Y$ **ii** $2X - 4Y$

c **i** $\dfrac{X - 3Y + 1}{5}$ **ii** $\dfrac{X + 2Y - 2}{3}$

d **i** $X_1 + X_2 + X_3$ **ii** $Y_1 + Y_2$

e **i** $X_1 - X_2 - 2Y_3$ **ii** $3X_1 - (Y_1 + Y_2 - Y_3)$.

2 If X is the random variable 'mass of a gerbil', explain the difference between $2X$ and $X_1 + X_2$.

3 Let X and Y be two independent variables with $E(X) = 4$, $\text{Var}(X) = 2$, $E(Y) = 1$ and $\text{Var}(Y) = 6$. Find:

a $E(3X)$ **b** $\text{Var}(3X)$ **c** $E(3X - Y + 1)$ **d** $\text{Var}(3X - Y + 1)$.

4 The average mass of a man in an office is 85 kg with standard deviation 12 kg. The average mass of a woman in the office is 68 kg with standard deviation 8 kg. The empty lift has a mass of 500 kg. What is the expectation and standard deviation of the total mass of the lift when three women and four men are inside?

5 A weighted dice has mean outcome 4 with standard deviation 1. Brian rolls the dice once and doubles the outcome. Camilla rolls the dice twice and adds the results together. What is the expected mean and standard deviation of the difference between their scores?

6 Exam scores at a large school have mean 62 and standard deviation 28. Two students are selected at random. Find the expected mean and standard deviation of the difference between their exam scores.

7 Adrian cycles to school with a mean time of 20 minutes and a standard deviation of 5 minutes. Pamela walks to school with a mean time of 30 minutes and a standard deviation of 2 minutes. They each calculate the total time it takes them to get to school over a five-day week. What is the expected mean and standard deviation of the difference in the total weekly journey times, assuming journey times are independent?

Section 2: Expectation and variance of the sample mean

When calculating the mean of a random sample of size n of the variable X you have to add up n independent observations of X, then divide by n. You give this sample mean the symbol $\bar{X}$ and it is itself a random variable (i.e. it might change each time it is observed).

$$\bar{X} = \frac{X_1 + X_2 + \ldots + X_n}{n}$$

$$= \frac{1}{n}X_1 + \frac{1}{n}X_2 + \ldots + \frac{1}{n}X_n$$

This is a linear combination of independent observations of X, so you can apply the rules of the previous section to get the very important results in Key point 8.2.

 Key point 8.2

$$\mathrm{E}(\bar{X}) = \mathrm{E}(X)$$

$$\mathrm{Var}(\bar{X}) = \frac{\mathrm{Var}(X)}{n}$$

The first of these results seems very obvious – the average of a sample is, on average, the average of the original variable.

The second result demonstrates why means are so important – their standard deviation, which can be thought of as a measure of the error caused by randomness, is smaller than the standard deviation of a single observation. This proves mathematically what you probably already knew instinctively – that finding an average of several results produces a more reliable outcome than just looking at one result.

 Explore

The result actually goes further than that: it contains what economists call 'the law of diminishing returns': The standard deviation of the mean is proportional to $\frac{1}{\sqrt{n}}$, so going from a sample of 1 to a sample of 20 has a much bigger impact than going from a sample of 101 to a sample of 120. Investigate the implications of this.

PROOF 5

Prove that if $\bar{X}$ is the average of n independent observations of X then $\mathrm{Var}(\bar{X}) = \frac{\mathrm{Var}(X)}{n}$.

$$\bar{X} = \frac{X_1 + X_2 + \ldots + X_n}{n}$$
Write $\bar{X}$ in terms of X_i.

$$= \frac{1}{n}X_1 + \frac{1}{n}X_2 + \ldots + \frac{1}{n}X_n$$

$$\mathrm{Var}(\bar{X}) = \mathrm{Var}\left(\frac{1}{n}X_1 + \frac{1}{n}X_2 + \ldots + \frac{1}{n}X_n\right)$$

$$= \frac{1}{n^2}\mathrm{Var}(X_1) + \frac{1}{n^2}\mathrm{Var}(X_2) \ldots + \frac{1}{n^2}\mathrm{Var}(X_n)$$
Use Key point 8.2.

$$= \frac{1}{n^2}(\mathrm{Var}(X_1) + \mathrm{Var}(X_2) + \ldots + \mathrm{Var}(X_n))$$

Continues on next page ...

$$= \frac{1}{n^2} \left(\overbrace{\text{Var}(X) + \text{Var}(X) + \ldots + \text{Var}(X)}^{n \text{ times}} \right)$$

Since $X_1, X_2, \ldots$ are all observations of X.

$$= \frac{1}{n^2} n \text{Var}(X)$$

$$= \frac{\text{Var}(X)}{n}$$

EXERCISE 8B

1 A sample is obtained from n independent observations of a random variable X. Find the expected value and the variance of the sample mean in the following situations:

a **i** $E(X) = 5$, $\text{Var}(X) = 1.2$, $n = 7$ **ii** $E(X) = 6$, $\text{Var}(X) = 2.5$, $n = 12$

b **i** $E(X) = -4.7$, $\text{Var}(X) = 0.8$, $n = 20$ **ii** $E(X) = -15.1$, $\text{Var}(X) = 0.7$, $n = 15$

c **i** $X \sim N(12, 3^2)$, $n = 10$ **ii** $X \sim N(8, 0.6^2)$, $n = 14$

d **i** $X \sim N(21, 6.25)$, $n = 7$ **ii** $X \sim N(14, 0.64)$, $n = 15$

e **i** $X \sim B(6, 0.5)$, $n = 10$ **ii** $X \sim B(12, 0.3)$, $n = 8$

f **i** $X \sim Po(6.5)$, $n = 20$ **ii** $X \sim Po(8.2)$, $n = 15$.

2 Eggs are packed in boxes of 12. The mass of the box itself is exactly 50 g. The mass of one egg has mean 12.4 g and standard deviation 1.2 g. Find the mean and the standard deviation of the mass of a box of eggs.

3 A machine produces chocolate bars so that the mean mass of a bar is 102 g and the standard deviation is 8.6 g. As a part of the quality control process, a sample of 20 chocolate bars is taken and the mean mass is calculated. Find the expectation and variance of the sample mean mass of these 20 chocolate bars.

4 Prove that $\text{Var}\left(\sum_{i=1}^{n} X_i\right) = n\text{Var}(X)$.

5 The standard deviation of the mean mass of a sample of two aubergines is 20 g smaller than the standard deviation in the mass of a single aubergine. Find the standard deviation of the mass of an aubergine.

6 A random variable X takes values 0 and 1 with probability $\frac{1}{4}$ and $\frac{3}{4}$ respectively.

a Calculate $E(X)$ and $\text{Var}(X)$.

A sample of three observations of X is taken.

b List all possible samples of size 3 and calculate the mean of each.

c Hence complete the probability distribution table for the mean of a sample of size 3:

$\bar{x}$	0	$\frac{1}{3}$	$\frac{2}{3}$	1
$P(\bar{X} = \bar{x})$	$\frac{1}{64}$			

d Show that $E(\bar{X}) = E(X)$ and $\text{Var}(\bar{X}) = \frac{\text{Var}(X)}{3}$.

7 A laptop manufacturer believes that their laptop battery life follows a normal distribution with mean 4.8 hours and variance 1.7 hours². They wish to take a sample to estimate the mean battery life. If they want the standard deviation of the sample mean to be less than 0.3 hours, what is the minimum sample size needed?

8 When the sample size is increased by 80, the standard deviation of the sample mean decreases to a third of its original size. Find the original sample size.

Section 3: Unbiased estimates of the mean and the variance

You saw in Key point 8.2 that the expected value of the sample mean equals the population mean. This property means that the sample mean is an **unbiased estimate** of the population mean.

However, measures of spread work in a different way. If you were to take lots of samples and measure the range of each sample then it is highly likely all of your values would be smaller than the true range. It turns out that all measures of spread will tend to be underestimated by a sample. However, in the case of the variance there is a formula that will provide an estimate that does not systematically underestimate the population variance. This is called the unbiased estimate of variance and it is usually given the symbol s^2 (see Key point 8.3).

 Key point 8.3

When estimating the variance of a population from a sample, use

$$s^2 = \frac{n}{n-1}\left(\frac{\Sigma x^2}{n} - \left(\frac{\Sigma x}{n}\right)^2\right)$$

> **Tip**
>
> You should check that you know how to find both types of variance on your calculator.

Notice that Key point 8.3 is the familiar formula for variance multiplied by $\frac{n}{n-1}$.

WORKED EXAMPLE 8.3

A sample is summarised by $\Sigma x^2 = 100$, $\Sigma x = 20$, $n = 10$. Find unbiased estimates of

a the population mean **b** the population variance.

a Unbiased estimate of the mean

$$= \frac{\Sigma x}{n} = \frac{20}{10} = 2$$

The unbiased estimate of the population mean is just the sample mean.

b Unbiased estimate of the variance

$$= \frac{n}{n-1}\left(\frac{\Sigma x^2}{n} - \left(\frac{\Sigma x}{n}\right)^2\right)$$

$$= \frac{10}{9}\left(\frac{100}{10} - \left(\frac{20}{10}\right)^2\right)$$

$$= \frac{20}{3} \approx 6.67$$

To find the unbiased estimate of the population variance you need to use the formula from Key point 8.3.

If you had calculated the sample variance you would have got 6. The unbiased estimate of the variance reflects the fact that the population probably has a larger variance than this sample. If the sample size had been larger the sample variance is likely to be closer to the population variance, so a smaller correction factor would be applied.

EXERCISE 8C

1 Calculate unbiased estimates for the population mean and variance based on the following data:

    a   **i**   1, 5, 8, 10   **ii**   12, 15, 28, 34, 60

    b   **i**   −2, 0, 1, 1, 6   **ii**   −3, −1, 0, 5, 10

    c   **i** $\Sigma x = -9$, $\Sigma x^2 = 135$, $n = 5$ **ii** $\Sigma x = 25$, $\Sigma x^2 = 439$, $n = 5$.

2 In order to find out the mean and standard deviation of masses of a particular breed of cat, Ben measures a random sample of 20 cats. The results are summarised as follows:

$$\Sigma w = 51, \quad \Sigma w^2 = 138.32.$$

    a Find the mean mass, and show that the unbiased estimate of the variance is 0.435 to three significant figures.

    b Ben hopes to obtain a more accurate estimate for the mean by taking a sample of size 100. The mean of this sample is 2.63. Is this necessarily a better estimate of the population mean than the one found in part **a**? Explain your answer.

3 A sample is summarised by $\Sigma(x - \bar{x})^2 = 501.5$, $n = 6$. Find the unbiased estimate of the variance of the population from which these data were drawn.

4 For the data 1, 2, 5, 8:

    a Calculate the variance using the formula $\sigma^2 = \dfrac{\Sigma(x - \bar{x})^2}{n}$.

    b Calculate the variance using the formula $s^2 = \dfrac{n}{n-1}\left(\dfrac{\Sigma x^2}{n} - \left(\dfrac{\Sigma x}{n}\right)^2\right)$.

    c When would it be appropriate to use the formula in part **b** rather than the one in part **a**?

5 If s^2 is the unbiased estimate of the variance, does that imply that s is the unbiased estimate of the standard deviation?

Section 4: Linear combinations of normal variables

Although the proof is beyond the scope of this course, it turns out that any linear combination of normal variables will also follow a normal distribution. You use the methods of Section 2 to find out the parameters of this distribution.

Key point 8.4

If X and Y are random variables following a normal distribution and $Z = aX + bY + c$ then Z also follows a normal distribution.

WORKED EXAMPLE 8.4

If $X \sim N(12,15)$, $Y \sim N(1,18)$ and $Z = X + 2Y + 3$ find $P(Z > 20)$.

$E(Z) = E(X) + 2 \times E(Y) + 3 = 17$

$Var(Z) = Var(X) + 2^2 \times Var(Y) = 87$

Use expectation algebra.

$Z \sim N(17,87)$

State the distribution of Z.

$P(Z > 20) = 0.374$

Use a calculator to find the normal probability.

WORKED EXAMPLE 8.5

If $X \sim N(15,12^2)$ and four independent observations of X are made, find $P(\bar{X} < 14)$.

$\bar{X} = \dfrac{X_1 + X_2 + X_3 + X_4}{4}$

Express $\bar{X}$ in terms of observations of X.

$E(\bar{X}) = \dfrac{1}{4}(E(X) + E(X) + E(X) + E(X))$

$= 15$

Use expectation algebra.

$Var(\bar{X}) = \left(\dfrac{1}{4}\right)^2 (Var(X) + Var(X) + Var(X) + Var(X))$

$= 36$

$\bar{X} \sim N(15,36)$

State the distribution of $\bar{X}$.

$P(\bar{X} < 14) = 0.434$

Use a calculator to find the normal probability.

Rewind

In Chapter 3 you met the idea that the Poisson distribution is scalable. You can now interpret this as meaning that the sum of two Poisson variables is also Poisson. The Poisson and the normal distributions are the only distributions in this course that have this property. However, unlike the normal distribution, a multiple of a Poisson distribution is *not* Poisson and the difference of two Poisson distributions is *not* Poisson.

WORK IT OUT 8.1

The distance Lily throws a javelin is distributed normally with mean 27 m and standard deviation 3 m. Find the probability that in two throws her total distance is more than 50 m.

Which is the correct solution? Can you identify the errors made in the incorrect solutions?

Solution 1	A total of 50 m is equivalent to 25 m in each throw, so if $X \sim N(27, 3)$ then $P(X > 25) = 0.748$
Solution 2	If $X \sim N(27, 9)$ then $2X \sim N(54, 36)$ so $P(2X > 50) = 0.748$ (3 s.f.)
Solution 3	If $X \sim N(27, 3^2)$ then $X_1 + X_2 \sim N(54, 18)$ so $P(X_1 + X_2 \geqslant 50) = 0.827$

EXERCISE 8D

1. If $X \sim N(12,16)$ and $Y \sim N(8,25)$ find:

   a i $P(X - Y > -2)$ ii $P(X + Y < 24)$

   b i $P(3X + 2Y > 50)$ ii $P(2X - 3Y > -2)$

   c i $P(X > 2Y)$ ii $P(2X < 3Y)$

   d i $P(X > 2Y - 2)$ ii $P(3X + 1 < 5Y)$

   e i $P(X_1 + X_2 > 2X_3 + 1)$ ii $P(X_1 + Y_1 + Y_2 < X_2 + 12)$

   f i $P(\bar{X} > 13)$ where $\bar{X}$ is the mean of twelve independent observations of X

        ii $P(\bar{Y} < 6)$ where $\bar{Y}$ is the mean of nine independent observations of Y.

2. An airline has found that the mass of their passengers follows a normal distribution with mean 82.2 kg and variance 10.7 kg². The mass of a passenger's hand luggage follows a normal distribution with mean 9.1 kg and variance 5.6 kg².

   a State the distribution of the total mass of a passenger and their hand luggage and find any necessary parameters.

   b What is the probability that the total mass of a passenger and their luggage exceeds 100 kg?

3. Evidence suggests that the times Aaron takes to run 100 m are normally distributed with mean 13.1 seconds and standard deviation 0.4 seconds. The times Bashir takes to run 100 m are normally distributed with mean 12.8 seconds and standard deviation 0.6 seconds.

   a Find the mean and standard deviation of the difference (Aaron – Bashir) between Aaron's and Bashir's times.

   b Find the probability that Aaron finishes a 100 m race before Bashir.

   c What is the probability that Bashir beats Aaron by more than 1 second?

4 A machine produces metal rods so that their length follows a normal distribution with mean 65 cm and variance 0.03 cm². The rods are checked in batches of six, and a batch is rejected if the average length is less than 64.8 cm or more than 65.3 cm.

   a Find the mean and the variance of a random sample of six rods.

   b Hence find the probability that a batch is rejected.

5 The distribution of lengths of pipes produced by a machine is normal with mean 40 cm and standard deviation 3 cm.

   a What is the probability that a randomly chosen pipe has a length of 42 cm or more?

   b What is the probability that the average length of a randomly chosen set of ten pipes of this type is 42 cm or more?

6 The masses, X kg, of male birds of a certain species are normally distributed with mean 4.6 kg and standard deviation 0.25 kg. The masses, Y kg, of female birds of this species are normally distributed with mean 2.5 kg and standard deviation 0.2 kg.

   a Find the mean and variance of $2Y - X$.

   b Find the probability that the mass of a randomly chosen male bird is more than twice the mass of a randomly chosen female bird.

   c Find the probability that the total mass of three male birds and four female birds (chosen independently) exceeds 25 kg.

7 A shop sells apples and pears. The masses, in grams, of the apples can be assumed to have a N(180, 12²) distribution and the masses of the pears, in grams, can be assumed to have a N(100, 10²) distribution.

   a Find the probability that the mass of a randomly chosen apple is more than double the mass of a randomly chosen pear.

   b A shopper buys two apples and a pear. Find the probability that the total mass is greater than 500 grams.

8 The length of a cornsnake is normally distributed with mean 1.2 m. The probability that a randomly selected sample of five cornsnakes has a mean above 1.4 m is 5 per cent. Find the standard deviation of the length of a cornsnake.

9 **a** Boys have scores in a test that follow the distribution N(50, 25). Girls' scores follow N(60, 16). What is the probability that a randomly chosen boy and a randomly chosen girl differ in score by less than five?

   b What is the probability that a randomly chosen boy scores less than three-quarters of the mark of a randomly chosen girl?

10 The daily rainfall in Algebraville follows a normal distribution with mean μ mm and standard deviation σ mm. The rainfall each day is independent of the rainfall on other days.

On a randomly chosen day, there is a probability of 0.1 that the rainfall is greater than 8 mm.

In a randomly chosen seven-day week, there is a probability of 0.05 that the *mean* daily rainfall is less than 7 mm.

Find the value of μ and of σ.

11 Anu uses public transport to go to school each morning. The time she waits each morning for the transport is normally distributed with a mean of 12 minutes and a standard deviation of 4 minutes.

a On a specific morning, what is the probability that Anu waits more than 20 minutes?

b During a particular week (Monday to Friday), calculate the probability that:

i her total morning waiting time does not exceed 70 minutes

ii she waits less than 10 minutes on exactly two mornings of the week

iii her mean morning waiting time is more than 10 minutes.

c Given that the total morning waiting time for the first four days is 50 minutes, find the probability that the mean for the week is over 12 minutes.

d Given that Anu's mean morning waiting time in a week is over 14 minutes, find the probability that it is less than 15 minutes.

 Tip

Only consider the last day.

Section 5: The distribution of means of large samples

In this section you will look at how to find the distribution of the sample mean or the sample total, even if you do not know the original distribution.

Focus on ...

Focus on ... Modelling 2 shows you how to simulate many of the results in this section.

The following graph shows 1000 observations of the roll of a fair dice.

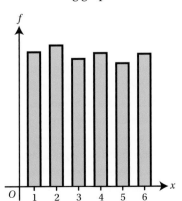

It seems to follow a uniform distribution quite well, as you would expect.

However, if you look at the sum of two dice 1000 times, the distribution looks quite different:

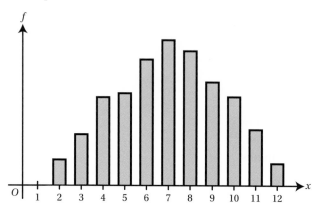

The sum of 20 dice forms a familiar shape:

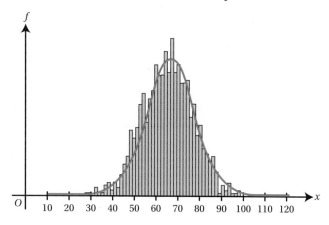

The sum seems to form a normal distribution.

This is more than a coincidence. If you sum enough independent observations of any random variable with finite variance, the result will approximate a normal distribution. Since the mean is the sum divided by a constant, this will also follow a normal distribution. This is called the central limit theorem or CLT (see Key point 8.5). You generally take 26 to be a sufficiently large sample size to apply the CLT.

Using Key point 8.5, you can predict which normal distribution is being followed.

🔑 Key point 8.5

CLT:

For *any* distribution you will meet, if $E(X) = \mu$, $Var(X) = \sigma^2$ and $n > 25$, then the approximate distributions are given by:

$$\bar{X} \sim N\left(\mu, \frac{\sigma^2}{n}\right)$$

🔍 Explore

Consider the following game: Eric flips two coins, and repeats until he flips at least one head. If this takes n tries, he scores 2^n points.
What is the expected score from this game?
Try simulating the game and investigate the distribution of the mean score of 50 games. Does the CLT apply here? If not, why not?
Try varying the game; the result is very different if one or three coins are used.

Since $\sum_1^n X_i = n\bar{X}$ you can apply Key point 2.3 to find the distribution of the sum. You find that $\sum_1^n X_i \sim N(n\mu, n\sigma^2)$.

 Did you know?

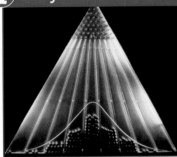

This a working replica of a version of Sir Francis Galton's 'bean machine', developed in the 19th century. It is a physical way of visualising the average of many 50–50 binomial trials, and so the CLT. You can see that it takes up the predicted bell-shaped curve associated with the normal distribution.

WORKED EXAMPLE 8.6

Esme eats an average of 1900 kcal each day with a standard deviation of 400 kcal. What is the probability that in a 31-day month she eats more than 2000 kcal per day on average?

Since you are finding an average over 31 days you can use the CLT (as $n > 25$)

Check conditions for CLT are met.

$$\bar{X} \sim N\left(1900, \frac{400^2}{31}\right)$$

State the distribution of the mean.

$P(\bar{X} > 2000) = 0.0820$ (3 s.f. from calculator)

Tip

You saw in non-parametric tests that when a discrete random variable is approximated by a continuous random variable a continuity correction improves the accuracy of the calculated probabilities. When using the Central Limit Theorem you could also use a continuity correction. However, since the CLT is only applied when the sample size is large, the effect of a continuity correction would be small and so it can be ignored in these questions.

EXERCISE 8E

1 The random variable X has mean 80 and standard deviation 20. State where possible the approximate distribution of:

a **i** $\bar{X}$ if the sample has size 2

ii $\bar{X}$ if the sample has size 3

b **i** $\bar{X}$ if the average is taken from 100 observations

ii $\bar{X}$ if the average is taken from 400 observations

c **i** $\sum_{i=1}^{i=50} X_i$ **ii** $\sum_{i=1}^{i=150} X_i$

2 The random variable Y has mean 200 and standard deviation 25. A sample of size n is taken. Find, where possible, the probability that:

a i $P(\bar{Y}<198)$ if $n=100$ **ii** $P(\bar{Y}<198)$ if $n=200$

b i $P(\bar{Y}<190)$ if $n=2$ **ii** $P(\bar{Y}<190)$ if $n=3$

c i $P(|\bar{Y}-195|>10)$ if $n=100$ **ii** $P(|\bar{Y}-201|>3)$ if $n=400$

d i $P\left(\sum_{i=1}^{i=50} Y_i>10\,500\right)$ **ii** $P\left(\sum_{i=1}^{i=150} Y_i \leqslant 29\,500\right)$

3 A random variable X has mean 12 and standard deviation 3.5. A sample of 40 independent observations of X is taken. Use the CLT to calculate the probability that the mean of the sample is between 13 and 14.

4 Masses of pomegranates, in grams, have mean 145 and variance 96. A crate is filled with 70 pomegranates. What is the probability that the total mass of the pomegranates in the crate is less than 10 kg?

5 Given that $X \sim \text{Po}(6)$, find the probability that the mean of 35 independent observations of X is greater than seven.

6 The average mass of a sheet of A4 paper is 5 g, and the standard deviation of the masses is 0.08 g.

a Find the mean and standard deviation of the mass of a ream of 500 sheets of A4 paper.

b Find the probability that the mass of a ream of 500 sheets is within 5 g of the expected mass.

c Explain how you have used the CLT in your answer.

7 The times Markus takes to answer multiple choice questions are normally distributed with mean 1.5 min and standard deviation 0.6 min. He has one hour to complete a test consisting of 35 questions.

a Assuming the times taken to answer questions are independent, find the probability that Markus does not complete the test in time.

b Explain why you did not need to use the CLT in your answer to part **a**.

8 A random variable has mean 15 and standard deviation 4. A large number of independent observations of the random variable is taken. Find the minimum sample size so that the probability that the sample mean is more than 16 is less than 0.05.

Checklist of learning and understanding

- Expectation of combinations of random variables:
$$E(aX+bY+c)=aE(X)+bE(Y)+c$$

- Variance of combinations of independent random variables:
$$\text{Var}(aX+bY+c)=a^2\text{Var}(X)+b^2\text{Var}(Y)$$

- For a sample of n independent observations of a random variable X, the sample mean $\bar{X}$ is a random variable with mean $E(X)$ and variance $\dfrac{\text{Var}(X)}{n}$.

- When you combine different variables you do not generally know the resulting distribution. However, there are two important exceptions:
  - A linear combination of normal variables also follows a normal distribution.
  - The sum or mean of a large sample ($n>25$) of observations of a variable with finite variance approximately follows a normal distribution, irrespective of the original distribution – this is called the CLT.

Mixed practice 8

1 X is a random variable with mean μ and variance σ^2. Y is a random variable with mean m and variance s^2. Find in terms of μ, σ, m and s:

a $E(X - 2Y)$

b $Var(X - 2Y)$

c $Var(4X)$

d $Var(X_1 + X_2 + X_3 + X_4)$ where X_i is the ith observation of X.

2 The heights of trees in a forest have mean 16 m and variance 60 m². A sample of 35 trees is measured.

a Find the mean and variance of the average height of the trees in the sample.

b Use the CLT to find the probability that the average height of the trees in the sample is less than 12 m.

3 The number of cars arriving at a car park in a five-minute interval follows a Poisson distribution with mean 7, and the number of motorbikes follows Poisson distribution with mean 2. Find the probability that exactly ten vehicles arrive at the car park in a particular five-minute interval.

4 The number of announcements posted by a head teacher in a day follows a distribution with mean 4 and standard deviation 2. Find the mean and standard deviation of the total number of announcements she posts in a five-day week. State any assumptions required.

5 A sample is found to have values 0, 1, 1, 6, 10. Find unbiased estimates for the mean and variance of the population based on this sample.

6 A random sample of 50 observations of the random variable X is summarised by

$$n = 50, \ \Sigma x = 182.5, \ \Sigma x^2 = 739.625.$$

Calculate unbiased estimates of the expectation and variance of X.

© OCR, GCE Mathematics, Paper 4733, January 2012

7 The masses of men in a factory are known to be normally distributed with mean 80 kg and standard deviation 6 kg. There is a lift with a maximum recommended load of 600 kg. With seven men in the lift, calculate the probability that their combined mass exceeds the maximum recommended load.

8 Davina makes bracelets by threading purple and yellow beads. Each bracelet consists of seven randomly selected purple beads and four randomly selected yellow beads. The diameters of the beads are normally distributed with standard deviation 0.4 cm. The average diameter of a purple bead is 1.5 cm and the average diameter of a yellow bead is 2.1 cm. Find the probability that the length of the bracelet is less than 18 cm.

9 The masses of the parents at a primary school are normally distributed with mean 78 kg and variance 30 kg², and the masses of the children are normally distributed with mean 33 kg and variance 62 kg². Let the random variable P represent the combined mass of two randomly chosen parents, and the random variable C the combined mass of four randomly chosen children.

a Find the mean and variance of $C - P$.

b Find the probability that four children weigh more than two parents.

10 X is a random variable with mean μ and variance σ^2. Prove that the expectation of the mean of three observations of X is μ but the standard deviation of the mean is $\dfrac{\sigma}{\sqrt{3}}$.

11 An animal scientist is investigating the lengths of a particular type of fish. It is known that the lengths have standard deviation 4.6 cm. She wishes to take a sample to estimate the mean length. She requires that the standard deviation of the sample mean is smaller than 1 cm, and that the standard deviation of the total length of the sample is less than 22 cm. What sample size should she take?

12 The marks students scored in a Maths test follow a normal distribution with mean 63 and variance 64. The marks of the same group of students in an English test follow a normal distribution with mean 61 and variance 71.

    a Find the probability that a randomly chosen student scored a higher mark in English than in Maths.

    b Find the probability that the average English mark of a class of twelve students is higher than their average Maths mark.

13 The masses of loaves of bread have mean 802 g and standard deviation σ. The probability that a light box containing 40 loaves of bread has mass under 32 kg is 0.146. Find the value of σ.

14 X is a continuous random variable with the distribution $N(48.5, 12.5^2)$. The values of X are transformed to standardised values of Y, using the equation $Y = aX + b$, where a and b are constants with $a > 0$.

    i Find values of a and b for which the mean and standard deviation of Y are 40 and 10 respectively.

    ii State the distribution of Y.

Two randomly chosen standardised values are denoted by Y_1 and Y_2.

    iii Calculate the probability that Y_2 is at least 10 greater than Y_1.

© OCR, GCE Mathematics, Paper 4734, January 2012

9 Further hypothesis tests and confidence intervals

A This chapter is for A Level students only.

In this chapter you will learn:

- about more situations where the normal distribution can be used in hypothesis testing
- how to estimate an interval that a population parameter lies in, called a confidence interval.

Before you start…

A Level Mathematics Student Book 2, Chapter 17	You should know how to conduct calculations with the normal distribution.	1	If $X \sim N(12, 100)$ find $P(X < 5)$.
A Level Mathematics Student Book 2, Chapter 18	You should know how to conduct hypothesis tests with the normal distribution.	2	A sample of 10 objects drawn from a normal distribution with a standard deviation of 3 has a mean of 12.3. Conduct a two-tailed test at 5% significance to decide if this provides significant evidence of a change from a mean of 11.
Chapter 8	You should know how to apply the CLT.	3	An unknown distribution has mean 100 and standard deviation 30. Find the probability that the mean of 400 observations of this distribution is above 102.
Chapter 8	You should know how to calculate unbiased estimates of the population variance.	4	Provide an unbiased estimate of the variance of a population based on the following sample: 2, 8, 8, 9, 9.

What is the best way to describe an estimate?

If you want to estimate a population parameter, which is better: having a single value that is very unlikely to be correct or having a range of values that is very likely to contain the population statistic? Most people prefer the latter, and it is called a **confidence interval**.

In this chapter you will extend your knowledge of the normal distribution to find new situations in which you can conduct hypothesis tests. In each of these situations you will also see that confidence intervals can be constructed.

Section 1: Hypothesis testing for the mean of a large sample

You should have already met, in A Level Mathematics Student Book 2, the idea of using a normal distribution to test a sample for evidence of a change in the mean from a previously believed value. The sample mean $\bar{X}$ follows the distribution $N\left(\mu, \dfrac{\sigma^2}{n}\right)$ and this can be used to conduct the hypothesis test.

However, this requires two assumptions:

A   The data is drawn from a normal distribution.
B   The variance of the population is known.

In reality, both of these assumptions might be dubious. However, if the sample size is large (bigger than 25) you can use tools from Chapter 8 to bypass these assumptions.

For large samples you can use the CLT to claim that the mean follows a normal distribution irrespective of the original distribution, and so bypass assumption A.

WORKED EXAMPLE 9.1

Standard light bulbs have an average lifetime of 800 hours and a standard deviation of 100 hours. A low energy light bulb manufacturer claims that the lifetimes of low energy light bulbs have the same standard deviation but that they last longer. A sample of 50 low energy light bulbs has an average lifetime of 829.4 hours. Test the manufacturer's claim at the 5% significance level.

$X =$ 'Lifetime of a bulb (hours)'	Define the variables (including units).
$H_0 : \mu = 800$ $H_1 : \mu > 800$	State hypotheses.
Using the CLT: $\bar{X} \sim N\left(800, \dfrac{100^2}{50}\right)$	State the distribution of the mean. You are using the CLT because you do not know the distribution of X, but the mean of 50 observations will be normally distributed.
$p\text{-value} = P\left(\bar{X} \geqslant 829.4\right)$ $= 0.0188$ (3 s.f.)	Use the calculator to find the p-value.
< 0.05 Therefore reject H_0 – there is evidence to support the manufacturer's claim.	Compare the p-value to the significance level and make a conclusion.

For large samples the unbiased estimate of the population variance will be a very good estimate of the population variance, so you can use that as the variance of the sample and bypass assumption B.

Explore

$N\left(\mu, \dfrac{\sigma^2}{n}\right)$ is in fact not the correct distribution for $\bar{X}$. Instead, the standardised

variable $\dfrac{\bar{X} - \mu}{s/\sqrt{n}}$ follows a t-distribution, where s^2 is the unbiased estimate of the population variance. However, when n is large it is approximately the same as the normal distribution, so you do not need to worry about the t-distribution in this course. Research how you can use a t-distribution to conduct tests using small samples taken from a normal distribution with unknown variance.

WORKED EXAMPLE 9.2

It is known that a species of monkey has a mean adult mass of 21 kg. A new group of similar monkeys is found. A sample of 100 adult monkeys from this group has an average mass of 20 kg and a sample variance of 63 kg². Does this provide evidence, at the 10% significance level, that the mean mass of the new group of monkeys is different from the rest of the species?

$X = $ 'Mass of a monkey (kg)'

> Define the variables (including units).

$H_0 : \mu = 21$
$H_1 : \mu \neq 21$

> State hypotheses.

$s^2 = \dfrac{100}{99} \times 63 = \dfrac{700}{11}$

> The population variance is not given, so use s^2 as an estimate.

Using CLT, $\bar{X} \sim N\left(21, \dfrac{7}{11}\right)$

> You are not told that the distribution of masses is normal, but the sample size is large enough to use the CLT.
> Remember to divide the variance by 100.

$p\text{-value} = 2 \times P(\bar{X} \leqslant 20)$

> For a two-tailed test, double the probability in one tail.

$\qquad = 2 \times 0.105$

$\qquad = 0.21 > 0.1$

The p-value is larger than the 10% significance level so you do not reject H_0. There is insufficient evidence to say that monkeys in the new group have a different mass.

EXERCISE 9A

1 In each of the following situations it is believed that the population standard deviation is 10. Find the acceptance region for the sample mean in each case.

a **i** $H_0: \mu = 60$; $H_1: \mu \neq 60$; 5% significance; $n = 160$

    ii $H_0: \mu = 120$; $H_1: \mu \neq 120$; 10% significance; $n = 300$

b **i** $H_0: \mu = 80$; $H_1: \mu > 80$; 1% significance; $n = 180$

    ii $H_0: \mu = 750$; $H_1: \mu \neq 750$; 2% significance; $n = 55$

c **i** $H_0: \mu = 80.4$; $H_1: \mu < 80.4$;   10% significance; $n = 120$

  ii $H_0: \mu = 93$; $H_1: \mu < 93$;   5% significance; $n = 400$

2 In each of the following situations it is believed that the variance of the population is 400. Find the p-value of the observed sample mean. Hence decide the result of the test if it is conducted at the 5% significance level

a **i** $H_0: \mu = 85$; $H_1: \mu \neq 85$; $n = 64$; $\bar{x} = 90$

  ii $H_0: \mu = 44$; $H_1: \mu \neq 44$; $n = 50$; $\bar{x} = 50$

b **i** $H_0: \mu = 85$; $H_1: \mu > 85$; $n = 80$; $\bar{x} = 95$

  ii $H_0: \mu = 144$; $H_1: \mu > 144$; $n = 140$; $\bar{x} = 148$

c **i** $H_0: \mu = 265$; $H_1: \mu < 265$; $n = 96$; $\bar{x} = 263.8$

  ii $H_0: \mu = 377$; $H_1: \mu < 377$; $n = 100$; $\bar{x} = 374.9$

d **i** $H_0: \mu = 95$; $H_1: \mu < 95$; $n = 20$; $\bar{x} = 96.4$

  ii $H_0: \mu = 184$; $H_1: \mu > 184$; $n = 50$; $\bar{x} = 183.2$

3 In each of the following situations, conduct a hypothesis test at the 5% significance level.

a **i** $H_0: \mu = 85$; $H_1: \mu \neq 85$; $n = 100$; $s = 100$; $\bar{x} = 90$

  ii $H_0: \mu = 0.4$; $H_1: \mu \neq 0.4$; $n = 80$; $s = 0.6$; $\bar{x} = 0.6$

b **i** $H_0: \mu = 40$; $H_1: \mu > 40$; $n = 60$; $s = 20$; $\bar{x} = 50$

  ii $H_0: \mu = 0.9$; $H_1: \mu < 0.9$; $n = 64$; $s = 0.8$; $\bar{x} = 0.8$

4 The average height of 18-year-olds in England is 168.8 cm. Caroline believes that the students in her school are taller than average. To test her belief she measures the heights of 30 students in her class.

a State the hypotheses for Caroline's test.

The students in Caroline's class have an average height of 171.4 cm and a standard deviation of 12 cm.

b State an assumption required to conduct a normal hypothesis test on this data.

c Test Caroline's belief at the 5% level of significance.

d Has Caroline used the CLT? Explain your answer.

5 All students in a large school are given a typing test and it was found that the times taken to type one page of text have a mean of 10.3 minutes and a standard deviation of 3.7 minutes. The students are given a month-long typing course and then a random sample of 40 students was asked to take the typing test again. The mean time was 9.2 minutes.

a Test at 10% significance level whether there is evidence that the time the students take to type a page of text has decreased.

b State an assumption made in your answer to part **a**.

6 A farmer knows from experience that the average height of apple trees is 2.7 m with standard deviation 0.7 m. He buys a new orchard and wants to test whether the average height of apple trees is different. He assumes that the standard deviation of heights is still 0.7 m.

Rewind

You learned about critical regions in A Level Mathematics Student Book 1, Chapter 18.

a State the hypotheses he should use for his test.

The farmer measures the heights of 45 trees and finds their average.

b Find the critical region for the test at 10% level of significance.

c If the average height of the 45 trees is 2.3 m, state the conclusion of the hypothesis test.

7 A doctor has a large number of patients starting a new diet in order to lose weight. Before the diet the mass of the patients was normally distributed with mean 82.4 kg and standard deviation 7.9 kg. The doctor assumes that the diet does not change the standard deviation of the masses. After the patients have been on the diet for a while, the doctor takes a sample of 40 patients and finds their average mass.

a The doctor believes that the average mass of the patients has decreased following the diet. He wishes to test his belief at the 5% level of significance. State suitable null and alternative hypotheses.

b Find the critical region for this test.

c Did you use the CLT in your answer to part **a**? Justify your answer.

d The average mass of the 40 patients after the diet was 78.4 kg. State the conclusion of the test.

8 A study from the 1990s showed that 15-year-olds in the UK spent an average of 1.8 hours each week playing computer games. A study of time spent playing computer games in 2017 is summarised by the following data:

$$\Sigma t = 78, \ \Sigma t^2 = 448, \ n = 30$$

(t is the time spent by each 15-year-old in hours)

a Find the unbiased estimate of the population variance from the data, giving your answer to three significant figures.

b Conduct a hypothesis test at the 5% significance level to see if the mean time spent playing computer games has increased.

c State one other fact you need to know about your sample before you would be confident in your conclusion.

9 The school canteen sells coffee in cups claiming to contain 250 ml. It is known that the amount of coffee in a cup is normally distributed with standard deviation 6 ml. Adam believes that on

average the cups contain less coffee than claimed. He wishes to test his belief at the 5% significance level.

a Adam measures the amount of coffee in 36 randomly chosen cups and finds the average to be 248.8 ml. Show that he cannot conclude that the average amount of coffee in a cup is less than 250 ml.

b Adam decides to collect a larger sample. He finds the average to be 248.8 ml again, but this time this is sufficient evidence to conclude that the average amount of coffee in a cup is less than 250 ml. What is the minimum sample size he must have used?

Section 2: Confidence intervals

A single value calculated from the sample used to estimate a population parameter is called a **point estimate**. You are trying to find an interval that has a specified probability of including the true population value of the statistic you are interested in. This interval is called a confidence interval and the specified probability is called the **confidence level**.

When doing quality control on the diameter of washers produced by a machine, a valid assumption based on long experience might be that the washers are normally distributed with a standard deviation of 0.8 mm.

In the quality control process a random sample of five washers is taken and the results in mm are:

    21.1   21.4   21.8   22.6   23.0

The sample mean is 21.98 mm and this provides an unbiased estimate of the population mean; however, it is very unlikely that the population mean is exactly 21.98 mm. In this section you will learn about a method that will allow you to say with 95% confidence that the population mean is somewhere between 21.28 mm and 22.68 mm. This does not mean that there is a probability of 95% that the population mean is between 21.28 mm and 22.68 mm, but rather that if you were to take lots more random samples from the population and each time construct a confidence interval then 95% of them would contain the population mean.

To develop the theory, it helps to start by looking at 95% intervals, which are the most common choice. Suppose that you have a sample of size n from a normal distribution with known standard deviation σ. Then the sample mean satisfies $\bar{X} \sim N\left(\mu, \dfrac{\sigma^2}{n}\right)$, where μ is the population mean (the thing you are trying to estimate).

You want to find an interval $[a, b]$, where the numbers a and b depend on the value of $\bar{X}$, which has a 95% probability of containing μ. Perhaps surprisingly, this can be achieved by starting with an interval symmetrical about μ which has a 95% probability of containing $\bar{X}$.

Tip

Confidence intervals can be constructed for any population parameter; however, in this course you will only be asked about confidence intervals for the population mean.

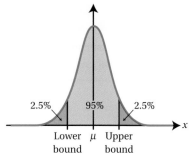

Since μ is unknown you need to use the Z-score of $\overline{X}$, $Z = \dfrac{\overline{X} - \mu}{\sigma/\sqrt{n}}$.

The z-value corresponding to the upper bound (see previous diagram) is $\Phi^{-1}(0.975) = 1.96$ (3 s.f.), so

$$P\left(-1.96 < \frac{\overline{X} - \mu}{\sigma/\sqrt{n}} < 1.96\right) = 0.95$$

You can rearrange the inequalities to focus on μ:

$$P\left(\overline{X} - 1.96\,\frac{\sigma}{\sqrt{n}} < \mu < \overline{X} + 1.96\,\frac{\sigma}{\sqrt{n}}\right) = 0.95$$

Be warned: although this looks like it is a statement about the probability of μ, in your derivation you treated μ as a constant so it is meaningless to talk about a probability of μ. This statement is still concerned with the probability distribution of $\overline{X}$.

So if the sample mean is $\overline{x}$, your 95% confidence interval for μ is

$$\left(\overline{x} - 1.96\,\frac{\sigma}{\sqrt{n}},\, \overline{x} + 1.96\,\frac{\sigma}{\sqrt{n}}\right).$$

You can generalise this method to other confidence levels. To find a $c\%$ confidence interval you can calculate the critical z-value using the formula in Key point 9.1 or find it geometrically using the properties of this graph.

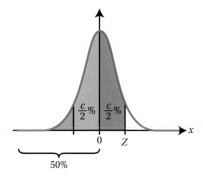

From this diagram you can see that the critical z-value is the one where there is a probability of $0.5 + \dfrac{\frac{1}{2}c}{100}$ of being below it.

> ### ◄◄ Rewind
>
> You saw in A Level Mathematics Student Book 2, Chapter 17 that $\Phi^{-1}(p)$ is the inverse normal distribution that tells you the Z-score that results in the cumulative probability p.

Key point 9.1

A $c\%$ confidence interval for μ is $\left(\bar{x} - z\dfrac{\sigma}{\sqrt{n}}, \bar{x} + z\dfrac{\sigma}{\sqrt{n}}\right)$ where $z = \Phi^{-1}\left(0.5 + \dfrac{\frac{1}{2}c}{100}\right)$

 Tip

Some calculators can find these confidence intervals for you.

WORKED EXAMPLE 9.3

The masses of fish in a pond is known to have standard deviation 150 g. The average mass of 96 fish from the pond is found to be 806 g.

a Find a 90% confidence interval for the average mass of all the fish in the pond.
b State, with a reason, whether or not you used the CLT in your previous answer.

a For a 90% confidence interval

$z = \Phi^{-1}(0.95)$

$= 1.64$

> Find the z-value associated with a 90% confidence interval using your calculator.

So the confidence interval is $806 \pm 1.64 \times \dfrac{150}{\sqrt{96}}$
which is $[781, 831]$

b You did need to use the CLT as you are not told that the mass of fish is normally distributed.

You do not need to know the centre of the interval to find the width of the confidence interval (see Key point 9.2).

 Key point 9.2

The width of a confidence interval is $2z\dfrac{\sigma}{\sqrt{n}}$

WORKED EXAMPLE 9.4

The results in a test are known to be normally distributed with a standard deviation of 20. How many people need to be tested to find a 80% confidence interval with a width of less than five?

For a 80% confidence interval

$z = \Phi^{-1}(0.9) = 1.28$

> Find the z-value associated with a 80% confidence interval.

$2 \times 1.28 \times \dfrac{20}{\sqrt{n}} < 5$

> Set up an inequality.

$\dfrac{2 \times 1.28 \times 20}{5} < \sqrt{n}$

$104.9 < n$

At least 105 people need to be tested.

As in Section 1, if the sample size is sufficiently large (greater than 25) you can use the CLT to drop the requirement that the random variable is drawn from a normal distribution. You can also use the unbiased estimate of the population variance as a substitute for the population variance.

Confidence intervals can be used to conduct hypothesis tests. For example, if a 95% confidence interval is found, it can be used to conduct a 5% significance two-tailed hypothesis test. This is illustrated in Worked example 9.5.

WORKED EXAMPLE 9.5

A vet is measuring the masses of a breed of dog (w kg). Her data are summarised as follows.

$$\Sigma w = 808, \ \Sigma w^2 = 20\,145, \ n = 40$$

a Find a 90% confidence interval for the population mean.

b A textbook claims that the average mass of this breed is 18 kg. Conduct a hypothesis test at the 10% significance level to decide if this sample suggests that the textbook figure is incorrect.

a $\bar{w} = \dfrac{808}{40} = 20.2$ First of all you need to work out the sample statistics.

$\sigma^2 = \dfrac{20145}{40} - 20.2^2 = 95.585$

$s^2 = \dfrac{40}{39} \times \sigma^2 \approx 98.0$ You need to find the unbiased variance.

$s \approx 9.90$

$z = \Phi^{-1}\left(0.5 + \dfrac{0.5 \times 90}{100}\right) = \Phi^{-1}(0.95) \approx 1.645$ You can use the formula from Key point 9.1 to find the appropriate z-value.

So   You can then use the expression in Key point 9.1, substituting s for σ.

$$\bar{w} - z\dfrac{s}{\sqrt{n}} < \mu < \bar{w} + z\dfrac{s}{\sqrt{n}}$$

$$20.2 - 1.645 \times \dfrac{9.90}{\sqrt{40}} < \mu < 20.2 + 1.645 \times \dfrac{9.90}{\sqrt{40}}$$

$$17.6 < \mu < 22.8$$

b $H_0: \mu = 18 \quad H_1: \mu \neq 18$

The true mean being 18 kg is consistent with the confidence interval found, so you do not reject H_0 at the 10% significance level. There is not significant evidence that the textbook is incorrect.

EXERCISE 9B

1 Find z for the following confidence levels:

a 80% **b** 99%

2 Find the required confidence interval for the population mean for the following summarised data. You can assume that the data are taken from a normal distribution with known variance.

a **i** $\bar{x} = 42.1$, $\sigma^2 = 18.4$, $n = 8$, 95% confidence interval

   ii $\bar{x} = 42.1$, $\sigma^2 = 18.4$, $n = 20$, 80% confidence interval

b **i** $\bar{x} = 350$, $\sigma^2 = 105$, $n = 15$, 90% confidence interval

   ii $\bar{x} = -1.8$, $\sigma^2 = 14$, $n = 6$, 99% confidence interval.

3 Fill in the missing values for the following table. You can assume that the data are taken from a normal distribution with known variance.

		$\bar{x}$	σ	n	Confidence level	Lower bound of interval	Upper bound of interval
a	**i**	58.6	8.2	4	90		
	ii	0.178	0.01	12	80		
b	**i**		4	4		39.44	44.56
	ii		1.2	900		30.30	30.50
c	**i**		18		95	115.59	124.41
	ii		25		88	1097.3	1102.7
d	**i**			100	75	−0.601	8.601
	ii			400	90	15.967	16.033
e	**i**	8	12	14		0.539	
	ii	0.4	0.01		80		0.403

4 The blood oxygen level (measured in per cent) of an individual is known to be normally distributed with a standard deviation of 3%. Based upon six readings, Niamh finds that her blood oxygen level is on average 88.2%. Find a 95% confidence interval for Niamh's true blood oxygen level.

5 The masses of newborn male babies in a hospital are known to be normally distributed with variance 2 kg². Find a 90% confidence interval for the average mass if a random sample of ten newborn male babies have an average mass of 3.8 kg.

6 A data set is summarised as follows:

$$\Sigma x = 40, \ \Sigma x^2 = 1246, \ n = 50.$$

Find a 90% confidence interval for the population mean.

7 **a** A sample of 50 people in a town has an average wage of £24 506 with an unbiased estimation of population variance of 144 million. Find a 95% confidence interval for the mean wage in the town.

b Is there significant evidence (at 5% significance) that the mean wage in this town is different from £25 000?

c Have you used the CLT in your answer to parts **a** and **b**? Justify your answer.

8 When a scientist measures the concentration of a solution, the measurement obtained can be assumed to be a normally distributed random variable with standard deviation 0.2.

    a He makes 18 independent measurements of the concentration of a particular solution and correctly calculates the confidence interval for the population mean as [43.908, 44.092]. Determine the confidence level of this interval.

    b He is now given a different solution and is asked to determine a 90% confidence interval for its population mean concentration. The confidence interval is required to have a width less than 0.05. Find the minimum number of measurements required.

9 A supermarket wishes to estimate the average amount spent shopping each week by single men. It is known that the amount spent has a normal distribution with standard deviation €22.40. What is the smallest sample required so that the margin of error (the difference between the centre of the interval and the boundary) for an 80% confidence interval is less than €10?

10 A physicist wishes to find a confidence interval for the population mean voltage of some batteries. He therefore randomly selects n batteries and measures their voltages. Based on his results, he obtains the 90% confidence interval [8.884, 8.916]. The voltages of batteries are known to be normally distributed with a standard deviation of 0.1 V.

    a Find the value of n.

    b Assuming that the same confidence interval had been obtained from measuring 49 batteries, what would be its level of confidence?

11 **a** A set of 40 data items produces a confidence interval for the population mean of (94.93, 105.07). If $\Sigma x^2 = 424\,375$, find the confidence level, giving your answer to two significant figures.

    b Jasmine wants to test the following hypotheses:

$$H_0: \mu = 94, \ H_1: \mu > 94.$$

    Use the given confidence interval to conduct a hypothesis test, stating the significance level.

12 From experience, you know that the variance in the increase between marks in a beginning-of-year test and an end-of-year test is 64. A random sample of four students in Mr Jack's class was selected and the results in the two tests were recorded:

	Alma	Brenda	Ciaran	Dominique
Beginning of year	98	62	88	82
End of year	124	92	120	116

    a Assuming that the difference can be modelled by a normal distribution with variance 64, find a 90% confidence interval for the population mean increase.

    b How could the width of the confidence interval be decreased?

    c Do these data provide evidence at the 5% significance level that Mr Jack's class is doing better than the school average of a 20-mark increase?

13 Which of the following statements are true for 90% confidence intervals of the population mean?

   a If a 90 per cent confidence interval is found to be 15.3 to 16.8, then there is a probability of 90 per cent that the true mean is between 15.3 and 16.8.

   b If you were to repeat the sampling process 100 times, 90 of the intervals would contain the true mean.

   c Once the interval has been created there is a 90 per cent chance that the next sample mean will be within the interval.

   d On average 90 per cent of intervals created in this way contain the true mean.

   e 90 per cent of sample means will fall within this interval.

 14 For a given sample, which will be larger: an 80% confidence interval for the mean or a 90% confidence interval for the mean?

 15 Give an example of a statistic for which the confidence interval would not be symmetric about the sample statistic.

✏ Checklist of learning and understanding

- A c% confidence interval for the population mean is an interval constructed from the data which captures the population mean for c% of samples.
- If the true population variance is known and the sample mean follows a normal distribution then the confidence interval takes the form:

$$\bar{x} - z\frac{\sigma}{\sqrt{n}} < \mu < \bar{x} + z\frac{\sigma}{\sqrt{n}}$$

  where:

$$z = \Phi^{-1}\left(0.5 + \frac{\frac{1}{2}c}{100}\right)$$

- The width of the confidence interval is given by $2z\frac{\sigma}{\sqrt{n}}$.

- When doing a hypothesis test or finding a confidence interval for the mean, if the sample size is sufficiently large (greater than 25) you can use the CLT to drop the requirement that the random variable is drawn from a normal distribution. You can also use the unbiased estimate of the variance as a substitute for the true variance.

Mixed practice 9

1 A data set is summarised as follows:

$$\Sigma x = 240, \Sigma x^2 = 1250, n = 50.$$

   a Calculate the unbiased estimate of the population variance based on this data set.

   b Find a 95% confidence interval for the population mean.

   c Conduct a two-tailed test at 5% significance to determine if there is a change from $\mu = 5$.

   d Do you need to use the CLT in your answers to parts **b** and **c**? Justify your answer.

2 The masses of bananas are investigated. The masses of a random sample of 100 of these bananas were measured and the mean was found to be 168 g with an unbiased variance of 200 g^2.

   a Find a 95% confidence interval for μ.

   b State, with a reason, whether or not your answer requires the assumption that the masses are normally distributed.

3 Gordon is a cricketer. Over a long period he knows that his population mean score, in number of runs per innings, is 28, and the population standard deviation is 12. In a new season he adopts a different batting style and he finds that in 30 innings using this style his mean score is 28.98.

   i Stating a necessary assumption, test at the 5% significance level whether his population mean score has increased.

   ii Explain whether it was necessary to use the Central Limit Theorem in part **i**.

© OCR, GCE Mathematics, Paper 4733, January 2013

4 A shopkeeper knows from experience that the average number of customers each day is 145 with standard deviation 25. He invests in a new advertising campaign and wants to know if this has had a significant positive effect on the numbers entering his shop.

   a State the hypotheses he should use for his test.

   The shopkeeper records the number of customers on 30 days and finds their average.

   b Find the critical region for the test at 10% level of significance.

   c If the average number of customers is 150, state the conclusion of the hypothesis test.

5 A new computer was bought by a local council to search council records and was tested by an employee. She searched a random sample of 500 records and the sample mean search time was found to be 2.18 milliseconds and an unbiased estimate of variance was 1.58^2 milliseconds^2.

   i Calculate a 98% confidence interval for the population mean search time μ milliseconds.

   ii It is required to obtain a sample mean time that differs from μ by less than 0.05 milliseconds with probability 0.95. Estimate the sample size required.

   iii State why it is unnecessary for the validity of your calculations that search time has a normal distribution.

© OCR, GCE Mathematics, Paper 4734, June 2013

6 The pH of a river is believed to be normally distributed with a standard deviation of 0.1. What is the smallest number of samples which should be taken to get a 90% confidence interval for the population mean with a width of less than 0.05?

7 From experience you know that the variance in the mass decrease during a diet is 9 kg². A random sample of four people was selected and their masses before and after their diets were recorded.

	Bobby	Sam	Francis	Alex
Before diet	82	77	86	80
After diet	78	77	87	75

a Assuming that the mass loss follows a normal distribution, find a 95% confidence interval for the population mean mass loss during the diet.

b Hence conduct a test at 5% significance to see if the diet results in a change in mass.

8 The random variable X is normally distributed with mean μ and standard deviation 5.

A random sample of 40 observations of X has a mean of 24.

a Find a 95% confidence interval for μ.

b It is believed that $P(X \leqslant 20) = 0.421$. Determine whether or not this is consistent with your confidence interval for μ.

Proving the formula for Spearman's rank correlation coefficient

Spearman's rank correlation coefficient is actually the ppmcc for the ranks. In this section you will see how the formula for Spearman's rank correlation coefficient can be derived from the formula for ppmcc. This derivation makes use of the fact that the ranks are integers from 1 to n where n is the number of data items. You will use the following standard mathematical formulae:

$$\sum_1^n r = \frac{n(n+1)}{2}, \qquad \sum_1^n r^2 = \frac{n(n+1)(2n+1)}{6}$$

Questions

1. Explain why the mean of the ranks is $\frac{n+1}{2}$ and hence show that the variance of the ranks is $\frac{n^2-1}{12}$.

2. Show that if x_i and y_i are ranks from 1 to n,

$$\sum_1^n (x_i - \bar{x})(y_i - \bar{y}) = \sum_1^n x_i y_i - n\left(\frac{n+1}{2}\right)^2$$

3. Hence use the identity $x_i y_i = -\frac{1}{2}\left((x_i - y_i)^2 - (x_i^2 + y_i^2)\right)$ to show that

$$\sum_1^n (x_i - \bar{x})(y_i - \bar{y}) = \frac{n(n^2-1)}{12} - \frac{1}{2}\sum_1^n d_i^2$$

   where $d_i = x_i - y_i$

4. Use the formula

$$r = \frac{\frac{1}{n}\sum_1^n (x_i - \bar{x})(y_i - \bar{y})}{\sigma_x \sigma_y}$$

   to prove that if x_i and y_i are ranks from 1 to n then

$$r = 1 - \frac{6\sum_1^n d_i^2}{n(n^2-1)}$$

Justifying the formula for Pearson's product moment correlation coefficient

One important aspect of solving real-world problems is coming up with a mathematical measure of the concept you are investigating. For example, when investigating correlation between two variables you need to come up with a single number to describe its strength. There may be several reasonable options and you need to be able to evaluate which one is the best measure to use.

Consider the following data:

(3,4)   (5,4)   (8,6)   (10,10)   (15,14).

Questions

1 Plot the data as points on a scatter diagram. Intuitively, do they appear to have a positive or a negative correlation?

2 Find the mean of all the x values and the mean of all the y values. Plot the lines $x = \bar{x}$ and $y = \bar{y}$ on your scatter diagram, splitting it into four regions.

3 If TR = number of dots in the top right region, BL = number of dots in the bottom left regions etc, explain why $r_c = \text{TR} + \text{BL} - \text{TL} - \text{BR}$ gives a measure of the linear correlation of the data.

What are the strengths and weaknesses of this measure? Can you suggest any alternative measures based on the number of points in each region?

4 The covariance of n data items is calculated as

$$\sigma_{xy} = \frac{1}{n}\Sigma(x_i - \bar{x})(y_i - \bar{y})$$

a Calculate the covariance of the given data.

b Explain why $(x_i - \bar{x})(y_i - \bar{y})$ is positive if it lies in the top right or bottom left regions from question 3.

A **c** Why might $(y_i - \bar{y})$ be described as a 'moment'?

d Explain why the covariance gives a measure of the linear correlation of the data. What are the strengths and weaknesses of this measure?

5 ppmcc can be defined as $r = \dfrac{\sigma_{xy}}{\sigma_x \sigma_y}$

a Show that this formula is equivalent to the one given in the formula book (Key point 5.1).

b Find the value of r for your data.

c What are the advantages and disadvantages of this measure? Try researching other potential measures of correlation.

Generating random numbers and the central limit theorem

Ⓐ This section is for A Level students only.

Most spreadsheets include a random number generator. This typically generates random numbers between 0 and 1. You can use other functions to generate random numbers from different distributions. For example, in Microsoft Excel or other spreadsheet software, you can create a random number from the N(0, 1) distribution using the syntax '=NORMINV(RAND(),0,1)'.

Questions

1 Prove that if U follows a continuous uniform distribution between 0 and 1 then $X = F^{-1}(U)$ is a random variable with cdf $F(x)$.

Although this provides an advanced way of simulating random variables from a given distribution, if you are using Excel there is a simpler way. The Data Analysis toolpak provides a way of generating random numbers from several standard and user-generated distributions. It also provides a way of creating histograms.

2 Use a spreadsheet to create a list of 200 random numbers taken from a uniform distribution between 0 and 1 in column A. Create a histogram with 10 groups to illustrate these data.

3 Now create another list of 200 random numbers taken from a uniform distribution between 0 and 1 in column B. In column K, calculate the row average of columns A and B. Plot a histogram illustrating the data in column K.

4 Now create 8 further lists of 200 random numbers from the same distribution in columns C to J. In column K, calculate the row average of columns A to J. Plot a histogram illustrating the data in column K.

5 Repeat questions 2 to 4 using a Poisson (0.8) distribution. You might need to choose your histogram groups carefully.

6 Repeat questions 2 to 4 using the following distribution:

x	0	1	2	3
$P(X=x)$	0.4	0.1	0.1	0.4

You might need to choose your histogram groups carefully.

From questions 4, 5 and 6 you should find that means of samples taken from all these distributions produce bell-shaped curves. You could conduct a chi-squared test to check that this is plausibly a normal distribution.

🔍 Explore

If you repeated this simulation using the Cauchy distribution (using the cdf $\frac{1}{\pi}$ arctan) $\left(x + \frac{1}{2} \right)$ you would find that although it produces a bell-shaped curve it is not close to a normal distribution. This is because the Cauchy distribution is an example of a distribution that does not satisfy all the conditions of the CLT. Which properties of the Cauchy distribution mean that it does not follow the CLT?

1 Two judges placed 7 dancers in rank order. Both judges placed dancers A and B in the first two places, but in opposite orders. The judges agreed about the ranks for all the other 5 dancers. Calculate the value of Spearman's rank correlation coefficient.

© OCR, AS GCE Mathematics, Paper 4732, June 2009

2 **i** When should Yates' correction be applied when carrying out a χ^2 test?

Two vaccines against typhoid fever, A and B, were tested on a total of 700 people in Nepal during a particular year. The vaccines were allocated randomly and whether or not typhoid had developed was noted during the following year. The results are shown in the table.

	Vaccines	
	A	B
Developed typhoid	19	4
Did not develop typhoid	310	367

ii Carry out a suitable χ^2 test at the 1% significance level to determine whether the outcome depends on the vaccine used. Comment on the result.

© OCR, GCE Mathematics, Paper 4734, January 2011

3 In a test of association of two factors, A and B, a 2×2 contingency table yielded 5.63 for the value of χ^2 with Yates' correction.

  i State the null hypothesis and alternative hypothesis for the test.

  ii State how Yates' correction is applied, and whether it increases or decreases the value of χ^2.

  iii Carry out the test at the $2\frac{1}{2}$% significance level.

© OCR, GCE Mathematics, Paper 4734, January 2012

4 The continuous random variable x has probability density function

$$f(x) = ax(b - x), \qquad 0 \le x \le b$$

If the mode of the distribution is at $x = 4$ find the values of the constants a and b.

5 A continuous random variable X has probability density function given by

$$f(x) = \begin{cases} \dfrac{2x}{5} & 0 \le x < 1, \\[2mm] \dfrac{2}{5\sqrt{x}} & 1 < x \le 4, \\[2mm] 0 & \text{otherwise.} \end{cases}$$

Find

  i $E(X)$,
                            ii $P(X \ge E(X))$.

© OCR, GCE Mathematics, Paper 4734, June 2009

6 The function F(t) is defined as follows.

$$F(t)=\begin{cases}0 & t<0,\\ \sin^4 t & 0\leqslant t\leqslant \frac{1}{2}\pi,\\ 1 & t>\frac{1}{2}\pi.\end{cases}$$

i Verify that F is a (cumulative) distribution function.

The continuous random variable T has (cumulative) distribution function F(t).

ii Find the lower quartile of T.

iii Find the (cumulative) distribution function of Y, where $Y=\sin T$, and obtain the probability density function of Y.

iv Find the expected value of $\dfrac{1}{Y^3+2Y^4}$.

© OCR, GCE Mathematics, Paper 4734, June 2009

7 80 randomly chosen people are asked to estimate a time interval of 60 seconds without using a watch or clock. The mean of the 80 estimates is 58.9 seconds. Previous evidence shows that the population standard deviation of such estimates is 5.0 seconds. Test, at the 5% significance level, whether there is evidence that people tend to underestimate the time interval.

© OCR, GCE Mathematics, Paper 4733, January 2010

8 The continuous random variable X has probability density function given by

$$f(x)=\begin{cases}\dfrac{2}{5} & -a\leqslant x<0,\\ \dfrac{2}{5}e^{-2x} & x\geqslant 0.\end{cases}$$

Find

i the value of the constant a, **ii** E(X).

© OCR, GCE Mathematics, Paper 4734, January 2010

9 Two random variables S and T have probability density functions given by

$$f_S(x)=\begin{cases}\dfrac{3}{a^3}(x-a)^2 & 0\leqslant x\leqslant a,\\ 0 & \text{otherwise,}\end{cases}$$

$$f_T(x)=\begin{cases}c & 0\leqslant x\leqslant a,\\ 0 & \text{otherwise,}\end{cases}$$

where a and c are constants.

i On a single diagram sketch both probability density functions.

ii Calculate the mean of S, in terms of a.

iii Use your diagram to explain which of S or T has the bigger variance. (Answers obtained by calculation will score no marks.)

© OCR, GCE Mathematics, Paper 4733, June 2013

10 Five dogs, A, B, C, D and E, took part in three races. The order in which they finished the first race was $ABCDE$.

   i Spearman's rank correlation coefficient between the orders for the five dogs in the first two races was found to be -1. Write down the order in which the dogs finished the second race.

   ii Spearman's rank correlation coefficient between the orders for the five dogs in the first race and the third race was found to be 0.9.

     a Show that, in the usual notation (as in the List of Formulae), $\Sigma d^2 = 2$.

     b Hence or otherwise find a possible order in which the dogs could have finished the third race.

© OCR, AS GCE Mathematics, Paper 4732, January 2011

11 The random variable H has the distribution $N(\mu, 5^2)$. The mean of a sample of n observations of H is denoted by $\overline{H}$. It is given that $P(\overline{H} > 53.28) = 0.0250$ and $P(\overline{H} < 51.65) = 0.0968$, both correct to 4 decimal places. Find the values of μ and n.

© OCR, GCE Mathematics, Paper 4733, January 2011

12 The continuous random variable X has mean μ and standard deviation 45. A significance test is to be carried out of the null hypothesis $H_0: \mu = 230$ against the alternative hypothesis $H_1: \mu \neq 230$, at the 1% significance level. A random sample of size 50 is obtained, and the sample mean is found to be 213.4.

   i Carry out the test.

   ii Explain whether it is necessary to use the Central Limit Theorem in your test.

© OCR, GCE Mathematics, Paper 4733, January 2011

13 A random variable X has the cumulative probability density function given by:

$$F(x) = \begin{cases} 0, & x < 0 \\ \dfrac{1}{30}x^2, & 0 \leqslant x \leqslant 3 \\ -\dfrac{1}{70}x^2 + \dfrac{2}{7}x - \dfrac{3}{7}, & 3 < x \leqslant 10 \\ 1, & x > 10 \end{cases}$$

The diagram shows the graph of $y = F(x)$.

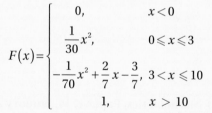

   a Find $P(X > 5)$.

   b Find the median of X.

   c Find the probability density function for X.

   d Show that the mean of X is $\dfrac{13}{3}$.

     You are given that the variance of X is $\dfrac{79}{18}$.

   e Find the probability that the mean of a random sample of 60 values of X is greater than 5.

14 The random variable X follows Poisson distribution with mean μ. Let $\rho = P(X = 1 \text{ or } X = 2)$.

   a Write down an expression for ρ in terms of μ.

   b Find the exact value of μ for which ρ is the largest possible.

15 The probability distribution of a discrete random variable X is given by $P(X=x)=\dfrac{5(p)^x}{4}$ for $x \in \mathbb{Z}, x \geqslant 0$. Find the value of ρ.

16 A continuous random variable X follows a Cauchy distribution with probability density function

$$f(x)=\frac{1}{\pi(x^2+3)}, \text{for } x \in \mathbb{R}.$$

Find the $P(-1 < x < 1)$, giving your answer in a form without π.

17 The continuous random variable X has (cumulative) distribution function given by

$$F(x)=\begin{cases} 0 & x < \dfrac{1}{2}, \\ \dfrac{2x-1}{x+1} & \dfrac{1}{2} \leqslant x \leqslant 2, \\ 1 & x > 2. \end{cases}$$

i Given that $Y=\dfrac{1}{X}$, find the (cumulative) distribution function of Y, and deduce that Y and X have identical distributions.

ii Find $E(X+1)$ and deduce the value of $E\left(\dfrac{1}{X}\right)$.

© OCR, GCE Mathematics, Paper 4734, January 2011

18 A chef wished to ascertain her customers' preference for certain vegetables. She asked a random sample of 120 customers for their preferred vegetable from asparagus, broad beans and cauliflower. The responses, classified according to the gender of the customer, are shown in the table.

	Asparagus	Broad beans	Cauliflower
Female preference	31	9	25
Male preference	17	21	17

i Test, at the 5% significance level, whether vegetable preference and gender are independent.

ii Determine whether, at the 10% significance level, the vegetables are equally preferred.

© OCR, GCE Mathematics, Paper 4734, January 2010

19 A certain type of particle is emitted at random from a radioactive source. A physicist assumes that the time between two successive emissions can be modelled by a random variable T with the pdf

$f(t)=\dfrac{4t}{9}-\dfrac{4t^3}{81}$ for $t \in [0, 3]$ and $f(t)=0$ elsewhere.

She carries out 50 experiments to measure the times between successive emissions and records how often the times fall into each of the five equal intervals:

$I_1 = [0, 0.6)$

$I_2 = [0.6, 1.2)$

$I_3 = [1.2, 1.8)$

$I_4 = [1.8, 2.4)$

$I_5 = [2.4, 3)$.

The results are shown in the following table:

I_1	I_2	I_3	I_4	I_5
2	11	11	20	6

a Assuming that the physicist's assumption is correct, for each value of k find $p_k = P(T \in I_k)$.

b At the 5% significance level can her assumption be accepted?

20 Three skaters, A, B and C, are placed in rank order by four judges. Judge P ranks skater A in 1st place, skater B in 2nd place and skater C in 3rd place.

i Without carrying out any calculation, state the value of Spearman's rank correlation coefficient for the following ranks. Give a reason for your answer.

Skater	A	B	C
Judge P	1	2	3
Judge Q	3	2	1

ii Calculate the value of Spearman's rank correlation coefficient for the following ranks.

Skater	A	B	C
Judge P	1	2	3
Judge R	3	1	2

iii Judge S ranks the skaters at random. Find the probability that the value of Spearman's rank correlation coefficient between the ranks of judge P and judge S is 1.

© OCR, AS GCE Mathematics, Paper 4732, June 2010

21 A statistician suggested that the weekly sales X thousand litres at a petrol station could be modelled by the following probability density function.

$$f(x) = \begin{cases} \dfrac{1}{40}(2x+3) & 0 \leqslant x < 5, \\ 0 & \text{otherwise.} \end{cases}$$

i Show that, using this model, $P(a \leqslant X < a+1) = \dfrac{a+2}{20}$ for $0 \leqslant a \leqslant 4$.

Sales in 100 randomly chosen weeks gave the following grouped frequency table.

x	$0 \leqslant x < 1$	$1 \leqslant x < 2$	$2 \leqslant x < 3$	$3 \leqslant x < 4$	$4 \leqslant x < 5$
Frequency	16	12	18	30	24

ii Carry out a goodness of fit test at the 10% significance level of whether $f(x)$ fits the data.

© OCR, GCE Mathematics, Paper 4734, January 2012

22 The amount of tomato juice, X ml, dispensed into cartons of a particular brand has a normal distribution with mean 504 and standard deviation 3. The juice is sold in packs of 4 cartons, filled independently. The total amount of juice in one pack is Y ml.

i Find $P(Y < 2000)$.

The random variable V is defined as $Y - 4X$.

ii Find E(V) and Var(V).

iii What is the probability that the amount of juice in a randomly chosen pack is more than 4 times the amount of juice in a randomly chosen carton?

© OCR, GCE Mathematics, Paper 4734, January 2010

 23 The heights, h m, and masses, m kg, of five men were measured. The results are plotted on the diagram.

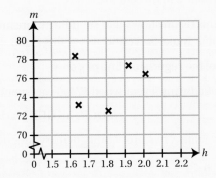

The results are summarised as follows.

$$n = 5 \qquad \Sigma h = 9.02 \qquad \Sigma m = 377.7 \qquad \Sigma h^2 = 16.382 \qquad \Sigma m^2 = 28\,558.67 \qquad \Sigma hm = 681.612$$

i Use the summarised data to calculate the value of the product moment correlation coefficient, r.

ii Comment on your value of r in relation to the diagram.

iii It was decided to re-calculate the value of r after converting the heights to feet and the masses to pounds. State what effect, if any, this will have on the value of r.

iv One of the men had height 1.63 m and mass 78.4 kg. The data for this man were removed and the value of r was re-calculated using the original data for the remaining four men. State in general terms what effect, if any, this will have on the value of r.

© OCR, AS GCE Mathematics, Paper 4732, January 2010

 24 In an experiment the temperature, x °C, of a rod was gradually increased from 0 °C, and the extension, y mm, was measured nine times at 50 °C intervals. The results are summarised as follows.

$$n = 9 \qquad \Sigma x = 1800 \qquad \Sigma y = 14.4 \qquad \Sigma x^2 = 510\,000 \qquad \Sigma y^2 = 32.6416 \qquad \Sigma xy = 4080$$

i Show that the gradient of the regression line of y on x is 0.008 and find the equation of this line.

ii Use your equation to estimate the temperature when the extension is 2.5 mm.

iii Use your equation to estimate the extension for a temperature of –50 °C.

iv Comment on the meaning and the reliability of your estimate in part **c**.

© OCR, AS GCE Mathematics, Paper 4732, June 2010 [Abridged]

25 A firm wishes to assess whether there is a linear relationship between the annual amount spent on advertising, £x thousand, and the annual profit, £y thousand. A summary of the figures for 12 years is as follows.

$$n = 12 \quad \Sigma x = 86.6 \quad \Sigma y = 943.8 \quad \Sigma x^2 = 658.76 \quad \Sigma y^2 = 83\,663.00 \quad \Sigma xy = 7351.12$$

i Calculate the product moment correlation coefficient, showing that it is greater than 0.9.

ii Comment briefly on this value in this context.

iii A manager claims that this result shows that spending more money on advertising in the future will result in greater profits. Make two criticisms of this claim.

iv Calculate the equation of the regression line of y on x.

v Estimate the annual profit during a year when £7400 was spent on advertising.

© OCR, AS GCE Mathematics, Paper 4732, January 2011

26 The continuous random variable X has probability density function given by

$$f(x) = \begin{cases} \dfrac{2}{9}x(3-x) & 0 \leqslant x \leqslant 3, \\ 0 & \text{otherwise.} \end{cases}$$

i Find the variance of X.

ii Show that the probability that a single observation of X lies between 0.0 and 0.5 is $\dfrac{2}{27}$.

iii 108 observations of X are obtained. Find the probability that at least 10 of the observations lie between 0.0 and 0.5.

iv The mean of 108 observations of X is denoted by $\overline{X}$. Write down the approximate distribution of $\overline{X}$, giving the value(s) of any parameter(s).

© OCR, GCE Mathematics, Paper 4733, June 2009 [Adapted]

27 The continuous random variable T is equally likely to take any value from 5.0 to 11.0 inclusive.

i Sketch the graph of the probability density function of T.

ii Write down the value of $E(T)$ and find by integration the value of $\text{Var}(T)$.

iii A random sample of 48 observations of T is obtained. Find the approximate probability that the mean of the sample is greater than 8.3, and explain why the answer is an approximation.

© OCR, GCE Mathematics, Paper 4733, January 2010

Time allowed: 1 hour and 15 minutes

The total mark for this paper is 60.

1 The letters of the word ARRANGE are written on seven separate cards, shuffled and randomly arranged in a line.

    a How many different arrangements are possible? **[2 marks]**

    b What is the probability that an arrangement has all the vowels together? **[3 marks]**

2 The following table shows the probability distribution of a discrete random variable X.

x	1	2	3	4
$P(X=x)$	0.5	0.1	a	b

    a If $E(X) = 2.15$ find the value of a and b. **[3 marks]**

    b Find the value of $\text{Var}(1 - 2X)$. **[3 marks]**

3 The outcome on a six-sided dice is thought to follow a uniform distribution. When it was rolled 600 times the following frequencies were observed:

Outcome	1	2	3	4	5	6
Frequency	95	91	109	102	105	98

    a State appropriate null and alternative hypotheses to test if this dice is biased. **[2 marks]**

    b Conduct a chi-squared test at the 10% significance level to determine if there is evidence that this dice is biased. **[4 marks]**

4 A market researcher knows that in a certain town 40 per cent of people vote for Party X. He stops people in the street and asks them about their voting intentions.

    a Give, in context, two further assumptions required to model the number of people up to and including the Party X voter by a $\text{Geo}(0.4)$ distribution. **[2 marks]**

You can assume that the conditions for a $\text{Geo}(0.4)$ distribution are met.

    b Find the probability that the market researcher must stop more than four people before finding a Party X voter. **[2 marks]**

    c Find the standard deviation in the number of people the market researcher must stop before finding a Party X voter. **[2 marks]**

5 The following table shows the results of a survey in a school about weekly hours spent watching TV.

Test at the 5% significance level whether school year and hours spent watching TV are independent.

		School year		
		7–9	10–11	12–13
Hours	< 5	16	12	17
	5–10	18	15	10
	10–20	26	20	14
	> 20	14	9	6

[8 marks]

6 Sarah models the number of buses arriving at a bus stop using a Poisson distribution. A is the number of Route 1 buses arriving in an hour and B is the number of Route 2 buses arriving. Sarah models these as being independent with $A \sim \text{Po}(3)$ and $B \sim \text{Po}(4.5)$.

a If $T = A + B$ state in context an interpretation of the variable T and write down its distribution, including any parameters.

[2 marks]

b Find the probability that three or fewer buses arrive in an hour.

[2 marks]

c Give one reason why the assumption that A and B are independent is unlikely to be the case.

[1 mark]

d To check her model Sarah counts the number of buses arriving in eleven randomly selected hours.

$$11, 2, 4, 11, 6, 3, 7, 7, 8, 10, 13$$

Use suitable calculations to determine if a Poisson model is feasible.

[4 marks]

7 The following data shows the marks (out of 10) given to six dancers in a competition by two judges:

	Judge 1	Judge 2
Dancer A	10	8
Dancer B	8	5
Dancer C	9	4.5
Dancer D	6	1
Dancer E	1	2
Dancer F	7	1.5

a Calculate Spearman's rank correlation coefficient between the two judges.

[4 marks]

b Explain why Spearman's rank correlation coefficient would be a better measure than Pearson's product moment correlation coefficient (ppmcc) in this situation.

[1 mark]

8 The following table gives the advertising budget, x million dollars, and sales income, y million dollars, of eight companies.

x	5.0	1.5	7.4	3.4	3.8	1.4	2.3	4.9
y	20	8	36	16	18	7	17	16

a Calculate the product moment correlation coefficient. **[1 mark]**

b Explain whether your answer to part **a** would have been different if x had been measured in pounds rather than dollars. **[1 mark]**

c i Assuming that the data is a random sample of all companies, carry out a test at the 5% significance level to determine if there is a correlation between the advertising budget and sales income of companies. **[6 marks]**

ii Explain whether your conclusion suggests that raising the advertising budget will raise the sales income of a company. **[1 mark]**

d Calculate the equation of the regression line of y on x. **[2 marks]**

e Explain whether the line found in part **d** should be used to estimate the sales income of a company with an advertising budget of:

i 6.2 million dollars **[2 marks]**

ii 22 million dollars. **[2 marks]**

Time allowed: 1 hour and 30 minutes

The total mark for this paper is 75.

1 A sample of ten data items is used to find a least squares regression line. It is found to have the equation $y = -1.5x + 2.1$.

    a Explain what is meant by the term 'least squares' in the context of finding regression lines. **[2 marks]**

    b Write down an inequality describing the possible values of the correlation coefficient for the ten data items. **[2 marks]**

    c It is found that all the values of x had been recorded incorrectly. They were all a factor of ten too small. Find the equation of the regression line that would be found when this error is corrected. **[2 marks]**

2 **a** What is meant by the term '99% confidence interval for the mean'? **[2 marks]**

    b The energy of a beta particle is measured in a unit called electron volts or eV. It is known that the energy of a beta particle emitted by a radioactive sample follows a normal distribution with a standard deviation of 1600 eV. How many observations are required so that the average energy of the emitted beta particles can be quoted as a symmetric 99% confidence interval with a width of less than 10 eV? Give your answer to two significant figures. **[4 marks]**

3 The discrete random variable X is modelled by the following distribution:

x	1	2	3
$P(X=x)$	$\frac{1}{2}$	$\frac{1}{3}$	$\frac{1}{6}$

    a Find $E(X)$. **[1 mark]**

    b Find $Var(X)$. **[3 marks]**

    c 125 independent observations of X are made. What is the probability that the mean of these observations is less than 1.5? **[4 marks]**

4 The following contingency table shows information about whether a random sample of people have music lessons, and their gender.

	Music lessons	No music lessons
Female	24	20
Male	15	35

    a State the null and alternative hypotheses when conducting a chi-squared test for independence. **[2 marks]**

    b Write down the number of degrees of freedom in this test. **[1 mark]**

    c Conduct a chi-squared test at the 5% significance level to see if there is a link between gender and choice of lessons. **[5 marks]**

5 The reading ages of children in two different classes are compared.

Class 1	11.2	11.5	12.3	10.7	
Class 2	10.9	10.8	12.1	9.8	11.0

Conduct a suitable non-parametric test at the 5% significance level to determine
if there is difference between the reading ages in the two classes. **[8 marks]**

6 In a game, five numbers are drawn at random from the integers from 1 to 20 inclusive.
Numbers cannot be drawn more than once. Before the numbers are drawn you write
down five integers from 1 to 20 inclusive.

  a Find the probability that the numbers you have written down are the same as the
numbers drawn:

  i in the order the numbers are drawn **[2 marks]**

  ii in any order. **[2 marks]**

  b Find the probability that the numbers you have written down include, in any
order, exactly three of the numbers drawn. **[4 marks]**

7 The time taken for a junior athlete to run the 100 metres is modelled by a normal
distribution with mean 12.2 seconds and standard deviation 0.5 seconds. The time taken
for a senior athlete to run the 400 m is independently modelled by a normal distribution
with mean 52.1 seconds and standard deviation 1.3 seconds.

  a In a race four junior athletes run consecutive 100 metres and a senior athlete
runs 400 m. What is the probability that the senior athlete wins the race? **[3 marks]**

  b A senior athlete runs 400 m and a junior athlete runs 100 m. What is the probability
that the senior athlete takes less than four times as long as the junior athlete? **[3 marks]**

  c The junior athlete takes two independent attempts at running the 100 m and
a senior athlete runs the 400 m once. What is the probability that the senior
athlete takes less than four times as long as the junior athlete's slower time?
Give your answer to three significant figures. **[3 marks]**

8 A bus company claims that there should be three buses arriving every 20 minutes on average.

  a State, in context, one assumption required to model the number of buses arriving
using a Poisson distribution. **[1 mark]**

To monitor their claim the bus company instructs researchers to monitor one hundred
ten-minute intervals. The number of buses arriving in these ten minutes is shown in
the table as follows:

Buses	0	1	2	$\geqslant 3$
Frequency	20	30	25	25

b If the data did follow the Poisson distribution described by the bus company, what would be the expected frequencies? Give your answers to three significant figures. **[4 marks]**

c Do the data shown follow the Poisson distribution suggested by the bus company?

Test this claim at the 10% significance level. **[5 marks]**

9 A crv X has a pdf given by

$$f(x) = \begin{cases} \dfrac{k}{x} & 1 < x < 2 \\ 0 & \text{otherwise.} \end{cases}$$

a Find the exact value of k. **[3 marks]**

b Find $E(X)$ and $Var(X)$, giving your answer to three significant figures. **[4 marks]**

c Find $F(x)$, the cdf of x. **[2 marks]**

d Hence find the pdf of $Y = \dfrac{1}{X}$. **[3 marks]**

FORMULAE

Vectors and 3-D coordinate geometry

Cartesian equation of the line through the point A with position vector $\mathbf{a} = a_1\mathbf{i} + a_2\mathbf{j} + a_3\mathbf{k}$ in direction

$\mathbf{u} = u_1\mathbf{i} + u_2\mathbf{j} + u_3\mathbf{k}$ is $\dfrac{x - a_1}{u_1} = \dfrac{y - a_2}{u_2} = \dfrac{z - a_3}{u_3}(=\lambda)$

Vector product: $\mathbf{a} \times \mathbf{b} = \begin{pmatrix} a_1 \\ a_2 \\ a_3 \end{pmatrix} \times \begin{pmatrix} b_1 \\ b_2 \\ b_3 \end{pmatrix} = \begin{vmatrix} \mathbf{i} & a_1 & b_1 \\ \mathbf{j} & a_2 & b_2 \\ \mathbf{k} & a_3 & b_3 \end{vmatrix} = \begin{pmatrix} a_2 b_3 & - & a_3 b_2 \\ a_3 b_1 & - & a_1 b_3 \\ a_1 b_2 & - & a_2 b_1 \end{pmatrix}$

Standard deviation

$\sqrt{\dfrac{\sum (x - \bar{x})^2}{n}} = \sqrt{\dfrac{\sum x^2}{n} - \bar{x}^2}$ **or** $\sqrt{\dfrac{\sum f (x - \bar{x})^2}{\sum f}} = \sqrt{\dfrac{\sum f x^2}{\sum f} - \bar{x}^2}$

Discrete distributions

X is a random variable taking values x_i in a discrete distribution with $\mathrm{P}(X = x_i) = p_i$

Expectation: $\mu = \mathrm{E}(X) = \sum x_i p_i$

Variance: $\sigma^2 = \mathrm{Var}(X) = \sum (x_i - \mu)^2 p_i = \sum x_i^2 p_i - \mu^2$

	$P(X = x)$	$\mathrm{E}(X)$	$\mathrm{Var}(X)$
Binomial B(n, p)	$\binom{n}{x} p^x (1-p)^{n-x}$	np	$np(1-p)$
Uniform distribution over 1, 2, …, n U(n)	$\dfrac{1}{n}$	$\dfrac{n+1}{2}$	$\dfrac{1}{12}(n^2 - 1)$
Geometric distribution Geo(p)	$(1-p)^{x-1} p$	$\dfrac{1}{p}$	$\dfrac{1-p}{p^2}$
Poisson Po(λ)	$e^{-\lambda} \dfrac{\lambda^x}{x!}$	λ	λ

Non-parametric tests

Goodness-of-fit test and contingency tables: $\sum \dfrac{(O_i - E_i)^2}{E_i} \sim \chi_\nu^2$

Correlation and regression

For a sample of n pairs of observations (x_i, y_i)

$S_{xx} = \sum (x_i - \bar{x})^2 = \sum x_i^2 - \dfrac{(\sum x_i)^2}{n}, S_{yy} = \sum (y_i - \bar{y})^2 = \sum y_i^2 - \dfrac{(\sum y_i)^2}{n},$

$S_{xy} = \sum (x_i - \bar{x})(y_i - \bar{y}) = \sum x_i y_i - \dfrac{\sum x_i \sum y_i}{n}$

Product moment correlation coefficient: $r = \dfrac{S_{xy}}{\sqrt{S_{xx} S_{yy}}} = \dfrac{\sum x_i y_i - \dfrac{\sum x_i \sum y_i}{n}}{\sqrt{\left[\left(\sum x_i^2 - \dfrac{(\sum x_i)^2}{n} \right) \left(\sum y_i^2 - \dfrac{(\sum y_i)^2}{n} \right) \right]}}$

The regression coefficient of y on x is $b = \dfrac{S_{xy}}{S_{xx}} = \dfrac{\sum(x_i - \bar{x})(y_i - \bar{y})}{\sum(x_i - \bar{x})^2}$

Least squares regression line of y on x is $y = a + bx$ where $a = \bar{y} - b\bar{x}$

Spearman's rank correlation coefficient: $r_s = 1 - \dfrac{6\sum d_i^2}{n(n^2 - 1)}$

Critical values for the product moment correlation coefficient, r

	5%	2½%	1%	½%	1-Tail Test		5%	2½%	1%	½%
	10%	5%	2%	1%	2-Tail Test		10%	5%	2%	1%
n						n				
1	-	-	-	-		31	0.3009	0.3550	0.4158	0.4556
2	-	-	-	-		32	0.2960	0.3494	0.4093	0.4487
3	0.9877	0.9969	0.9995	0.9999		33	0.2913	0.3440	0.4032	0.4421
4	0.9000	0.9500	0.9800	0.9900		34	0.2869	0.3388	0.3972	0.4357
5	0.8054	0.8783	0.9343	0.9587		35	0.2826	0.3338	0.3916	0.4296
6	0.7293	0.8114	0.8822	0.9172		36	0.2785	0.3291	0.3862	0.4238
7	0.6694	0.7545	0.8329	0.8745		37	0.2746	0.3246	0.3810	0.4182
8	0.6215	0.7067	0.7887	0.8343		38	0.2709	0.3202	0.3760	0.4128
9	0.5822	0.6664	0.7498	0.7977		39	0.2673	0.3160	0.3712	0.4076
10	0.5494	0.6319	0.7155	0.7646		40	0.2638	0.3120	0.3665	0.4026
11	0.5214	0.6021	0.6851	0.7348		41	0.2605	0.3081	0.3621	0.3978
12	0.4973	0.5760	0.6581	0.7079		42	0.2573	0.3044	0.3578	0.3932
13	0.4762	0.5529	0.6339	0.6835		43	0.2542	0.3008	0.3536	0.3887
14	0.4575	0.5324	0.6120	0.6614		44	0.2512	0.2973	0.3496	0.3843
15	0.4409	0.5140	0.5923	0.6411		45	0.2483	0.2940	0.3457	0.3801
16	0.4259	0.4973	0.5742	0.6226		46	0.2455	0.2907	0.3420	0.3761
17	0.4124	0.4821	0.5577	0.6055		47	0.2429	0.2876	0.3384	0.3721
18	0.4000	0.4683	0.5425	0.5897		48	0.2403	0.2845	0.3348	0.3683
19	0.3887	0.4555	0.5285	0.5751		49	0.2377	0.2816	0.3314	0.3646
20	0.3783	0.4438	0.5155	0.5614		50	0.2353	0.2787	0.3281	0.3610
21	0.3687	0.4329	0.5034	0.5487		51	0.2329	0.2759	0.3249	0.3575
22	0.3598	0.4227	0.4921	0.5368		52	0.2306	0.2732	0.3218	0.3542
23	0.3515	0.4132	0.4815	0.5256		53	0.2284	0.2706	0.3188	0.3509
24	0.3438	0.4044	0.4716	0.5151		54	0.2262	0.2681	0.3158	0.3477
25	0.3365	0.3961	0.4622	0.5052		55	0.2241	0.2656	0.3129	0.3445
26	0.3297	0.3882	0.4534	0.4958		56	0.2221	0.2632	0.3102	0.3415
27	0.3233	0.3809	0.4451	0.4869		57	0.2201	0.2609	0.3074	0.3385
28	0.3172	0.3739	0.4372	0.4785		58	0.2181	0.2586	0.3048	0.3357
29	0.3115	0.3673	0.4297	0.4705		59	0.2162	0.2564	0.3022	0.3328
30	0.3061	0.3610	0.4226	0.4629		60	0.2144	0.2542	0.2997	0.3301

Critical values for Spearman's rank correlation coefficient, r_s

5%	2½%	1%	½%	1-Tail Test	5%	2½%	1%	½%
10%	5%	2%	1%	2-Tail Test	10%	5%	2%	1%
n					n			
1	-	-	-	-	31	0.3012	0.3560	0.4185	0.4593
2	-	-	-	-	32	0.2962	0.3504	0.4117	0.4523
3	-	-	-	-	33	0.2914	0.3449	0.4054	0.4455
4	1.0000	-	-	-	34	0.2871	0.3396	0.3995	0.4390
5	0.9000	1.0000	1.0000	-	35	0.2829	0.3347	0.3936	0.4328
6	0.8286	0.8857	0.9429	1.0000	36	0.2788	0.3300	0.3882	0.4268
7	0.7143	0.7857	0.8929	0.9286	37	0.2748	0.3253	0.3829	0.4211
8	0.6429	0.7381	0.8333	0.8810	38	0.2710	0.3209	0.3778	0.4155
9	0.6000	0.7000	0.7833	0.8333	39	0.2674	0.3168	0.3729	0.4103
10	0.5636	0.6485	0.7455	0.7939	40	0.2640	0.3128	0.3681	0.4051
11	0.5364	0.6182	0.7091	0.7545	41	0.2606	0.3087	0.3636	0.4002
12	0.5035	0.5874	0.6783	0.7273	42	0.2574	0.3051	0.3594	0.3955
13	0.4835	0.5604	0.6484	0.7033	43	0.2543	0.3014	0.3550	0.3908
14	0.4637	0.5385	0.6264	0.6791	44	0.2513	0.2978	0.3511	0.3865
15	0.4464	0.5214	0.6036	0.6536	45	0.2484	0.2974	0.3470	0.3822
16	0.4294	0.5029	0.5824	0.6353	46	0.2456	0.2913	0.3433	0.3781
17	0.4142	0.4877	0.5662	0.6176	47	0.2429	0.2880	0.3396	0.3741
18	0.4014	0.4716	0.5501	0.5996	48	0.2403	0.2850	0.3361	0.3702
19	0.3912	0.4596	0.5351	0.5842	49	0.2378	0.2820	0.3326	0.3664
20	0.3805	0.4466	0.5218	0.5699	50	0.2353	0.2791	0.3293	0.3628
21	0.3701	0.4364	0.5091	0.5558	51	0.2329	0.2764	0.3260	0.3592
22	0.3608	0.4252	0.4975	0.5438	52	0.2307	0.2736	0.3228	0.3558
23	0.3528	0.4160	0.4862	0.5316	53	0.2284	0.2710	0.3198	0.3524
24	0.3443	0.4070	0.4757	0.5209	54	0.2262	0.2685	0.3168	0.3492
25	0.3369	0.3977	0.4662	0.5108	55	0.2242	0.2659	0.3139	0.3460
26	0.3306	0.3901	0.4571	0.5009	56	0.2221	0.2636	0.3111	0.3429
27	0.3242	0.3828	0.4487	0.4915	57	0.2201	0.2612	0.3083	0.3400
28	0.3180	0.3755	0.4401	0.4828	58	0.2181	0.2589	0.3057	0.3370
29	0.3118	0.3685	0.4325	0.4749	59	0.2162	0.2567	0.3030	0.3342
30	0.3063	0.3624	0.4251	0.4670	60	0.2144	0.2545	0.3005	0.3314

Critical values for the χ^2 distribution

If X has a χ^2 distribution with v degrees of freedom then, for each pair of values of p and v, the table gives the value of x such that

$$P(X \leqslant x) = p.$$

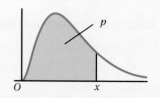

P	0.01	0.025	0.05	0.90	0.95	0.975	0.99	0.995	0.999
$v=1$	0.0^31571	0.0^39821	0.0^23932	2.706	3.841	5.024	6.635	7.879	10.83
2	0.02010	0.05064	0.1026	4.605	5.991	7.378	9.210	10.60	13.82
3	0.1148	0.2158	0.3518	6.251	7.815	9.348	11.34	12.84	16.27
4	0.2971	0.4844	0.7107	7.779	9.488	11.14	13.28	14.86	18.47
5	0.5543	0.8312	1.145	9.236	11.07	12.83	15.09	16.75	20.51
6	0.8721	1.237	1.635	10.64	12.59	14.45	16.81	18.55	22.46
7	1.239	1.690	2.167	12.02	14.07	16.01	18.48	20.28	24.32
8	1.647	2.180	2.733	13.36	15.51	17.53	20.09	21.95	26.12
9	2.088	2.700	3.325	14.68	16.92	19.02	21.67	23.59	27.88
10	2.558	3.247	3.940	15.99	18.31	20.48	23.21	25.19	29.59
11	3.053	3.816	4.575	17.28	19.68	21.92	24.73	26.76	31.26
12	3.571	4.404	5.226	18.55	21.03	23.34	26.22	28.30	32.91
13	4.107	5.009	5.892	19.81	22.36	24.74	27.69	29.82	34.53
14	4.660	5.629	6.571	21.06	23.68	26.12	29.14	31.32	36.12
15	5.229	6.262	7.261	22.31	25.00	27.49	30.58	32.80	37.70
16	5.812	6.908	7.962	23.54	26.30	28.85	32.00	34.27	39.25
17	6.408	7.564	8.672	24.77	27.59	30.19	33.41	35.72	40.79
18	7.015	8.231	9.390	25.99	28.87	31.53	34.81	37.16	42.31
19	7.633	8.907	10.12	27.20	30.14	32.85	36.19	38.58	43.82
20	8.260	9.591	10.85	28.41	31.41	34.17	37.57	40.00	45.31
21	8.897	10.28	11.59	29.62	32.67	35.48	38.93	41.40	46.80
22	9.542	10.98	12.34	30.81	33.92	36.78	40.29	42.80	48.27
23	10.20	11.69	13.09	32.01	35.17	38.08	41.64	44.18	49.73
24	10.86	12.40	13.85	33.20	36.42	39.36	42.98	45.56	51.18
25	11.52	13.12	14.61	34.38	37.65	40.65	44.31	46.93	52.62
30	14.95	16.79	18.49	40.26	43.77	46.98	50.89	53.67	59.70
40	22.16	24.43	26.51	51.81	55.76	59.34	63.69	66.77	73.40
50	29.71	32.36	34.76	63.17	67.50	71.42	76.15	79.49	86.66
60	37.48	40.48	43.19	74.40	79.08	83.30	88.38	91.95	99.61
70	45.44	48.76	51.74	85.53	90.53	95.02	100.4	104.2	112.3
80	53.54	57.15	60.39	96.58	101.9	106.6	112.3	116.3	124.8
90	61.75	65.65	69.13	107.6	113.1	118.1	124.1	128.3	137.2
100	70.06	74.22	77.93	118.5	124.3	129.6	135.8	140.2	149.4

Arithmetic series

$$S_n = \frac{1}{2}n(a+l) = \frac{1}{2}n\{2a+(n-1)d\}$$

Geometric series

$$S_n = \frac{a(1-r^n)}{1-r}$$

$$S_\infty = \frac{a}{1-r} \text{ for } |r| < 1$$

Binomial series

$$(a+b)^n = a^n + {}^nC_1 a^{n-1}b + {}^nC_2 a^{n-2}b^2 + \ldots + {}^nC_r a^{n-r}b^r + \ldots + b^n \qquad (n \in \mathbb{N}),$$

where $\displaystyle {}^nC_r = \binom{n}{r} = \frac{n!}{r!(n-r)!}$

$$(1+x)^n = 1 + nx + \frac{n(n-1)}{2!}x^2 + \ldots + \frac{n(n-1)\ldots(n-r+1)}{r!}x^r + \ldots \left(|x|<1, n \in \mathbb{R}\right)$$

Series

$$\sum_{r=1}^{n} r^2 = \frac{1}{6}n(n+1)(2n+1), \quad \sum_{r=1}^{n} r^3 = \frac{1}{4}n^2(n+1)^2$$

Maclaurin series

$$f(x) = f(0) + f'(0)x + \frac{f''(0)}{2!}x^2 + \ldots + \frac{f^{(r)}(0)}{r!}x^r + \ldots$$

$$e^x = \exp(x) = 1 + x + \frac{x^2}{2!} + \ldots + \frac{x^r}{r!} \ldots \text{ for all } x$$

$$\ln(1+x) = x - \frac{x^2}{2} + \frac{x^3}{3} - \ldots + (-1)^{r+1}\frac{x^r}{r} + \ldots \left(-1 < x \leqslant 1\right)$$

$$\sin x = x - \frac{x^3}{3!} + \frac{x^5}{5!} - \ldots + (-1)^r \frac{x^{2r+1}}{(2r+1)!} + \ldots \text{ for all } x$$

$$\cos x = 1 - \frac{x^2}{2!} + \frac{x^4}{4!} - \ldots + (-1)^r \frac{x^{2r}}{(2r)!} + \ldots \text{ for all } x$$

$$(1+x)^n = 1 + nx + \frac{n(n-1)}{2!}x^2 + \ldots + \frac{n(n-1)\ldots(n-r+1)}{r!}x^r + \ldots \left(|x|<1, n \in \mathbb{R}\right)$$

Differentiation

$f(x)$	$f'(x)$
$\tan kx$	$k\sec^2 kx$
$\sec x$	$\sec x \tan x$
$\cot x$	$-\operatorname{cosec}^2 x$
$\operatorname{cosec} x$	$-\operatorname{cosec} x \cot x$

$f(x)$	$f'(x)$
$\arcsin x$ or $\sin^{-1} x$	$\dfrac{1}{\sqrt{1-x^2}}$
$\arccos x$ or $\cos^{-1} x$	$-\dfrac{1}{\sqrt{1-x^2}}$
$\arctan x$ or $\tan^{-1} x$	$\dfrac{1}{1+x^2}$

Quotient rule $y = \dfrac{u}{v}, \dfrac{dy}{dx} = \dfrac{v\dfrac{du}{dx} - u\dfrac{dv}{dx}}{v^2}$

Integration

$$\int \frac{f'(x)}{f(x)}\,dx = \ln|f(x)| + c$$

$$\int f'(x)\big(f(x)\big)^n\,dx = \frac{1}{n+1}\big(f(x)\big)^{n+1} + c$$

Integration by parts $\displaystyle\int u\frac{dv}{dx}\,dx = uv - \int v\frac{du}{dx}\,dx$

The mean value of $f(x)$ on the interval $[a, b]$ is $\dfrac{1}{b-a}\displaystyle\int_a^b f(x)\,dx$

Area of sector enclosed by polar curve is $\dfrac{1}{2}\displaystyle\int r^2\,d\theta$

$f(x)$	$\int f(x)\,dx$
$\dfrac{1}{\sqrt{a^2-x^2}}$	$\sin^{-1}\left(\dfrac{x}{a}\right)\;(|x| < a)$
$\dfrac{1}{a^2+x^2}$	$\dfrac{1}{a}\tan^{-1}\left(\dfrac{x}{a}\right)$
$\dfrac{1}{\sqrt{a^2+x^2}}$	$\sinh^{-1}\left(\dfrac{x}{a}\right)$ or $\ln\left(x+\sqrt{x^2+a^2}\right)$
$\dfrac{1}{\sqrt{x^2-a^2}}$	$\cosh^{-1}\left(\dfrac{x}{a}\right)$ or $\ln\left(x+\sqrt{x^2-a^2}\right)\;(x > a)$

Numerical methods

Trapezium rule: $\displaystyle\int_a^b y\,dx \approx \frac{1}{2}h\big\{(y_0 + y_n) + 2(y_1 + y_2 + \ldots + y_{n-1})\big\}$, where $h = \dfrac{b-a}{n}$

The Newton-Raphson iteration for solving $f(x) = 0$: $x_{n+1} = x_n - \dfrac{f(x_n)}{f'(x_n)}$

De Moivre's Theorem: $\big\{r(\cos\theta + i\sin\theta)\big\}^n = r^n(\cos n\theta + i\sin n\theta)$

Roots of unity: The roots of $z^n = 1$ are given by $z = \text{Exp}\left(\dfrac{2\pi k}{n}i\right)$ for $k = 0, 1, 2, ..., n-1$

Cartesian equation of a plane is $n_1 x + n_2 y + n_3 z + d = 0$

The distance between skew lines is $D = \dfrac{|(\mathbf{b}-\mathbf{a})\cdot\mathbf{n}|}{|\mathbf{n}|}$, where $\mathbf{a}$ and $\mathbf{b}$ are position vectors of points on each line and $\mathbf{n}$ is a mutual perpendicular to both lines

The distance between a point and a line is $D = \dfrac{|ax_1 + by_1 - c|}{\sqrt{a^2 + b^2}}$, where the coordinates of the point are (x_1, y_1) and the equation of the line is given by $ax + by = c$

The distance between a point and a plane is $D = \dfrac{|\mathbf{b}\cdot\mathbf{n} - p|}{|\mathbf{n}|}$, where $\mathbf{b}$ is the position vector of the point and the equation of the plane is given by $\mathbf{r}\cdot\mathbf{n} = p$

Small angle approximations

$\sin\theta \approx \theta$, $\cos\theta \approx 1 - \dfrac{1}{2}\theta^2$, $\tan\theta \approx \theta$ where θ is small and measured in radians

Trigonometric identities

$\sin(A \pm B) = \sin A \cos B \pm \cos A \sin B$

$\cos(A \pm B) = \cos A \cos B \mp \sin A \sin B$

$\tan(A \pm B) = \dfrac{\tan A \pm \tan B}{1 \mp \tan A \tan B}\ \left(A \pm B \neq \left(k + \dfrac{1}{2}\right)\pi\right)$

Hyperbolic functions

$\cosh^2 x - \sinh^2 x = 1$

$\sinh^{-1} x = \ln\left[x + \sqrt{(x^2 + 1)}\right]$

$\cosh^{-1} x = \ln\left[x + \sqrt{(x^2 - 1)}\right], x \geqslant 1$

$\tanh^{-1} x = \dfrac{1}{2}\ln\left(\dfrac{1+x}{1-x}\right), -1 < x < 1$

Simple harmonic motion

$x = A\cos(\omega t) + B\sin(\omega t)$

$x = R\sin(\omega t + \phi)$

Probability

$P(A \cup B) = P(A) + P(B) - P(A \cap B)$

$P(A \cap B) = P(A)P(B|A) = P(B)P(A|B)$ **or** $P(A|B) = \dfrac{P(A \cap B)}{P(B)}$

Sampling distributions

For any variable X, $E(\bar{X}) = \mu$, $\text{Var}(\bar{X}) = \dfrac{\sigma^2}{n}$ and $\bar{X}$ is approximately normally distributed when n is large enough (approximately $n > 25$).

If $X \sim N(\mu, \sigma^2)$ then $\bar{X} \sim N\left(\mu, \dfrac{\sigma^2}{n}\right)$ and $\dfrac{\bar{X} - \mu}{\sigma/\sqrt{n}} \sim N(0,1)$.

Unbiased estimates of the population mean and variance are given by $\dfrac{\sum x}{n}$ and $\dfrac{n}{n-1}\left(\dfrac{\sum x^2}{n} - \left(\dfrac{\sum x}{n}\right)^2\right)$.

Expectation algebra

Use the following results, including the cases where $a = b = \pm 1$ and/or $c = 0$:

1 $E(aX + bY + c) = aE(X) + bE(Y) + c,$
2 if X and Y are independent then $\text{Var}(aX + bY + c) = a^2\text{Var}(X) + b^2\text{Var}(Y)$.

Continuous distributions

X is a continuous random variable (crv) with probability density function (pdf) $f(x)$

Expectation: $\mu = E(X) = \displaystyle\int_{-\infty}^{\infty} x f(x)\,dx$

Variance: $\sigma^2 = \text{Var}(X) = \displaystyle\int_{-\infty}^{\infty} (x-\mu)^2 f(x)\,dx = \int_{-\infty}^{\infty} x^2 f(x)\,dx - \mu^2$

Cumulative distribution function (cdf) $F(x) = P(X \leqslant x) = \displaystyle\int_{-\infty}^{x} f(t)\,dt$

	pdf	$E(X)$	$\text{Var}(X)$
Continuous uniform distribution over $[a, b]$	$\dfrac{1}{b-a}$	$\dfrac{1}{2}(a+b)$	$\dfrac{1}{12}(b-a)^2$
Exponential	$\lambda e^{-\lambda x}$	$\dfrac{1}{\lambda}$	$\dfrac{1}{\lambda^2}$
Normal $N(\mu, \sigma^2)$	$\dfrac{1}{\sigma\sqrt{2\pi}} e^{-\frac{1}{2}\left(\frac{x-\mu}{\sigma}\right)^2}$	μ	σ^2

Percentage points of the normal distribution

If Z has a normal distribution with mean 0 and variance 1 then, for each value of p, the table gives the value of z such that $P(Z \leqslant z) = p$.

p	0.75	0.90	0.95	0.975	0.99	0.995	0.9975	0.999	0.9995
z	0.674	1.282	1.645	1.960	2.326	2.576	2.807	3.090	3.291

Approximate distributions for large samples

Wilcoxon signed-rank test: $T \sim N\left(\dfrac{1}{4}n(n+1), \dfrac{1}{24}n(n+1)(2n+1)\right)$

Wilcoxon rank-sum test (samples of sizes m and n, with $m \leqslant n$): $W \sim N\left(\dfrac{1}{2}m(m+n+1), \dfrac{1}{12}mn(m+n+1)\right)$

Wilcoxon signed-rank test

W_+ is the sum of the ranks corresponding to the positive differences,

W_- is the sum of the ranks corresponding to the negative differences,

T is the smaller of W_+ and W_-.

For each value of n the table gives the **largest** value of T that will lead to rejection of the null hypothesis at the level of significance indicated.

Critical values of T

	Level of significance			
One Tail	0.05	0.025	0.01	0.005
Two Tail	0.10	0.05	0.02	0.01
$n = 6$	2	0		
7	3	2	0	
8	5	3	1	0
9	8	5	3	1
10	10	8	5	3
11	13	10	7	5
12	17	13	9	7
13	21	17	12	9
14	25	21	15	12
15	30	25	19	15
16	35	29	23	19
17	41	34	27	23
18	47	40	32	27
19	53	46	37	32
20	60	52	43	37

For larger values of n, each of W_+ and W_- can be approximated by the normal distribution with mean $\frac{1}{4}n(n+1)$ and variance $\frac{1}{24}n(n+1)(2n+1)$.

Wilcoxon rank-sum test

The two samples have sizes m and n, where $m \leqslant n$.

R_m is the sum of the ranks of the items in the sample of size m.

W is the smaller of R_m and $m(m+n+1) - R_m$.

For each pair of values of m and n, the table gives the **largest** value of W which will lead to rejection of the null hypothesis at the level of significance indicated.

Critical values of W

	Level of significance											
One Tail	0.05	0.025	0.01	0.05	0.025	0.01	0.05	0.025	0.01	0.05	0.025	0.01
Two Tail	0.1	0.05	0.02	0.1	0.05	0.02	0.1	0.05	0.02	0.1	0.05	0.02
n	$m=3$			$m=4$			$m=5$			$m=6$		
3	6	-	-									
4	6	-	-	11	10	-						
5	7	6	-	12	11	10	19	17	16			
6	8	7	-	13	12	11	20	18	17	28	26	24
7	8	7	6	14	13	11	21	20	18	29	27	25
8	9	8	6	15	14	12	23	21	19	31	29	27
9	10	8	7	16	14	13	24	22	20	33	31	28
10	10	9	7	17	15	13	26	23	21	35	32	29

	Level of significance											
One Tail	0.05	0.025	0.01	0.05	0.025	0.01	0.05	0.025	0.01	0.05	0.025	0.01
Two Tail	0.1	0.05	0.02	0.1	0.05	0.02	0.1	0.05	0.02	0.1	0.05	0.02
n	$m=7$			$m=8$			$m=9$			$m=10$		
7	39	36	34									
8	41	38	35	51	49	45						
9	43	40	37	54	51	47	66	62	59			
10	45	42	39	56	53	49	69	65	61	82	78	74

For larger values of m and n, the normal distribution with mean $\frac{1}{2}m(m+n+1)$ and variance $\frac{1}{12}mn(m+n+1)$ should be used as an approximation to the distribution of R_m.

Answers

Chapter 1

Before you start...

1 42

2 0.5

Exercise 1A

1 a i 30   **ii** 57
  b i 13   **ii** 29

2 a 140   **b** 16

3 a 6   **b** 2   **c** 12

4 48

5 a 90   **b** 48   **c** 63

6 15

7 a 15 637 960   **b** 10 104 528

8 115 316 136

9 8

10 a 720   **b** 648

11 a 60   **b** 125

12 a 81   **b** 125

Exercise 1B

1 a i 120   **ii** 720
  b i 48   **ii** 360
  c i 600   **ii** 240

2 a i 40 320   **ii** 39 916 800
  b i 1080   **ii** 1 814 400
  c i 475 372 800   **ii** 357 840

3 a 720   **b** 40 320
  c $26! = 4.03 \times 10^{26}$ (3 s.f.)

4 a 5040   **b** 720

5 a 120   **b** 24

6 a $17! = 3.56 \times 10^{14}$ (3 s.f.)
  b $16! = 2.09 \times 10^{13}$ (3 s.f.)

7 2880

8 360

9 a 720   **b** 240

10 $30! \approx 2.65 \times 10^{32}$

11 $6 \times 5! \times 4! = 17\,280$

Exercise 1C

1 a i 21   **ii** 792
  b i 60   **ii** 60
  c i 126   **ii** 135
  d i 136   **ii** 36

2 a i 28   **ii** 126
  b i 912   **ii** 14
  c i 1176   **ii** 980

3 5005

4 a 35   **b** 15

5 15 380 937

6 36 960

7 31 500

8 $\binom{140}{12}\binom{128}{10}\binom{118}{10} \approx 1.61 \times 10^{45}$

9 a 14 950   **b** 14 674

10 a 43 680   **b** 78 000

11 a 35   **b** 35
  c 31   **d** 33

12 a 126   **b** 120

13 a 120   **b** 210

14 $\binom{45}{15}\binom{30}{15} \approx 5.35 \times 10^{19}$

Exercise 1D

1 560

2 600

3 a 120   **b** 1320

4 a 4920   **b** 4800

5 19 557

6 270 200

7 65 559

8 a 11 082   **b** 48 378

9 504

Exercise 1E

1 a 5040   **b** 5040

2 a 60   **b** 210

3 7.75×10^{10} (3 s.f.)

4 255 024

5 504

6 336

7 3 276 000

8 186

9 84

10 4624

Exercise 1F

1 $13! \times 2 = 1.25 \times 10^{10}$

2 2 488 320

3 30 240

4 1.50×10^{14}

5 a 32 432 400   **b** 45 360

6 a 17 280   **b** 5760

   c 43 200   **d** 2880

Exercise 1G

1 360

2 2520

3 3 326 400

4 24

5 15 120

6 12

7 120

8 a 24   **b** 144

9 36

10 14

11 Proof

Exercise 1H

1 $\dfrac{1}{8}$

2 $\dfrac{4}{7}$

3 a 0.359   **b** 0.375

4 a 0.0476   **b** 0.119

5 a $\dfrac{1}{15}$ **b** $\dfrac{1}{3}$

6 a 1.03×10^{-4} **b** 0.0102

Mixed practice 1

1 a $\dfrac{1}{120}$

  b i $\dfrac{3!}{210}$

    ii He is assuming that all results are equally likely. This is unlikely to be the case.

2 a 120   **b** $\dfrac{1}{120}$

3 $\dfrac{1}{120}$

4 a 729   **b** 0.81

5 $\dfrac{3}{14}$

6 $\dfrac{1}{3}$

7 a 2947   **b** $\dfrac{421}{429}$

8 $\dfrac{2}{3}$

9 $\dfrac{28}{33}$

10 a 921 164 400   **b** $\dfrac{1}{15\,600}$

11 $\dfrac{1}{40\,320}$

12 $\dfrac{1}{112}$

13 a i 48   **ii** 72

  b $\dfrac{21}{60}$

14 a $\dfrac{1}{32}$ **b** $\dfrac{15}{16}$

15 a 121 080 960   **b** 3 991 680

  c $\dfrac{3}{13}$

16 i a 5040   **b** $\dfrac{2}{7}$

  ii a $\dfrac{1}{35}$ **b** $\dfrac{1}{7}$

17 i a 3024   **b** 1680

  ii a $\dfrac{5}{14}$ **b** $\dfrac{1}{63}$

Chapter 2

Before you start...

1 0.12

2 $\dfrac{1}{6}$

3 6

Work it out 2.1

The correct answer is Solution 2.

Exercise 2A

1 a i $E(X) = 2, \text{Var}(X) = 1, \sigma = 1$

    ii $E(X) = 9, \text{Var}(X) = 1, \sigma = 1$

  b i $E(X) = 20, \text{Var}(X) = 100, \sigma = 10$

    ii $E(X) = 90, \text{Var}(X) = 100, \sigma = 10$

  c i $E(W) = 0.235, \text{Var}(W) = 0.0153, \sigma = 0.124$

    ii $E(V) = 0.18, \text{Var}(V) = 0.0096, \sigma = 0.0980$

  d i $E(X) = 2.57, \text{Var}(X) = 0.388, \sigma = 0.623$

    ii $E(X) = 3, \text{Var}(X) = 2, \sigma = 1.41$

2 a Proof   **b** 4.4

3 a $p = 10, q = 0.3$ **b** 0.4

4 a Proof   **b** $\dfrac{16}{9}$

5 a $\dfrac{1}{10}$ **b** 2

c 0.775

6 $E(X) = \dfrac{13}{6}$, $Var(X) = \dfrac{65}{36}$

7 a $p = 0.5$, $q = 0.2$ **b** 0.922

8 40

9 a

d	0	1	2	3	4	5
p	$\dfrac{1}{6}$	$\dfrac{5}{18}$	$\dfrac{2}{9}$	$\dfrac{1}{6}$	$\dfrac{1}{9}$	$\dfrac{1}{18}$

b 1.94 **c** 2.05

d $\dfrac{5}{9}$

10 a

Frequency of chosen number	0	1	2	3
Profit (£)	$-n$	$1-n$	$2n$	$3n$
Probability	$\dfrac{27}{64}$	$\dfrac{27}{64}$	$\dfrac{9}{64}$	$\dfrac{1}{64}$

b £0.82

Exercise 2B

1 a i $E(Y) = 27$, $Var\,(Y) = 225$
  ii $E(Y) = 36$, $Var\,(Y) = 400$
  b i $E(Y) = 8$, $Var\,(Y) = 25$
  ii $E(Y) = 11$, $Var\,(Y) = 25$
  c i $E(Y) = 19$, $Var\,(Y) = 100$
  ii $E(Y) = 22$, $Var\,(Y) = 225$
  d i $E(Y) = -17$, $Var\,(Y) = 225$
  ii $E(Y) = -10$, $Var\,(Y) = 100$
  e i $E(Y) = 2$, $Var\,(Y) = \dfrac{25}{16}$
  ii $E(Y) = 1.4$, $Var\,(Y) = 0.25$

2 a 20 **b** 36

3 $E(Y) = 10$, $Var(Y) = 16$

4 $E(F) = 392$, $\sigma_F = 9$.

5 $a = 0.2$, $b = -2$ or $a = -0.2$, $b = 2$

6 $E(Y) = 12$, $\sigma_Y = 10$.

7 Proof

8 Any value allowed, there is no upper limit.

Exercise 2C

1 a i $E(X) = 3$, $Var(X) = 2$
  ii $E(X) = 4.5$, $Var(X) = 5.25$
  b i $E(X) = \dfrac{2x+1}{2}$, $Var(X) = \dfrac{4x^2 - 1}{12}$
  ii $E(X) = \dfrac{x}{2}$, $Var(x) = \dfrac{x(x-2)}{12}$

2 $E(X) = 6$, $\sigma = 2.83$.

3 $E(X) = 2.5$, $\sigma = 1.71$

4 a $a = 1$, $b = -n - 1$ **b** $\dfrac{n^2 + n}{3}$

5 Mean = 202 cm, Variance = 13 332 cm².

6 833

7 $E(Y) = m + \dfrac{n}{2}$, $Var(Y) = \dfrac{n^2 + 2n}{12}$

8 11

9 Proof

10 Proof

Exercise 2D

1 a i $E(X) = 10$, $\sigma(X) = 3$
  ii $E(X) = 8$, $\sigma(X) = 2$
  b i $E(X) = 4.5$, $\sigma(X) = 1.77$
  ii $E(Y) = 7$, $\sigma(Y) = 2.13$
  c i $E(Z) = \dfrac{n-1}{n}$, $\sigma(Z) = \dfrac{n-1}{n}$
  ii $E(X) = 2$, $\sigma(X) = \sqrt{\dfrac{2(n-2)}{n}}$

2 a 2700 **b** 30

3 a 0.0231 **b** 2
  c 1.22 **d** 0.0273

4 a 4.8 **b** $\dfrac{12\sqrt{2}}{5}$

5 $p = 0.65$, $n = 30$

6 $p = \dfrac{2}{3}$, $n = 18$

Exercise 2E

1 a i 0.0658 **ii** 0.0531
  b i 0.763 **ii** 0.963
  c i 0.162 **ii** 0.309
  d i 0.0625 **ii** 0.0419
2 a i 3, 2.45 **ii** 6.67, 6.15
  b i 12, 11.5 **ii** 3, 2.45
3 a 0.144 **b** 2.5
  c Unlikely to be valid. People tend to get better over time so if one test is failed it might be the case that the next one has a greater probability of being passed. Alternatively, it might be that if the first test is failed there is added pressure and nerves so the second test is less likely to be passed.
4 a 2.5, 3.75 **b** 0.870
5 a For example, the probability of observing a motorbike has to be the same every day and different days have to be independent of each other.

b For example, the assumptions seem not very realistic – there are likely to be more motorbikes on sunny days.

c 6.67   **d** 0.108

e 0.444

6 1

7 0.3 or 0.7

8 0.25

9 a $x \geqslant 11$ **b** $x \geqslant 10$

10 Proof

Mixed practice 2

1 a

b	0	1	2
p	$\dfrac{6}{56}$	$\dfrac{30}{56}$	$\dfrac{20}{56}$

b 1.25

2 a

x	1	2	3	4	6
p	$\dfrac{1}{6}$	$\dfrac{1}{3}$	$\dfrac{1}{6}$	$\dfrac{1}{6}$	$\dfrac{1}{6}$

b 3   **c** $\dfrac{8}{3}$

3 a $E(X) = 7$, $Var(X) = 14$

  b $E(Y) = 20$, $Var(Y) = 14$

  c $E(Z) = 14$, $Var(Z) = 56$

4 a $a = 0.1$, $b = 0.3$ **b** 6.7

5 $E(Y) = 2$, $\sigma_Y = 4$

6 a Proof   **b** $E(X) = 6$, $Var(X) = 4$

7 $a = 2$, $b_1 = -14$ or $a = -2$, $b = 34$

8 a 0.4   **b** $E(Y) = 7.6$,

  $Var(Y) = 1.44$

9 a

t	1	2	3
p	$\dfrac{1}{6}$	$\dfrac{5}{36}$	$\dfrac{25}{36}$

b $\dfrac{91}{36}$

c 3   **d** 0.583

10

S	2	3	4	5	6	7	8
p	$\dfrac{1}{16}$	$\dfrac{2}{16}$	$\dfrac{3}{16}$	$\dfrac{4}{16}$	$\dfrac{3}{16}$	$\dfrac{2}{16}$	$\dfrac{1}{16}$

b $E(S) = 5$, $Var(S) = 2.5$ **c** $E(X) = 5$, $Var(X) = 5$

11 $\dfrac{5}{9}$

12 a 40   **b** 6.22

13 a Constant probability, independent. Neither is very likely. Probability of a nut cracking might depend on which type of nut is dropped. The squirrel might get more frustrated and throw harder if nuts are not breaking or perhaps get tired.

b i 4   **ii** $\dfrac{9}{16}$

14 i a $\dfrac{6561}{100\,000}$ **b** $\dfrac{59\,049}{100\,000}$

  c 0.028

ii a $\dfrac{9}{125}$ **b** 0.0052

15 a $\dfrac{2}{n(n+1)}$ **b** $\dfrac{2n+1}{3}$

  c $\dfrac{(n+2)(n-1)}{18}$

Chapter 3

Before you start...

1 0.211

2 $\dfrac{2}{3}$

3 $E(X) = 3.2$, $Var(X) = 0.96$

Work it out 3.1

The correct answer is Solution 1.

Exercise 3A

1 a i Po(36)   **ii** Po(9)

  b i Po(2.4)   **ii** Po(120)

  c i Po(3.6)   **ii** Po(48)

2 a i 0.180   **ii** 0.271

  b i 0.946   **ii** 0.592

  c i 0.201   **ii** 0.729

  d i 0.933   **ii** 0.997

  e i 0.215   **ii** 0.525

3

1	2	3	4	> 4
0.311	0.264	0.150	0.0636	0.0296

4 0.0116

5 a 0.0595   **b** 0.0548

6 a 0.298   **b** 0.973

7 a 0.616   **b** 0.351

  c 0.825   **d** 0.570

8 a 0.0537   **b** 0.321

9 a 0.916   **b** 0.0656

10 0.430

11 a 0.161, 0.0614   **b** 2.76×10^{-6}

   c There are other ways to get 42 emails in a week than 6 every day.

12 a 0.475

   b 1, because the probability (0.323) is highest

   c 0.004 13

13 a 0.273   **b** 0.143   **c** 201

14 $1 + \sqrt{3}$

15 a Proof   **b** 7

Mixed practice 3

1 a $B \sim \text{Po}(3.5)$, it must be assumed that the arrival of robins and the arrival of thrushes are independent.

   b 0.0302

   c 0.799

2 a Independent events. Constant rate of success.

   b 0.912

3 a 2.5   **b** 0.0821

4 a 10, 10   **b** 0.734

5 a Mean = 3, s.d. = 1.79   **b** Mean ≈ Variance

6 a 0.175   **b** 0.0195

7 a 0.0786   **b** 5.02×10^{-4}

8 a 0.511   **b** 0.0152

9 a 1.19   **b** 0.259, 2.54

   c $w = \lambda - 1$

10 a 0.362   **b** 0.279

   c 0.659   **d** 0.0464

   e 1.68×10^{6} litres   **f** 0.247

   g 0.641

11 a 0.547   **b** 3

12 a 0.189   **b** 0.372

13 a 0.219   **b** 4

   c 2.8   **d** 7

14 i a 0.133   **b** 0.0580

   ii e.g. Contagious so incidences do not occur independently, or more cases in winter so not at a constant average rate.

15 i Failures do not occur at regular or predictable intervals.

   ii Failures occur independently – might not happen if there is a power cut.

Failures occur at a constant average rate – might not happen if manipulated to change more rapidly at peak times.

   iii $\lambda = 8$, $P(Y = 7) = 0.140$

Chapter 4

Before you start...

1 0.678

2 Do not reject H_0. No significant evidence of a bias ($p = 0.0623$)

3 0.579

Exercise 4A

1 Do not reject H_0

2 Do not reject H_0

3 Do not reject H_0

4 a A non-parametric test does not assume that the data is drawn from a particular distribution.

   b Reject H_0 (i.e. there is significant evidence to support the teacher's belief)

5 Reject H_0.

6 15

Exercise 4B

1 a i Significant   **ii** Not significant

   b i Not significant   **ii** Significant

   c i Significant   **ii** Significant

2 Significant

3 Not significant

4 a When you do not know that the underlying distribution is normal.

   b Not significant

5 Reject H_0

Exercise 4C

1 Not significant

2 Significant

3 Not significant

4 Not significant

5 Significant

6 Not significant

7 a p-value = 3.52%. Significant evidence of an increase in productivity of more than 20 dollars per day per person.

   b It takes into account the size of the differences as well as the signs.

Exercise 4D

1 a H_0: The median number of eggs produced on the two farms is the same.

H_1: The median number of eggs produced on the two farms is different.

b Proof   **c** 13

d There is significant evidence that there is a difference between the median number of eggs produced on the two farms.

2 No

3 No significant evidence

4 Significant evidence

5 a e.g. Students form a representative sample of all students. Distributions of boys and girls differ only in location.

b 86

c No significant evidence of a difference between the number of books read by boys and girls.

Exercise 4E

1 Not significant

2 Not significant

3 Not significant

4 Not significant

Mixed practice 4

1 Do not reject H_0

2 Significant

3 Not significant

4 Not significant

5 a No significant difference

b No evidence that the data is taken from a normal distribution, so non-parametric is appropriate. Unpaired data so rank-sum.

6 a H_0: Median at beginning of year = median at end of year

H_1: Median at beginning of year < median at end of year

b $T = 10$, do not reject the null hypothesis.

7 No significant difference

8 No significant difference

9 i $T = 9$, Reject H_0

ii The data is paired, but the rank-sum test is for independent samples.

10 i We have a numerical data set consisting of two unpaired, independent groups that have the same general characteristics.

ii Significant, there is evidence that salinity affects growth.

Focus on ... 1

Focus on ... Proof 1

1 $\binom{n}{0}p^n + \binom{n}{1}p^{n-1}q + \binom{n}{2}p^{n-2}q^2 \ldots + \binom{n}{n}q^n$

2 Proof

3 Proof

4 Proof

5 Proof

6 Proof

Focus on ... Problem solving 1

1 0.613 or 0.168   **2** 0.199 or 0.416

3 8

4 0.325 or 0.184

5 a Proof   **b** Proof

c $\dfrac{1}{8}$

Focus on ... Modelling 1

1 Rate might not be constant in every part of the ocean. The presence of fish might not be independent, so not very appropriate.

2 Not a random process so Poisson not appropriate.

3 This is well modelled by a Poisson distribution.

4 This is not a number of events in a given interval, and the rate might not be constant throughout the day. Buses might not be independent.

5 The rate might not be constant, but the Poisson tends to work quite well in these situations.

6 The number of fish being caught is sufficient that it might have a significant effect on the number of fish remaining in the pond, so Poisson is not appropriate.

7 This is well modelled by the Poisson distribution (and indeed is used in a derivation of the chi-squared statistic later).

8 This is well modelled by the Poisson distribution. You might want to use technology to confirm this.

Cross-topic review exercise 1

1 i $2-2a$ **ii** Proof

2 a 2.4   **b** 0.558

3 a 1.12   **b i** 11   **ii** 5

4 a $\dfrac{13}{2}$ **b** 0.844

5 i 0.103   **ii** 0.240

   iii 0.832

6 a $E(Y)=10, \operatorname{Var}(Y)=1$ **b** $E(Z)=15, \operatorname{Var}(Z)=1$

7 i Proof   **ii** 6, 4

8 $\dfrac{1}{2}$

9 i 56   **ii** $\dfrac{3}{8}$

   iii $\dfrac{1}{336}$

10 a 7   **b** Proof

11 i Bricks scattered at constant average rate and independently of one another.

   ii 0.683   **iii** 0.305 cubic metres

12 No significant difference

13 a Use Wilcoxon matched-pairs signed-rank test. Significant difference.

   b Use Wilcoxon rank-sum test. No significant difference.

   c You do not know anything about the underlying distributions.

   d The matched-pairs design is better as it eliminates the variation between subjects.

14 a i 80   **ii** 8.85   **iii** 0.119

   b When someone is ill they might spread the disease, increasing the probability of other people visiting the doctor.

15 i Attempts independent and with constant probability of success in threading.

   ii a 0.0720   **b** 0.168

   iii e.g. Likely to improve with practice.

16 $T=17$ so there is sufficient evidence the drug II is linked with fewer sneezes.

17 i 60   **ii** 24

   iii $\dfrac{3}{5}$

18 $W=32$, so insufficient evidence of a difference between median mark of the two groups.

19 5.10

20 a p^2 **b** Proof   **c** Proof

21 a −1 or 4   **b** 16

22 i a 6   **b** 27   **c** 24

   ii 54

23 i 0.920

   ii e.g. Occurrence of bacteria should be independent in drugs.

24 i When the distribution of the variable in question is unknown.

   ii There is significant evidence using the Wilcoxon matched-pairs signed-rank test, and there is no significant evidence using a Wilcoxon rank-sum test.

   iii Wilcoxon matched-pairs (paired-sample) signed-rank test as it takes into account ranks.

Chapter 5

Before you start...

1 Strong positive correlation.

2 −0.5

3 2.75

4 Do not reject H_0. No significant evidence that the coin is biased.

Exercise 5A

1 a i 0.802   **ii** 0.770

   b i −0.942   **ii** −0.949

   c i 0.194   **ii** 0.441

   d i 1   **ii** −1

2 a i 0.364   **ii** −0.175

   b i −0.002 53   **ii** −0.567

   c i 0.541   **ii** −0.645

3 a Just because the sample coefficient is positive, this does not mean the population value will also be positive.

   b No significant evidence of a correlation between the number of doctorates awarded in America and the sales of comic books.

   c 0.0333 – Significant evidence of a correlation between the number of doctorates awarded in America and the sales of comic books.

4 a 0.990

   b Strong positive correlation

   c Significant evidence of correlation

   d No, correlation does not imply causation.

5 a 0.876   **b** Positive correlation

   c Significant evidence

   d Yes, that is a reasonable interpretation of positive correlation in this context.

6 a 0.162

   b No, from a hypothesis test the number is not significant (and the sample size is small).

Even if it were, there will be natural variation / other factors so the relationship is not directly causal.

7 a Reject H_0. Evidence of correlation.

b As well as the usual lack of causality, just because the country as a whole eats more chocolate does not mean that the Nobel prize winners do too. (This is called the 'ecological fallacy'.)

8 a −0.996   **b** −0.996

c They are the same because it is just a linear coding of the temperature.

9 There are three issues here:

The conclusion is too strong – it does not take into account the possibility of a false positive result.

Even if there is genuine correlation, the test is just for whether the true underlying correlation is non-zero. It might have a value of 0.01, which would not come from this perfect linear relationship.

Even if there was a perfect linear relationship, there is no reason to believe that it is proportional – i.e. it could be $Y = aX + b$.

Exercise 5B

1 a i 0.429   **ii** 0.771
  b i −0.829   **ii** −0.714

2 a i −0.607, no significant evidence
    ii −0.643, no significant evidence
  b i 0.6, significant evidence
    ii −0.588, significant evidence

3 a 0.643   **b** 0.643

4 −0.543. This suggests that athletes who are better at the 100 m are less good at the 1500 m.

5 −0.0857, no significant evidence

6 0.839, significant evidence

7 a $r_s = -0.829$. As the volume of CO_2 increases the volume of SO_2 tends to decrease.

b No significant evidence of correlation.

c If you do not know whether the variables are normally distributed then it is more appropriate to use Spearman's.

8 a If you fix the ranking of the x-coordinates then there are $3! = 6$ possible sets of rankings for the y-coordinates. Considering all these possibilities gets four possible values of r_s: −1, −0.5, 0.5 and 1.

  b $\dfrac{1}{3}$ **c** $\dfrac{2}{3}$

9 a

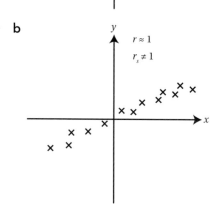

b

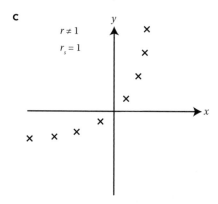

c

Work it out 5.1

The correct answer is Solution 2.

Exercise 5C

1 a i $y = 2.27x - 0.489$ **ii** $y = 1.48x + 0.296$
  b i $y = -0.258x + 15.1$ **ii** $y = -0.557x + 57.7$
  c i $y = 0.155x + 1.98$ **ii** $y = 1.09x - 5.37$
  d i $y = 2x + 1$ **ii** $y = 10 - x$

2 a i $y = 3x - 4.8$ **ii** $y = 5.10x + 1.62$
  b i $y = -2.44x - 0.724$ **ii** $y = -1.09x + 2.22$
  c i $y = -0.961x + 99.2$ **ii** $y = 4.78x + 4.36$

3 a 400   **b** Cannot be found

4 a 0.962   **b** d
  c 23.9   **d** Extrapolation

5 a −0.700   **b** T

  c $h = -0.0236T + 24.6$

  d Extrapolation and relatively poor correlation

  e $H = -0.000\,236T + 0.246$

6 a −0.660

  b e.g. Whether or not the day is on a weekend

  c The temperature is not dependent on the number of sales.

  d $y = -19.0x + 617$

  e £617 (The correlation coefficient was important in establishing that a linear relationship existed.)

  f Extrapolating from the data

7 a Proof   **b** ka

8 a i −0.328   **ii** 0.996

  b $y = 1.11x^2 - 3.55$

9 a False   **b** False

  c True   **d** False

Mixed practice 5

1 If $r = 1$ data lie in a perfect straight line so the ranks will also match perfectly. If $r_s = 1$, then the data might not lie in a straight line so r is not necessarily 1.

2 a 0.2

  b No significant evidence   **c** 0.2

3 i x because depths are fixed

  ii −0.926

  iii a $y = -0.752x + 75.0$

    b r close to −1; 25 is within range of data so reliable. 100 is outside range of data so unreliable.

4 a 0.945

  b Assuming that the distribution of temperatures and ice creams are both normal, this provides significant evidence of positive correlation.

  c This is just a linear transformation.

  d Equation is $y = 4.998x - 87.783$, so estimate is 37.

  e This is extrapolating from the given data. It is also using the dependent variable to predict the independent variable.

5 a −0.864   **b** −0.943

  c Since the diagram shows non-linear association, this will be detected more by Spearman's rank correlation coefficient.

6 i $n = 14$

  ii a True   **b** False

7 Greater than 0.68

8 $c = \dfrac{a}{b}$, $k = \dfrac{1}{b}$

9 a −0.733   **b** −0.771

  c No change

  d i Significant evidence

    ii No significant evidence

  e Because Spearman's is non-parametric it does not use the real values so it needs stronger evidence to show significance.

  f $c = -0.666q + 72.4$

  g i This is valid since the ppmcc shows significant evidence of linear behaviour and it is interpolating among the given data.

    ii This is not valid since it is extrapolating from the given data.

  h $C = -0.666Q + 72\,400\,000$

Chapter 6

Before you start...

1 Yes, the p-value is 1.93%

2 0.24

3 5

Exercise 6A

1 a i Independent, $v = 4$, $\chi^2_{calc} = 0.188$

    ii Dependent, $v = 2$, $\chi^2_{calc} = 14.1$

  b i Dependent, $v = 4$, $\chi^2_{calc} = 404$

    ii Dependent, $v = 2$, $\chi^2_{calc} = 10.4$

2 a H_0: Grades and Maths course are independent.

    H_1: Grades and Maths course are dependent.

  b

	D or lower	B or C	A or A*
Further Maths	62.1	209	143
Maths AS or A	62.0	208	143
No Maths	26.0	87.2	60.0

  c $\chi^2_{calc} = 195$, $v = 4$

  d Dependent. People studying a higher level of Mathematics tend to do better in Physics.

3 Dependent, $v = 6$, $\chi^2_{calc} = 14.8$. People who visit more tend to spend more on each visit.

4 Independent, $v = 6$, $\chi^2_{calc} = 16.0$. The drug does not appear to be effective in increasing the speed of recovery.

215

5 a

	Male	Female
$< £20\,000$	9.35	5.65
£20 000–30 000	16.2	9.79
£30 000–40 000	53.0	32.0
£40 000–60 000	20.0	12.0
$\geq 60\,000$	7.48	4.52

  b Independent, $v = 3$, $\chi^2_{calc} = 1.61$

6 a Proof   **b** 548
  c 542

7 a Proof   **b** $v = 2$, $\chi^2_{calc} = 0.867$
  c 346
  d There will be random variation within the sample.

8 a

		First factor				**Total**
		0	**1**	**2**	**3**	
Second factor	**A**	12	12	1	5	30
	B	10	1	4	5	20
	C	3	2	25	20	50
Total		25	15	30	30	100

  b Proof

9 a Proof   **b** Proof

Work it out 6.1

The correct solution is Solution 3.

Exercise 6B

1 a i Independent, $\chi^2_{Yates} = 0.435$
    ii Independent, $\chi^2_{Yates} = 1.36$
  b i Dependent, $\chi^2_{Yates} = 7.69$
    ii Dependent, $\chi^2_{Yates} = 18.2$

2 $\chi^2_{Yates} = 0.0513$

3 Independent, $\chi^2_{Yates} = 0.918$

4 Independent, $\chi^2_{Yates} = 0.000\,797$

5 Dependent, $\chi^2_{Yates} = 4.09$. It does not establish causality.

6 a $\chi^2_{Yates} = 81.6$. The acceptance patterns depend on department. A higher percentage of men are admitted (44% versus 30%). This appears to be evidence of bias.
  b $\chi^2_{calc} = 1690$, $v = 15$. Two out of six departments have a higher proportion of men accepted. The acceptance patterns depend on department.

7 You cannot do a calculation based on 'two factors are dependent' unless you know exactly what that dependency is.

Exercise 6C

1 a i $v = 5$ No fit, $17.6 > 11.1$
    ii $v = 4$.Fit, $5.25 < 9.49$
  b i $v = 3$.Fit, $7.54 < 7.82$
    ii $v = 4$.Fit, $4.86 < 9.49$

2 $\chi^2 = 12$, $v = 2$, Reject H_0

3 $\chi^2 = 40$, $v = 3$, Reject H_0

4 a $\dfrac{1}{95}$
  b $\chi^2_{calc} = 4.79$, $v = 4$; insufficient evidence to reject H_0

5 a $H_0 : X \sim N(167, 7^2)$, H_1: otherwise
  b 11.4, 6.33
  c 0.753, $v = 4$ **d** Fit, $0.753 < 4.61$

6 a 2.31
  b i $H_0 : X \sim P(\lambda)$, H_1: otherwise
    ii $v = 4$, $\chi^2 = 10.1 > 9.49$, Reject H_0

7 Accept claim as model is a feasible fit, $2.55 < 6.25$

8 a i 2.07   **ii** 0.413
  b $\chi^2_{calc} = 1.04 < 3.84$. No significant evidence that it does not follow a binomial distribution.

9 a Mean 27.5 minutes, standard deviation 6.25 minutes
  b 10.8, 6.56   **c** Fit, $0.692 < 5.99$

10 a Fit (coins might be fair), $9.58 < 11.1$
  b No fit (reject coins being fair), $9.58 > 9.24$

11 a 135, 28.6, 20.4, 12.2, 4.08; combine last two columns
  b $\chi^2_{calc} = 3.86$, $v = 3$; insufficient evidence to reject H_0

12 a $y = 31 - x$
  b $\chi^2_{test} = \dfrac{2352x^2 - 104\,160x + 1\,195\,205}{16\,800}$
  c $16 \leqslant x \leqslant 29$

13 a Total expected = Total observed
  b $x = 34$, $y = 32$

Mixed practice 6

1 $\chi^2 = 3.84$. No significant evidence that location affects economic status.

2 $\chi^2 = 0.825$. No significant evidence that ratio is not $1 : 1 : 2$.

3 a

57.1	32.8	11.1
55.9	32.2	10.9

b 4.34, 2   **c** Do not reject H_0.

4 $\chi^2 = 5.34$, do not reject H_0.

5 a H_0: same distribution, H_1: different distribution

  b Reject H_0, $12.6 > 9.49$ for a 5% significance test

6 A

7 $\chi^2 \approx 48.7$, $v = 9$, there is an association between age and department.

8 a i mean 17.5, variance 16.1
    ii Poisson has equal mean and variance.

  b H_0: distribution is $P(\lambda)$, H_1: otherwise. Reject H_0, $\chi^2_{\text{calc}} \approx 15.0 > 7.82$

9 a i Dice is not fair $(14.3 > 11.1)$
    ii Dice is fair $(14.3 < 15.1)$

  b Significance level indicates the acceptable probability that the observed data (or more extreme) could be found from the distribution proposed under H_0.

10 Data is compatible with the theory $(7.43 < 7.82)$

11 i

	Biology	Chemistry	Art
Male	17.5	4.2	6.3
Female	32.5	7.8	11.7

  ii Male Chemistry has an expected value below five. Combine the sciences.
  iii Reject hypothesised independence between subject and gender at 2.5% significance level $(5.56 > 5.02)$

12 a Proof   **b** $\chi^2_{\text{calc}} = 0.303$, $v = 2$
  c 3950

13 a i $X \sim \text{Geo}(p)$ **ii** $E(X) = p^{-1}$
  b i 2.4   **ii** $p = 2.4^{-1} = 0.417$
    iii Data can be modelled by geometric distribution, $\chi^2_{\text{calc}} \approx 3.21 < 7.82$

Chapter 7

Before you start...

1 4.5

2 $-\dfrac{1}{3}\cos 3x + c$

3 0.5

4 6

Exercise 7A

1 a i $\dfrac{4}{65}$ **ii** $\dfrac{3}{14}$

  b i $-\dfrac{2}{3}$ **ii** -1.3

  c i 1.41   **ii** $\dfrac{1+\sqrt{5}}{2}$

  d i 0.5   **ii** 0.754

  e i 1.32   **ii** 0.816

  f i $k = \infty$ **ii** 0

  g i -0.797 **ii** 0.210, 1.38

  h i $\dfrac{-1 \pm \sqrt{5}}{2}$ **ii** 0.582

  i i 51 100   **ii** 0.277

2 a i 0.48   **ii** 0.75

  b i 0.159   **ii** 0.5

  c i 0.301   **ii** 0.477

3 a i 0.632   **ii** 0.949

  b i 7.04   **ii** 7.48

  c i 0.4   **ii** 3.5

4 a 0.0968   **b** 370

5 0.5

6 e^{-6}

7 a $b = e^k$ **b** $a = \dfrac{2(e^k - 1)}{e^k + 1}$

8 $a = 0.5$, $b = 2$

9 0.560

10 $k = 0.5$

Exercise 7B

1 a i $E(X) = \dfrac{1}{3}$, median 0.293, mode 0

    $\text{Var}(X) = \dfrac{1}{18}$

    ii $E(X) = \dfrac{16}{3}$, median 5.66, mode 8

    $\text{Var}(X) = \dfrac{32}{9}$

  b i $E(X) = \dfrac{9}{\ln 10}$, median 3.16, mode 1

    $\text{Var}(X) = \dfrac{9(11\ln 10 - 18)}{2(\ln 10)^2}$

    ii $E(X) = 2\ln 2$, median 1.33, mode 1

    $\text{Var}(X) = 2 - 4(\ln 2)^2$

  c i $E(X) = \dfrac{\pi}{2} - 1$, median 0.524, mode 0

    $\text{Var}(X) = \pi - 3$

    ii $E(X) = 2\ln 2 - 1$, median 0.405, mode $\ln(2)$

    $\text{Var}(X) = 1 - 2(\ln 2)^2$

d i $E(X)=1.5$, median 1.26, mode 1

$Var(X)=0.75$

ii $E(X)=\dfrac{4}{3}$, median 1.19, mode 1

$Var(X)=\dfrac{2}{9}$

2 a i $k=1.21$ **ii** $k=12$

b i $k=\dfrac{3\pm\sqrt{7}}{2}$ **ii** $k=\dfrac{3}{e-2}$

3 a $\dfrac{36}{25}$ **b** $\dfrac{8}{3}$

4 a $a=\dfrac{3}{973}$ **b** $E(B)=\dfrac{4251}{556}$

5 a Proof   **b** $E(Y)=\dfrac{1}{k}$

6 a Proof   **b** $k=\dfrac{5\sqrt{3}}{3}$

7 0.339

8 $E(X)=0$

Exercise 7C

1 a i 12   **ii** 24

b i 2   **ii** 3

c i −4   **ii** −16

d i 9   **ii** 1

e i −3   **ii** 13

2 a i 54   **ii** 216

b i 1.5   **ii** 3.375

c i 6   **ii** 96

d i 6   **ii** 6

e i 24   **ii** 54

3 a i 0.5   **ii** 0.4

b i 10   **ii** 8

c i $2(\sin(1)-\cos(1))\approx 0.602$

    ii 2

d i −1.5   **ii** $\dfrac{22}{15}$

4 a £10.40   **b** £1.60

5 $a=0$ or $a=3$

6 a 4 hours   **b** 0.5 hours

7 a 2.25   **b** 13.5

8 a 0   **b** −1

c $\dfrac{1}{4}(\pi-2)$

9 a 0 if n is odd, $\dfrac{3}{n+3}$ if n is even

b $\dfrac{12}{175}$

Exercise 7D

1 a i $2x-x^2$ $0<x<1, \dfrac{2-\sqrt{2}}{2}$

ii $\dfrac{x^2-4}{32}$ $2<x<6, \sqrt{20}$

b i $1-\cos x$ $0<x<\dfrac{\pi}{2},\dfrac{\pi}{3}$

ii $\dfrac{\ln x}{\ln 10}$ $1<x<10, \sqrt{10}$

2 a i 1 $1\leqslant x<2, \dfrac{3}{2}$ **ii** 3 $0\leqslant x<\dfrac{1}{3},\dfrac{1}{6}$

b i $2x-1$ $1\leqslant x<\dfrac{1+\sqrt{5}}{2},\dfrac{1+\sqrt{3}}{2}$

ii $\cos x$ $0\leqslant x<\dfrac{\pi}{2},\dfrac{\pi}{6}$

3 $e^{0.8}$

4 a $\dfrac{1}{2}\ln 2$ **b** $2e^{2x}$ $0\leqslant x<\dfrac{1}{2}\ln 2$

c $x=\dfrac{1}{2}\ln\dfrac{3}{2}$

Exercise 7E

1 a

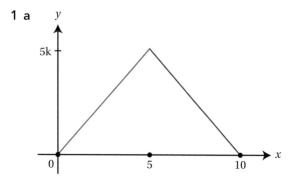

b $\dfrac{1}{25}$ **c** 6

2 a 1   **b** $\dfrac{7}{6},\dfrac{23}{36}$

3 a Proof

b

$$F(x)=\begin{cases} 0, & x\leqslant 0 \\ \dfrac{1}{8}x^2, & 0<x\leqslant 2 \\ 1+54(x-5)^2, & 2<x\leqslant 5 \\ 1, & x>5 \end{cases}$$

c $\dfrac{1}{2}$ **d** 2.62

4 a $f(w)$

b 7

c 3.64

d 3.54

e 3

5 a Proof

b $2 - (\ln 2)^2 - 2\ln 2$

6 a $\dfrac{4}{1 + 4\ln 2}$

b $\dfrac{24}{5 + 20\ln 2}$

c

$$F(X) = \begin{cases} 0, & x < 0 \\[2mm] \dfrac{x^4}{1 + 4\ln 2} & 0 \leqslant x < 1 \\[2mm] \dfrac{1 + 4\ln x}{1 + 4\ln 2} & 1 \leqslant x < 2 \\[2mm] 1 & x \geqslant 2 \end{cases}$$

d $e^{-\frac{1}{8}}\sqrt{2}$

e $\sqrt[4]{\dfrac{1}{4} + \ln 2} \approx 0.985$

Exercise 7F

1 a i $\dfrac{2}{7}$ **ii** $\dfrac{13}{20}$

b i $\dfrac{2}{3}$ **ii** 0.836

c i $\dfrac{2}{3}$ **ii** $\dfrac{13}{30}$

d i $\dfrac{5}{9}$ **ii** $\dfrac{7}{10}$

e i 0.1   **ii** 0.3

2 a i 2.5, 2.02   **ii** 6.05, 1.07

b i 17, 0.289   **ii** 18.5, 0.289

3 a $\dfrac{5}{16}$ **b** 4, 2.31

4 $\dfrac{2}{3}$

5 0.00742

6 a Proof   **b** $\sqrt{12}$

7 0.75, 0.433

Exercise 7G

1 a i 0.161   **ii** 0.0579

b i 0.432   **ii** 0.0183

c i 0.223   **ii** 0.528

2 a i 1.25, 1.25   **ii** 0.313, 0.313

b i 0.25 km, 0.25 km   **ii** 3 min, 3 min

3 0.442

4 a 0.184   **b** 0.368

c 10, 10

5 0.301

6 0.716

7 $\dfrac{-k}{\ln p}$

8 it equals e^{-1}

9 a exponential, $\lambda = \dfrac{1}{12}$

b 0.513

c Proof

10 Proof

11 a $Po(t\lambda)$ **b** $e^{-\lambda t}$

c Proof   **d** Proof

Exercise 7H

1 a $F(t) = 0.5(t-1)$ for $1 < t < 3$, 0 if $t \leqslant 1$ and 1 if $t \geqslant 3$

b Proof

c Proof

2 Proof

3 a

$$P(V \leqslant x) = \begin{cases} 0 & \text{for } x \leqslant 0 \\[2mm] \dfrac{x}{10} & \text{for } 0 < x < 10 \\[2mm] 1 & \text{for } 10 \leqslant x \end{cases}$$

b

$$\begin{cases} \dfrac{4\pi r^2}{10} & \text{for } 0 < r < 3\sqrt{\dfrac{15}{2\pi}} \\[2mm] 0 & \text{otherwise} \end{cases}$$

4 a

$$P(X \leqslant x) = \begin{cases} 0 & \text{for } x \leqslant 1 \\[2mm] \displaystyle\int_1^x \dfrac{3t^2}{26}\, dt = \dfrac{x^3 - 1}{26} & \text{for } 1 < x < 3 \\[2mm] 1 & \text{for } r \leqslant x \end{cases}$$

b $\dfrac{37}{702}$

5 a $f(x) = \begin{cases} 1 & \text{for } 0 < x < 1 \\ 0 & \text{otherwise} \end{cases}$

b $g(y) = 3y^2$ for $0 \leqslant y \leqslant 1$ **c** 0.75

Exercise 7I

1 $\chi^2_{calc} = 7.30$, $v = 3$; insufficient significant evidence to reject H_0

2 $\chi^2_{calc} = 4.8$, $v = 4$; insufficient evidence to reject H_0

3 a Proof $(\chi^2_{calc} = 3.48, v = 3)$

  b $\chi^2_{calc} = 1.52$, $v = 1$; insufficient evidence to reject H_0

4 $\chi^2_{calc} = 2.99 (3\text{s.f.})$, $v = 3$; insufficient evidence to reject H_0

5 a $\dfrac{2}{\ln 226}$

  b $\chi^2_{calc} = 7.92$, $v = 4$; insufficient evidence to reject H_0

Mixed practice 7

1 a
$$P(Y \leqslant y) = \begin{cases} 0 & \text{for } y \leqslant 0 \\ \int_0^y g(x)\,dx = 3y^2 - 2y^3 & \text{for } 0 < y < 1 \\ 1 & \text{for } 1 \leqslant y \end{cases}$$

  b 0.5   **c** 9

2 a $\dfrac{5}{4}$ **b** $\dfrac{11}{24}$

  c $\dfrac{47}{576}$

3 a £100   **b** £1300   **c** £141

4 a $a = \dfrac{3}{32}$, $b = \dfrac{-1}{32}$

  b i 11   **ii** 0.325

5 a $\dfrac{x^2 - 9x + 20}{2}$ $5 \leqslant x \leqslant 6$

  b $\dfrac{9 + \sqrt{5}}{2}$

6 0.695

7 a 0.25   **b** $\dfrac{13}{6}$

  c 18   **d** $\dfrac{1}{8}\ln 5$

8 a 2.18 hours   **b** 0.503   **c** 0.503

9 a Proof   **b** $0 \text{ if } X < a$

  c $\left(\dfrac{c-a}{b-a}\right)^2$ $\dfrac{x-a}{b-a} \text{ if } a \leqslant X \leqslant b$

                               $1 \text{ if } X > b$

10 0.519

11 $a = 0$, $b = 2$, $c = \dfrac{1}{8}$

12 a Proof   **b** $\dfrac{1}{4}e - e^{\frac{1}{2}} + e^{\frac{1}{4}}$

  c $E(X) = 0.5e - 1$, $\text{Var}(X) = \left(\dfrac{e}{3}\right) - \left(\dfrac{e^2}{4}\right)$

  d 0.290

  e i 0.0243   **ii** 0.179

13 i a $E(X) = \dfrac{7}{3}$ **b** $m = 2.25$

  ii Proof

14 i Values of X close to a are more likely than those close to 0.

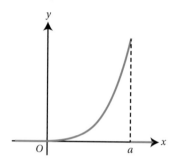

  ii a 6   **b** 1.35

Chapter 8

Before you start...

1 4.30

2 0.2

3 0.557

4 24

Exercise 8A

1 a i $-5, 6$ **ii** 3, 6

  b i 5, 34   **ii** $-18, 72$

  c i $-2.4, 1.52$ **ii** $\dfrac{5}{3}, 2$

  d i $-3, 6$ **ii** 8, 8

  e i $-8, 20$ **ii** $-7, 30$

2 $2X$ is twice the mass of a single gerbil, $X_1 + X_2$ is the sum of the masses of two different gerbils.

3 a 12   **b** 18

  c 12   **d** 24

4 1044 kg, 27.7 kg

5 0, 2.45

6 0, 39.6

7 50 minutes, 11.6 minutes

Exercise 8B

1 a i 5, 0.171   **ii** 6, 0.208

  b i $-4.7, 0.04$ **ii** $-15.1, 0.0467$

c i 12, 0.9 **ii** 8, 0.0257
d i 21, 0.893 **ii** 14, 0.0427
e i 3, 0.15 **ii** 3.6, 0.315
f i 6.5, 0.325 **ii** 8.2, 0.547

2 198.8, 4.16

3 102, 3.70

4 Proof

5 68.3 g

6 a $\dfrac{3}{4}, \dfrac{3}{16}$

b 000 (0); 001 $\left(\dfrac{1}{3}\right)$; 010 $\left(\dfrac{1}{3}\right)$; 100 $\left(\dfrac{1}{3}\right)$; 011 $\left(\dfrac{2}{3}\right)$;

101 $\left(\dfrac{2}{3}\right)$; 110 $\left(\dfrac{2}{3}\right)$; 111 (1)

c

$\bar{x}$	0	$\dfrac{1}{3}$	$\dfrac{2}{3}$	1
$P(X_3 = \bar{x})$	$\dfrac{1}{64}$	$\dfrac{9}{64}$	$\dfrac{27}{64}$	$\dfrac{27}{64}$

d Proof

7 19

8 10

Exercise 8C

1 a i Mean: 6, Variance: 15.3
ii Mean: 29.8, Variance: 367
b i Mean: 1.2, Variance: 8.7
ii Mean: 2.2, Variance: 27.7
c i Mean: −1.8, Variance: 29.7
ii Mean: 5, Variance: 78.5

2 a 2.55

b It is likely to be better, but with random fluctuations it is possible to be worse.

3 100

4 a 7.5 **b** 10

c If the data were a sample from a population and you wanted to estimate the variance of the population.

5 No, $E(S) \neq \sqrt{E(S^2)}$

Work it out 8.1

The correct answer is Solution 3.

Exercise 8D

1 a i 0.826 **ii** 0.734
b i 0.551 **ii** 0.547
c i 0.355 **ii** 0.5
d i 0.426 **ii** 0.543

e i 0.459 **ii** 0.329
f i 0.193 **ii** 0.115

2 a N(91.3,16.3) **b** 0.0156

3 a 0.3 s, 0.721 s **b** 0.339
c 0.166

4 a 65 cm, 0.005 cm² **b** 0.002 35

5 a 0.253 **b** 0.0175

6 a 0.4 kg, 0.223 kg² **b** 0.198
c 0.0209

7 a 0.196 **b** 0.0211

8 0.272 m

9 a 0.208

10 $\mu = 7.33$ mm, $\sigma = 0.525$ mm

11 a 0.0228
b i 0.868 **ii** 0.0315
iii 0.868
c 0.692 **d** 0.645

Exercise 8E

1 a i Cannot say **ii** Cannot say
b i N(80,4) **ii** N(80,1)
c i N(4000,20 000) **ii** N(12 000,60 000)

2 a i 0.212 **ii** 0.129
b i Cannot say **ii** Cannot say
c i 0.0228 **ii** 0.0555
d i 0.002 34 **ii** 0.0512

3 0.0352

4 0.0336

5 0.007 86

6 a 2500 g, 3.2 g **b** 0.995
c You could use normal distribution in part **b**.

7 a 0.0173
b The mean of normal variables is normal.

8 44

Mixed practice 8

1 a $\mu - 2m$ **b** $\sigma^2 + 4s^2$
c $16\sigma^2$ **d** $4\sigma^2$

2 a 16 m, 1.71 m² **b** 0.001 13

3 0.119

4 20, 4.47. The number of announcements on each day are independent of other days.

5 Mean: 3.6, Variance: 18.3

6 Mean: 3.65, Variance: 1.5

7 0.005 87

8 0.249

9 a -24 kg, 308 kg^2 **b** 0.0857

10 Proof

11 22

12 a 0.432 **b** 0.276

13 12.0 g

14 i $a = 0.8$, $b = 1.2$ **ii** $N(40, 100)$
iii 0.240

Chapter 9

Before you start...

1 0.242

2 Do not reject H_0

3 9.12%

4 8.7

Exercise 9A

1 a i 58.5 to 61.5 **ii** 119 to 121
b i $x > 81.7$ **ii** 747 to 753
c i $\bar{x} < 79.2$ **ii** $\bar{x} < 92.2$

2 a i 0.0455, reject H_0
ii 0.0339, reject H_0
b i 3.87×10^{-6}, reject H_0
ii $0.008\,98$, reject H_0
c i 0.278, do not reject H_0
ii 0.147, do not reject H_0
d i 0.623, do not reject H_0
ii 0.611, do not reject H_0

3 a i $p = 0.617$, do not reject H_0
ii $p = 0.002\,87$, reject H_0
b i $p = 5.38 \times 10^{-5}$, reject H_0
ii $p = 0.159$, do not reject H_0

4 a $H_0: \mu = 168.8$, $H_1: \mu > 168.8$
b That the sample standard deviation can be used as the population standard deviation for all 18-year-olds
c p-value $= 0.118$, do not reject H_0
d Yes, she used it when calculating probabilities from a normal distribution.

5 a p-value $= 0.0300$, reject H_0
b Assume that the standard deviation is unchanged.

6 a $H_0: \mu = 2.7$, $H_1: \mu \neq 2.7$.
b $\bar{x} < 2.53$ or $\bar{x} > 2.87$ **c** Reject H_0

7 a $H_0: \mu = 82.4$, $H_1: \mu < 82.4$ **b** $\bar{x} < 80.3$
c No, the data is already stated to be normally distributed.
d Reject H_0.

8 a 8.46
b p-value $= 0.0659$, do not reject H_0.
c The sampling method. The conclusion is only valid if the sample is representative of all 15-year-olds in the UK.

9 a p-value $= 0.115$ **b** 68

Exercise 9B

1 a 1.28 **b** 2.58

2 a i $[39.1, 45.1]$ **ii** $[40.9, 43.3]$
b i $[346, 354]$ **ii** $[-5.73, 2.13]$

3

	$\bar{x}$	σ	n	Confidence level	Lower bound of interval	Upper bound of interval
a i	58.6	8.2	4	90	51.9	65.3
ii	0.178	0.01	12	80	0.174	0.182
b i	42	4	4	80	39.44	44.56
ii	30.4	1.2	900	99	30.30	30.50
c i	120	18	64	95	115.59	124.41
ii	1100	25	207	88	1097.3	1102.7
d i	4	40	100	75	−0.601	8.601
ii	16	0.4	400	90	15.967	16.033
e i	8	12	14	98	0.539	15.46
ii	0.4	0.01	18	80	0.397	0.403

4 $(85.8, 90.6)$

5 $(3.06, 4.54)$

6 $(-0.358, 1.96)$

7 a $(21\,200, 27\,800)$

   b No, cannot reject H_0.

   c Yes, it was needed to justify that the sampling distribution of the mean was normal.

8 a 94.9%   **b** 173

9 9

10 a 106   **b** 73.7%

11 a 80%

   b Reject H_0 at the 10% significance level.

12 a $(23.9, 37.1)$

   b Increase the sample size

   c Yes

13 a False   **b** False

   c False   **d** True

   e False

14 90% interval

15 e.g. Range

Mixed practice 9

1 a 2   **b** $(4.41, 5.19)$

   c Do not reject H_0 **d** Yes

2 a $(165, 171)$

   b No, the large sample means that you can use the CLT.

3 i $H_0: \mu = 28.0$, $H_1: \mu > 28.0$; there is insufficient evidence of an increase in mean score. Assume that variance is unchanged.

   ii Yes

4 a $H_0: \mu = 145$, $H_1: \mu > 145$

   b $\bar{x} > 151$

   c Do not reject H_0

5 i $(2.05, 2.31)$ **ii** 2430

   iii n is large enough to use the CLT.

6 44

7 a $(-2.77, 6.77)$ **b** Do not reject H_0

8 a $(22.5, 25.5)$

   b No, the given probability suggest that $\mu = 21.7$ which does not fall in the confidence interval.

Focus on ... 2

Focus on ... Proof 2

1 Proof   **2** Proof

3 Proof   **4** Proof

Focus on ... Problem solving 2

1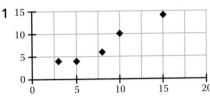

They seem to have a positive correlation.

2 $\bar{x} = 8.2$, $\bar{y} = 7.6$

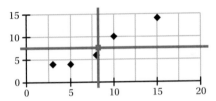

3 If it is a straight line with positive gradient you expect most points in TR and BL. If it is a straight line with negative gradient you expect most points in TL and BR. However, this does not take into account where the points are in the quadrants or how many points there are in total. You could divide by the number of points to improve this measure.

4 a 15.68

   b The factors are either both positive or both negative.

   c By analogy with turning moments in mechanics.

   d Similar to the measure in 3 but takes into account how far from the edges of the quadrants the points are. However, it depends on what units x and y are measured in, making comparisons between two different situations difficult.

5 a Proof

   b $r = 0.97$.

   c It must lie between -1 and 1, making comparisons possible. However, it only measures linear correlation.

Focus on ... Modelling 2

1 $P(X < x) = P(F^{-1}(U) < x) = P(U < F(x)) = F(x)$

2 Histogram should be quite flat.

3 It has a peak in the middle.

4 It should look very much like a normal distribution.

5 An initially skewed histogram becomes more and more symmetrical.

6 A U-shaped curve flattens then tends towards a bell-shaped curve.

Cross-topic review exercise 2

1 $\dfrac{27}{28}$

2 i When there is one degree of freedom

   ii $\chi^2 = 10.7$, so there is sufficient evidence that the outcome depends on the vaccine used.

3 i H_0: A and B are not associated, H_1: A and B are associated.

   ii $\chi^2 = \Sigma \dfrac{(|O - E| - 0.5)^2}{E}$, which decreases the value.

   iii Reject H_0. There is evidence of association between A and B.

4 a $\dfrac{3}{256}$ **b** 8

5 i 2   **ii** 0.469

6 i $F(0) = 0$, $F\left(\dfrac{\pi}{2}\right) = 1$, increasing

   ii $\dfrac{\pi}{4}$

   iii $G(y) = y^4$, $g(y) = 4y^3$ if $0 \leqslant y \leqslant 1$, 0 otherwise

   iv $2 \ln 3$

7 $z = -1.97$, $p = 0.0245$. Significant evidence that people underestimate time.

8 i 2   **ii** -0.7

9 i

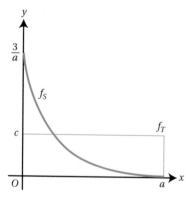

ii $\dfrac{a}{4}$

iii T has bigger variance since S is more concentrated towards 0.

10 i EDCBA

    ii a Proof   **b** e.g BACDE

11 52.3, 100

12 i $z = -2.61$, Significant evidence that the population mean is not 230.

    ii Yes, population is not known to be normal.

13 a $\dfrac{5}{14}$ **b** $10 - \sqrt{35}$

   c $f(x) = \begin{cases} \dfrac{1}{15}x, & 0 \leqslant x \leqslant 3, \\ -\dfrac{1}{35}x + \dfrac{2}{7}, & 3 < x \leqslant 10, \\ 0 & \text{otherwise} \end{cases}$

   d Proof   **e** 6.85×10^{-3}

14 a $e^{-\mu}\left(\mu + \dfrac{\mu^2}{2}\right)$ **b** $\sqrt{2}$

15 $\dfrac{1}{5}$

16 $\dfrac{1}{3\sqrt{3}}$

17 i $G(y) = \dfrac{(2y - 1)}{(y + 1)}$ for $\dfrac{1}{2} \leqslant y \leqslant 2$

   ii $3 \ln 2 - 1$

18 i $\chi^2 = 9.64$, sufficient evidence that vegetable preference and gender are not independent.

   ii $\chi^2 = 4.2$, insufficient evidence of a difference in proportion of preferred vegetables.

19 a

k	1	2	3	4	5
p_k	0.0784	0.216	0.296	0.280	0.130

   b Fit, $3.78 < 7.81$

20 i $r_s = -1$ **ii** $-\dfrac{1}{2}$ **iii** $\dfrac{1}{6}$

21 i Proof

   ii $\chi^2 = 6.60 < 7.78$, so not sufficient evidence that $f(x)$ does not fit the data.

22 i 0.003 83   **ii** 0, 180   **iii** 0.5

23 i $r = 0.139$

   ii Small, as points are not close to a line.

   iii Unchanged   **iv** Larger

24 i $y = 0.008x$ **ii** 313   **iii** −0.4
   iv Contraction, unreliable because of extrapolation

25 i 0.956
   ii Strong positive linear relationship
   iii Relationship might not continue. Correlation does not imply causation.
   iv $y = 16.0x − 36.7$ **v** About £81 600

26 i 0.45   **ii** Proof
   iii 0.278   **iv** $\overline{X} \sim N(1.5, \frac{1}{240})$

27 i $f(t)$

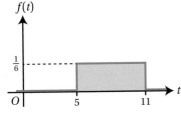

   ii 8, 3
   iii 0.115, CLT is only approximate

AS Level practice paper

1 a 1260   **b** $\frac{1}{7}$

2 a $a = 0.15$, $b = 0.25$ **b** 6.51

3 a H_0: The dice follows a uniform distribution.

     H_1: The dice does not follow a uniform distribution.

   b $\chi^2 = 2.2$. Do not reject H_0

4 a Any two from e.g. People in the street are representative of people in the whole town; people's voting intentions are independent of the people they are with; the population is large enough so that the probability does not change significantly if lots of non-Party X voters are approached; people answer honestly. Other examples can be valid answers.

   b 0.130   **c** 1.94

5 $\chi^2 = 4.22$, $v = 6$, accept H_0

6 a Total number of Route 1 and Route 2 buses in an hour: $T \sim Po(7.5)$

   b 0.0591
   c e.g. Both are dependent on traffic.
   d Mean = 7.45, Unbiased estimate of variance = 11.5. Mean is not close to variance, so Poisson is unlikely.

7 a 0.771
   b The numbers might mean different things to the two judges. The relative position of the dancers is more important.

8 a 0.917
   b No difference, r is unaffected by linear coding.
   c i Significant evidence of correlation
     ii No, correlation does not imply causation.
   d $y = 4.00x + 2.38$
   e i Yes: significant correlation and within the given data
     ii No: extrapolating from the given data

A Level practice paper

1 a The sum of the squares of the vertical distance between data points and the regression line is minimised.
   b $−1 \leqslant r < 0$ **c** $y = 0.15x + 2.1$

2 a An interval which would be expected to include the population mean in 99% of repetitions of the sample.
   b 680 000

3 a $\frac{5}{3}$ **b** $\frac{5}{9}$ **c** 0.621%

4 a H_0: Gender and lessons are independent, H_1: Gender and lessons are not independent
   b 1
   c $\chi^2 = 4.84$, reject H_0.

5 $W = 16$, so not significant evidence of a difference between the two classes.

6 a i $\frac{1}{1\,860\,480}$ **ii** $\frac{1}{15\,504}$

   b $\frac{1050}{15\,504} \approx 6.77\%$

7 a 2.21%   **b** 8.33%
   c 16.0%

8 a e.g. buses arrive independently of each other.

   b

Buses	0	1	2	$\geqslant 3$
Frequency	22.3	33.5	25.1	19.1

   c $\chi^2 = 2.41$. There is insufficient evidence to doubt the bus company's claim.

9 a $\frac{1}{\ln 2}$

   b $E(X) = 1.44$, $Var(X) = 0.0827$

   c $F(x) = \begin{cases} 0 & x \leqslant 1 \\ \dfrac{\ln x}{\ln 2} & 1 < x < 2 \\ 1 & x \geqslant 2 \end{cases}$

   d $g(y) = \dfrac{1}{y \ln 2}$ $\dfrac{1}{2} < y < 1$

Glossary

bivariate data: Data where for each item two properties are recorded, e.g. height and weight of a group of people.

confidence interval: A plausible interval for a population parameter based upon a sample. It is quoted with a specified confidence level.

confidence level: The proportion of confidence intervals that are expected to contain the true value of the population parameter.

contingency tables: A table showing the frequency of observations split among two different categorisations.

continuity correction: A change that is made to a discrete value when it is modelled by a continuous distribution.

continuous random variable (crv): A variable that can change each time it is observed and can take any value in a given interval.

controlled variable (see 'independent variable'): A variable that is predetermined in the design of an experiment, and is considered to have less error than the response variable.

critical value: A cut-off that determines whether a test statistic is sufficient to reject the null hypothesis.

cumulative distribution function (cdf): The probability of a variable being less than or equal to a given value.

dependent variable: A variable that is believed to be affected by changes in the independent variable.

discrete random variable: A variable that can change each time it is observed and but can only take a certain predetermined values.

discrete uniform distribution: A distribution where any value between 1 and n is equally likely.

domain: The set of possible inputs into a function.

expectation: The predicted mean of a distribution, assuming it can be sampled infinitely often.

exponential distribution: A distribution modelling the waiting time between Poisson events.

extrapolating: Making a prediction for a y value using an x value beyond the interval of the observed data.

geometric distribution: Models the number of independent trials until the first success, where the probability of success in any individual trial is constant.

hypothesis test: A method for making decisions in which the likelihood of observing the given data (or more extreme) while a null hypothesis is true is used to decide whether or not to reject this hypothesis.

independent variable: A variable whose value is thought to not depend causally upon another variable. In experimental design this is usually the controlled variable.

interpolating: Making a prediction for a y value using an x value within the interval of the observed data.

linear coding: A way of transforming data using a rule of the form $Y = aX + b$.

point estimate: A single value used to estimate a population parameter based on a sample. Usually considered inferior to a confidence interval.

Poisson distribution: A commonly used distribution measuring the number of successes for random events occurring independently at a constant average rate.

probability density function (pdf): A way of describing the probability of a discrete random variable. If f(x) is the pdf for the crv X then

$$P(a < X < b) = \int_a^b f(x)\,dx$$

probability distributions: A list of all possible outcomes along with their probabilities or probability densities.

p-value: The probability of getting the observed data or more extreme while the null hypothesis is true.

random variable: A variable that can change each time it is observed.

rank: Numerical value assigned to an observation, with the largest value being rank 1, the next, rank 2, etc. until all observations are ranked.

regression line: A line of best fit based on a given sample.

response variable (see 'dependent variable'): A variable whose change is caused by a controlled variable.

signed ranks: The rank of the magnitude of differences with a positive sign associated with differences in one direction and a negative sign associated with differences in the other direction.

unbiased estimate: An estimate that on average over many samples gives the true value of the population parameter.

variance: The square of the standard deviation.

Index

Acknowledgements

The authors and publishers acknowledge the following sources of copyright material and are grateful for the permissions granted. While every effort has been made, it has not always been possible to identify the sources of all the material used, or to trace all copyright holders. If any omissions are brought to our notice, we will be happy to include the appropriate acknowledgements on reprinting.

Thanks to the following for permission to reproduce images:

Cover image: huskyomega/Getty Images

Back cover: Fabian Oefner www.fabianoefner.com

HairFacePhoto/Getty Images; Filograph/Getty Images; Chris Hepburn/ Getty Images; Mark Newman/Getty Images; Mark Kolbe/Getty Images; Maremagnum/Getty Images; PM Images/Getty Images; aaaaimages/ Getty Images; Florian Fodermeyer/EyeEm/Getty Images; Ludgien Angeles/EyeEm/Getty Images